Palgrave Studies in Prisons and Penology

This is a unique and innovative series, the first of its kind dedicated entirely to prison scholarship. At a historical point in which the prison population has reached an all-time high, the series seeks to analyse the form, nature and consequences of incarceration and related forms of punishment. Palgrave Studies in Prisons and Penology provides an important forum for burgeoning prison research across the world.

Carol Robinson

Dying in Prison

Deaths from Natural Causes in Prison Culture, Regimes and Relationships

palgrave
macmillan

Carol Robinson
Department of Sociology
University of York
York, UK

ISSN 2753-0604 ISSN 2753-0612 (electronic)
Palgrave Studies in Prisons and Penology
ISBN 978-3-031-27102-1 ISBN 978-3-031-27103-8 (eBook)
https://doi.org/10.1007/978-3-031-27103-8

Cover illustration: Beth Achenbach/EyeEm

This Palgrave Macmillan imprint is published by the registered company Springer Nature Switzerland AG
The registered company address is: Gewerbestrasse 11, 6330 Cham, Switzerland

Foreword

Most people don't like thinking or talking about prisons much; and they certainly don't like thinking or talking about death. So Carol Robinson's coolly analytical study of deaths from natural causes in prisons confronts a topic from which we too often avert our gaze. There is, at one level, a savagery in her descriptions of the humiliations and spectacle imposed on dying prisoners: the escort chains that tether them to prison officers, mark them out and deny them privacy in their hospital death beds; the bureaucratic obstacles that prevent the compassionate release that might enable them to avoid the "ultimate failure" of dying in prison and die with dignity and comfort at home or in a hospice; the weight of security-heavy rules and regulations that smother human instincts of care and sympathy and the rigidity of post-death inquiry procedures that strip dignity from the body of the deceased. And yet. Robinson also tellingly describes how dying begins to blur the rigid prison boundaries between the locations of wing, health care and hospital; between identities as prisoner, patient and person and between the cultures of prison officer and health care staff. This blurring allows care, decency and tenderness to seep through into the treatment of some (deserving/sympathetic) dying prisoners from those same prison officers and health care staff, and from prisoners who may be their dying fellow's only friends. There is a desire from all of these to make a 'death as good as it can be' and despite the limits of that ambition, there is comfort in their efforts to achieve it. As Robinson points out, with an ageing prison population, natural cause deaths in prison will increase. This is a timely study of an overlooked subject. These deaths should be able to be much better than they are. I hope this book provides encouragement to no longer look away and in doing so provide a real impetus for making 'good as these can be' much, much better.

December 2022

Professor Nick Hardwick
Royal Holloway University of London
Egham, UK

Acknowledgements

I am grateful to the staff and prisoners at the two prisons studied, who made me feel welcome and so generously shared their stories, their experiences of dealing with death and dying in prison and their private joys and sorrows. I am especially grateful to the Safer Custody teams, healthcare professionals and chaplaincy teams in each prison, and to the staff and prisoners in the areas of the prison where I spent much of my time. It was a privilege to step into their lives for a while, and I wish them all the best for the future.

I am thankful for funding from the Economic and Social Research Council (ES/J500215/1) which enabled the research that informs this book, and fortunate to have been supervised by Dr. Ruth Penfold-Mounce, Professor Maggie O'Neill and Professor Dave Beer. Their insights, encouragement, wisdom, care, challenge and support were essential to this project.

Lastly, my thanks to Nick Perks, for his support, encouragement, patience and enthusiasm in all things.

Contents

1
Introduction

It is said that no one truly knows a nation until one has been inside its jails. A nation should not be judged by how it treats its highest citizens, but its lowest ones. Nelson Mandela.[1]

Care for the dying, those who are important to them, their carers and the bereaved, is the measure of a compassionate society. (National Palliative & end of life care partnership, 2015)

Background

England and Wales have the second highest imprisonment rate in Western Europe (132 prisoners per 100,000 of population) and a prison population which has increased by 70% in the last 30 years and is predicted to rise by 19,000 people by 2026 (Prison Reform Trust, 2022). What happens within prisons is more relevant than ever since it affects more of the population. However, at the same time as prisons have come

[1] Quoted in United Nations Office on Drugs and Crime (2015).

C. Robinson, *Dying in Prison*, Palgrave Studies in Prisons and Penology, https://doi.org/10.1007/978-3-031-27103-8_1

under pressure from overcrowding, reductions in staffing and the need to implement changing government strategies, demographic changes are presenting new challenges associated with meeting the needs of elderly prisoners. There are now more than three times the numbers of people aged over 60 in prison than there were 20 years ago (Ministry of Justice, 2022), with 17% of prisoners aged over 50 (Ministry of Justice, 2022) and as of 30 September 2020, 315 prisoners aged 80 or over (HL WA, 17 November 2020), most of whom had been sentenced after the age of 70 (HL WA, 27 October 2017). Ministry of Justice (2021a) projections for prison populations until 2026 suggest the number of prisoners over 60 years old will continue to increase. Forty-five per cent of men in prison aged over 50 have been convicted of sex offences (HL WA, 5 January 2017), a statistic which goes some way to explain these demographic changes. With an ageing prison population such as this, it is unsurprising that the year to June 2021 saw the highest ever number of deaths in prison in England and Wales, seventy per cent of which were due to natural causes, as opposed to suicide or homicide (Ministry of Justice, 2022). Pre-Covid-19 records show an increase in the rates of deaths from natural causes in prison, from 1.06 per 1,000 prisoners in 2006 to 2.43 per 1,000 prisoners in 2016 (Ministry of Justice, 2018b). Deaths from natural causes, those caused by illness or a malfunction of the body rather than an external intervention, are not limited to older prisoners. Thirty-six per cent of prisoners who died from natural causes in 2016 were under the age of 60 (Ministry of Justice, 2017b). Without changes in sentencing practice, or an overhaul of the compassionate release scheme for terminally ill prisoners, this trend for increasing numbers of prisoners to die of natural causes in custody seems likely to continue.

Despite the growing number of deaths of prisoners from natural causes, dying in prison is still an unusual experience. Across England and Wales, almost all deaths will be in other settings, typically hospitals, hospices, care homes or at home. Most people do not consider the possibility of dying in prison (Glamser & Cabana, 2003). If they were to do so, then they would probably conclude, with Aday and Wahidin (2016, p. 314):

> Behind bars one finds the possibility of dying alone, no family present to support you, no last goodbyes and no opportunity for reconciliations. For most people, dying in prison would be the least optimal environment on earth from which to choose.
>
> Studies of older men in prison have suggested dying in prison is seen as the ultimate failure (Bolger, 2004), an additional, unjustifiable punishment (Schaefer, 2022) and that prisoners yearn to die as a free persons (Crawley & Sparks, 2005).

Dying from natural causes in prison is not the same as dying from natural causes in other settings (Aday & Wahidin, 2016; Burles et al., 2016; Dawes, 2002; Handtke & Wangmo, 2014; Turner et al., 2011; Wood, 2007). Where age is a factor, older prisoners are in poorer health than their peers outside of the prison (Aday & Wahidin, 2016) and have poorer access to hospital services (Davies et al., 2020). The House of Commons Health and Social Care Committee's report on Prison Health found that deaths from natural causes in prison often reflected the poor physical health of the prison population and that prisoners sometimes experienced long delays in getting their health concerns addressed (Health and Social Care Committee, 2018). The select committee heard evidence from the charity INQUEST that prisoner deaths categorised as resulting from natural causes were often premature and avoidable and found that prisoners in England have a mortality rate 50% higher than the general public (Health and Social Care Committee, 2018).

Despite the higher mortality rate amongst prisoners, and the rise by more than 120% in deaths from natural causes in the last decade (Prison Reform Trust, 2022), they are rarely researched and receive little public attention. Current media discourses about the challenges faced by prisons in England and Wales focus on prison violence, radicalisation and the use of new forms of illegal drugs. Attention has understandably been paid by the media to self-inflicted deaths and the small number of prison homicides, but the greater number of deaths from natural causes is overlooked. Academic research about prisons has also traditionally overlooked questions around prisoners dying from natural causes. It has instead focussed on the majority of prisoners, those who will be released, and the circumstances in which they are kept until then. Classic studies such as Sykes (1958), Clemmer (1958) and Irwin (1970) describe the conditions and experience of imprisonment and the prison culture in the US, but share an assumption that the prisoners they describe will at some point be released. In the UK, another significant text, by Cohen and Taylor (1972), looks at the experience of long-term prisoners, addressing questions around their psychological survival, without considering the possibility of death in prison. More recent landmark studies, such as Crewe (2009), have shed new light on the experience of imprisonment, but have not addressed the experience of deaths from natural causes whilst imprisoned. When deaths of prisoners are considered, the emphasis has traditionally been on deaths resulting from suicide or occasionally as a result of homicide, not deaths from natural causes (see Carlton & Sims, 2018; Crighton, 2002; Dooley, 1990; Liebling, 1999; Liebling & Ludlow, 2016; Sattar, 2003). This oversight suggests a lack of awareness amongst researchers of deaths from natural causes in prisons and the questions they raise. It is this context, of a growing number of deaths from natural causes in prison custody overlooked in existing research, which informs the aims of this book.

Rationale and Aims

Given the increase in the number of prisoners dying of natural causes, the paucity of studies in this area is striking. In recent years, with an increasing use of whole life tariffs, primarily in the US, and a changing prisoner demographic in many countries, academic research has begun to pay attention to dying prisoners. However, the few studies that do exist typically focus on the experience of the dying prisoner (such as their fears about death or attitudes towards dying in prison [Aday & Wahidin, 2016]) or the provision of healthcare for the terminally ill prisoner (Turner et al., 2011) from the perspective of Health Sciences. The impact of such deaths on prison regimes, culture and relationships remains overlooked.

The aim of this book is therefore to critically engage with the impact on prison culture, prison regimes and prison relationships of the growing number of prisoners dying of natural causes, and to explore the factors influencing the responses within prisons towards dying prisoners. As Visser (2021) points out, "Dying in prison does not only affect the dying prisoner". Therefore, two key questions will be addressed:

- How do deaths from natural causes in prisons impact on prison regimes, culture and relationships?
- What determines the responses of prison regimes and personnel to dying prisoners?

In doing so, it is important to consider the extent to which deaths from natural causes challenge existing practices and assumptions within the prison and whether these challenges have repercussions for the wider prison. Of interest is how they might impact on the physical environment and resourcing of the prison, staff identities and staff well-being, perceptions of prisoners, the implementation of prison rules and the provision of services: in short, the very nature of prison. This book therefore has a wider interest than the care of the individual prisoner, as important as that is to all involved.

Whilst there may a lack of studies of deaths from natural causes in prison, the need for such research has been recognised. Liebling (2017, p. 27) proposes:

> deaths in custody are, and should be, controversial because they raise issues of accountability, legitimacy, and quality of life, including safety, as well as questions about the quality of death for those who die of natural causes in prison as a result of their age or sentence.

This controversy alone should provide sufficient reason to research deaths in prison custody from natural causes. In addition, Girling and Seal (2016) claim that the "prisoners' loss of liberty places a heavy responsibility on the State to ensure that they are adequately cared for" (p. 216). Arguably, the performance of this responsibility should be subject to scrutiny, through academic study as well as the investigations following individual deaths and the reviews by bodies such as the Prison and Probation Ombudsman. Although understanding the circumstances of individual deaths from natural causes in prison matters, considering the impact of deaths from natural causes on prison regimes, culture and relationships, all wider units of interest, helps to address more structural factors. Considering these aspects is important because as Arnold et al. (2007) suggest, "the prison as an *institution* tends to get less attention from researchers than prisoners" (p. 484). Similarly, as Sykes (1958) argued: "the custodial institution — as a special type of social system — is a significant object of study in its own right" (p. xiv). Prison regimes, culture and relationships are all key aspects of the prison as an institution.

Personal Story: Insider Status

My own awareness of prisoners dying of natural causes originates in having worked as a prison chaplain for nine years. Prison chaplains work in multi-faith teams to meet the faith, religious and pastoral needs of prisoners and are appointed to reflect the faith composition of the prison population. When I worked in a large category C prison, for those prisoners "who cannot be trusted in open conditions but who do not have the resources and will to make a determined escape attempt" (Garton Grimwood, 2015, p. 4), the prospect of a death from natural causes was extremely rare. Talk of death was limited to the few elderly prisoners who found themselves in a category C prison as they neared the conclusion of life sentences mostly served elsewhere. In a later role, at a high security prison for Category A and Category B prisoners, for whom the Ministry of Justice deems escape must be made impossible or at least very difficult (Garton Grimwood, 2015), significantly more of my time was spent on death-related matters.

In providing pastoral care for prisoners and staff, I found myself discussing funeral plans with healthy prisoners who expect never to be released, supporting the efforts of terminally ill prisoners to find lost family members before it is too late, and sharing memories with other prisoners when one of their peers has died. On several occasions I visited seriously ill prisoners who have been transferred to hospitals for treatment, chatting to them and to the prison officers accompanying them. I tried to meet their relevant practical and spiritual needs, within the constraints of the situation: everything from getting their reading glasses or favourite religious book sent out to them to discovering why they were refusing to eat. Once or twice, I left the hospital having said what I expected to be a final goodbye. I have facilitated memorial services, sometimes in my own faith tradition, but also memorial gatherings that have reflected the wide range of beliefs of the deceased's friends in prison. I have passed the private ambulance outside the prison as I come to work, and wondered which of the many seriously ill men inside it has come for. I have stood in cell doorways, accompanying prisoners in the shock of their grief for a man they cared for who had just died. I have attempted to offer support to officers trying to create a 'good death' for the next prisoner expected to die whilst processing the paperwork and the expectations of an inquest from previous deaths. And on one day as duty chaplain, I slipped away from my regular duties as often as I could to sit at the bedside and read aloud from the Bible of a dying prisoner, choosing yet another passage he had carefully bookmarked, unaware whether he could hear me or not. Eventually, on my final visit of the day, I was just in time to say prayers over his body before the cell door was locked pending the inevitable investigation. His death was the first I had witnessed.

Dying in prison is the "ultimate failure" (Bolger, 2004, p. 139) and the "ultimate punishment (Aday, 2006, p. 208), but it is one I was unaware of before working as a prison chaplain, despite it being a reality for a growing number of prisoners. Being a prison chaplain has given me a privileged insight, since chaplains occupy the space between prison officers (and arguably other staff) and prisoners (Craig, 2002; Hicks, 2012). It has also brought me closer to the dying and dead than I expected. This personal connection made me aware of circumstances not addressed by existing research and lead me to look for explanations that would assist in the work.

Boundaries and Definitions

Although the site of a prison has a clear boundary, the walls and fences that physically enclose it, deaths in prison custody are not so neatly boundaries. Of the deaths from natural causes in prison custody from 2016 to 2021, between 52 and 70% each year occurred in hospitals, hospices or nursing homes, with a small proportion occurring in the ambulance travelling to the hospital (Ministry of Justice, 2021b). Some of the prisoners who die in these locations, outside of the prison, will have been granted release on temporary licence (ROTL) for medical reasons, but remain the responsibility of the prison (Ministry of Justice, 2021b). Other prisoners, whose deaths occur within the prison buildings, may have received medical treatment prior to death in outside hospitals or hospices. In considering deaths from natural causes in prison custody, the limits of custody must therefore be extended to include prisoners in hospitals and hospices outside of the prison boundary.

Dying also has untidy boundaries. Glaser and Strauss (1968) are clear that the dying trajectory has a varying duration and different shapes, and is marked by critical junctures, with the dying person passing through transitional stages. The question remains for any individual: when do they start dying? As Glaser and Strauss (1968) point out, "dying must be defined in order to be reacted to as dying" (p. 242). Some of the deaths from natural causes within the prison will be unexpected, resulting from sudden catastrophic events such as strokes or heart attacks. In these circumstances, the prisoner will have been definable as 'dying', by themselves or others, for only a very short period. Other deaths will have been anticipated, resulting from a terminal diagnosis of conditions such as cancers, organ diseases or degenerative illnesses. In these circumstances, the individual or those around them may have regarded them as dying for weeks or months before death occurs. The definition of end of life included in the document *Ambitions for Palliative and End of Life Care; a national framework for local action 2015–2020* (National Palliative & End of Life Care Partnership, 2015) provides one useful framework:

> Patients are 'approaching the end of life' when they are likely to die within the next 12 months. This includes patients whose death is imminent (expected within a few hours or days) and those with: a) advanced, progressive, incurable conditions; b) general frailty and co-existing conditions that mean they are expected to die within 12 months; c) existing conditions if they are at risk of dying from a sudden acute crisis in their

> condition; d) life-threatening acute conditions caused by sudden catastrophic events. (National Palliative & End of Life Care Partnership, 2015, p. 38)

The National Palliative and End of Life Care Partnership definition of end of life helps set some limits on which prisoners' experiences are relevant when considering how the prison regime and personnel respond to dying prisoners. However, in this book, it is the participants' understandings of when someone was dying, to be discussed fully in Chapter 4, that is given priority. No attempt was made to identify which prisoners had a terminal diagnosis; the emphasis was on how participants defined dying.

Prison Culture, Regimes and Relationships

Given this research looks at how deaths from natural causes impact on prison regimes, culture and relationships, it is important to provide definitions of these terms. A prison regime is essentially how things are done in a particular prison, the ways in which the prison is organised and run, including both formal and less formal systems. There is a close link with the culture of the prison as a whole, but the prison regime is essentially about the system of order, governance or control in operation within the establishment, informed by the regulations, rules and guidance that shape prisons in general, but also by the informal practices present in the particular institution. In this respect, it closely matches the Oxford English Dictionary (2009) definition of a 'regime' as a:

> method or system of rule, governance, or control; a system of organization; a way of doing things, esp. one having widespread influence or prevalence.

Most studies of prisons refer to the 'prison regime' but the term is often used vaguely. Her Majesty's Chief Inspector of Prisons for England and Wales (1992, p. 2) provides a useful definition in the introduction to a report on prison regimes:

> The term 'regime' refers in the broadest sense to a system of overall administration. In the institutional setting it is generally taken to apply to the way in which daily life is organised to achieve the basic tasks and objectives. Within the prison setting, the broadest interpretation of regime is the impact of systems of administration upon those who occupy the institution. In common usage within the Prison Service regime means daily life for prisoners; in the narrowest sense it is taken to relate only to inmates' occupation….we take regime to mean the impact of systems of administration on all those who live and work in penal establishments. (HM Inspectorate of Prisons, 1993)
>
> This definition is notable for acknowledging staff as well as prisoners as being affected by the regime of a prison. There are other explicit explanations of what constitutes a prison regime. Dawes (2009) suggests "a prison regime is the system of government or rules applying within a prison and varies from prison to prison" (p. 263). This is a narrower definition, prioritising the importance of rules and perhaps underestimating the less formalised systems of government that other sources regard as key to the delivery of the prison. Liebling et al. (2011) suggest the daily work of prison officers, routines such as unlocking and locking doors, delivering meals, counting, moving, receiving, discharging and observing prisoners, is both the accomplishment of the regime and only achievable because the regime enables these actions. They argue the smooth delivery of these routines rests on the officers' ability to communicate with and manage prisoners. Crawley (2005a) widens the definition further, to include a prison's timetable, physical layout and activities, as well as its rules and practices. The vagueness of the term 'prison regime' permits very different definitions. Rodriguez (2006) argues for a 'meso' definition, between a macro- and micro-level understanding, which includes processes, structures and vernaculars. Rodriguez regards the parameters of the term as both including dominion in line with the conventional understanding of a discrete area of territory controlled by the ruling order or state, and the Latin concept of dominium as dominion over tangible things, in which prisoners are regarded as the property of the state. He regards this as a critical or radical understanding of the prison regime, as opposed to the more traditional approach usually taken by sociology.

In most prison research, prison regimes are recognised as varying between establishments (Crawley, 2004; Jenkins, 1993; Liebling et al.,

1999). Liebling, Price and Elliot equate the regime with how prisoners are 'policed' and observe that "the way in which prisons are 'policed' can vary from 'liberal-permissive' to near 'zero-tolerance' between wings, between establishments and over time" (p. 74). This notion that prison regimes vary is supported by Crawley (2004) in her study of prison officers, where she finds many officers feel a liberal regime presents them with more difficulties because when prisoners are out of their cells for longer, relationships between officers and prisoners become more informal. As will be shown later, differing regimes in the prisons studied informed differing situations for dying prisoners.

The regime attempts to set the culture of the prison, but as well as having their own regime, individual establishments also have their own culture (Arnold et al., 2007; Crewe, 2009; Leggett, 2002; Liebling, 2008) within which there are a number of subcultures, including prisoners' social structures and staff occupational cultures as well as forms of resistance to the regime. Different areas within a prison could also have their own cultures (Cohen & Taylor, 1972; Liebling et al., 1999; Nylander et al., 2011), prison culture being the informal and formal social organisation of the prison (Clemmer, 1958). Leggett (2002) identifies a number of determinants of a prison's culture, including its history, current condition and management style. The extent to which individuals follow the dominant culture within the prison may also vary (Arnold, 2016).

Crewe (2009) addresses US twentieth-century prison research which debated how far prisoner culture is derived from the deprivations of imprisonment (Sykes, 1958) or imported from outside criminal culture (Irwin & Cressey, 1962) to produce an ethnography of HMP Wellingborough which seeks to show how importation and deprivation models combine to produce prison cultures. He finds prisoners' social relationships and everyday culture are influenced by three main factors; the prison's inherent structural imperatives, the culture, function and policies of the particular prison and the ideologies and inclinations of the prisoners before imprisonment. As with earlier prison studies (see Clemmer, 1958; Giallombardo, 1966; Sykes, 1958, and many others), Crewe (2009) produces a typology of prisoners as a tool for providing a description of social life within the prison. However, he concludes: "one of the clear findings of this study is that there is no such thing as a typical prisoner or a single 'prison culture'" (p. 154).

The importance of relationships within the prison should not be understated. Crewe (2009) shows prisoners as distinguishing between their relationships with their peers as 'real friends', 'prison friends' and 'associates'. In Crewe's (2009) research, the strongest basis for a relationship with another prisoner is a shared home background, with shared race and ethnicity also being significant. Crewe describes the difficulties of prisoners in trusting each other, and suggests "for the majority of prisoners, the prison was a site of inauthenticity and a place where social conditions inhibited the formation of friendship" (p. 322). He finds friendship cliques were typically small, and on a wing a fifth of prisoners may choose to be solitary.

It is the relationship between prisoners and staff which is usually regarded as the most significant. The Home Office Control Review Committee (Home Office, 1984) statement is often quoted (Hay & Sparks, 1991; Liebling et al., 2011), to refer to prison officers' relationships with prisoners:

> At the end of the day, nothing else that we can say will be as important as the general proposition that relations between staff and prisoners are at the heart of the whole prison system and that control and security flow from getting that relationship right. Prisons cannot be run by coercion: they depend on staff having a firm, confident and humane approach that enables them to maintain close contact with prisoners without abrasive confrontation. (Home Office, 1984, para. 16)
>
> These relationships are central to the moral quality of prison life and decisive in shaping the climate of the prison (Liebling, 2011). Liebling et al., (1999) explain, "what 'goes on' in prisons goes on primarily through relationships" (p. 72) and that "relationships matter because they influence action. They frame, inform, constrain and facilitate staff and prisoner behaviour" (Liebling et al., 1999, p. 77). How they are affected by the circumstances of a dying prisoner is therefore highly relevant.

There is a certain inevitably to the existence of at least some form of relationship between prison officers, as Arnold (2016) argues: "as the two ever present groups within a prison, and those who have the most frequent contact, a relationship —whether good or bad — will exist in some form between uniformed staff and prisoners" (p. 267). Liebling et al. (1999) attempt a definition of 'relationship' in the context of the prison: "we mean (something like) sustained periods of interaction, including interaction of a non-rule enforcing — or rule-resisting — nature" (p. 72). What is less clear is what constitutes the appropriate relationship between staff and prisoners. It is recognised (Crawley, 2004; Liebling et al., 1999) that staff–prisoner relationships are complex. Liebling et al. (1999) suggest key characteristics of staff–prisoner relationships which continue to have currency in prison studies. They claim "there is a flow of interaction and dependence in two directions, although in the coercive environment of the prison, the relationship is invested with an unusual amount of power (the ability of one party to influence or determine the behaviour of another party)" (p. 71) but this power is mostly 'held in reserve'. The idea that prison officers underuse their power is reiterated in later work (Liebling, Price & Shefer, 2011) and the asymmetric nature of power inherent in the staff–prisoner relationship is reinforced by other scholars, (see Drake, 2008; Newell, 2002; Scott, 2008).

In Crewe's (2011) view, the prison service in England and Wales regards staff–prisoner relationships as central to ensuring decent, stable regimes and the rehabilitation of offenders. He argues these relationships are generally more positive in England and Wales than in other jurisdictions. Echoing this, Liebling et al. (2011) suggest in the British tradition of prison management, staff–prisoner relationships are the 'glue' holding the prison together. Similarly, Crawley (2004) finds in her study of the work of prison officers a consensus that control and order in the prison are best achieved through relationships. The influence of good relationships is such that Liebling et al. (2011) suggest "if officers treat prisoners fairly, prisoner will generally consider the prison regime to be fair as a whole" (p. 105).

The quality of relationships is evident in the terminology used by staff and prisoners towards each other. Throughout this book, those held in prison custody will be referred to as 'prisoners', or, since the prisoners in this research project were all male, by male pronouns. Coyle (2012) argues the terminology used in the context of prisons is often intended to soften reality, but is actually indicative of how people held in prison are regarded. He describes 'inmate', used in the late twentieth century as having medical overtones, and 'offender' as restricting understanding of all aspects of the person to one aspect of their behaviour. Instead, Coyle (2012) provides a strong case for the term 'prisoner' as the most appropriate, since it reflects the deprivation of liberty inherent in the punishment of imprisonment. The prisoners in one of the prisons studied for this book provide a further reason why 'prisoner' should be the term used. During the fieldwork, a poster in a busy area of the Centre in the LTHSE prison asked, "what would you like the prison to call you?" Plastic counters were provided to use to 'vote' in boxes labelled 'inmate', 'prisoner' or 'resident'. The results were 249 votes for 'prisoner', 229 for 'resident' and 62 for 'inmate'.

The Study

This book is based on data collected primarily in two prisons, one in the Long Term High Security Prisons Estate, and the other in a Local prison, accommodating sentenced and remanded prisoners. Data was also collected in the hospitals to which prisoners were transferred when healthcare services within these prisons could not meet their medical needs.

The Prisons

The use of two fieldwork sites was intended to benefit the research project by providing an opportunity for comparisons and contrasts (Fielding, 2001). The two fieldwork prisons were chosen based on their purposes and the characteristics of the prisoners they housed. Both prisons accommodated only male prisoners. Men typically constitute 95% of the prison population of England and Wales and in the twelve months to June 2022, 98.5% of the deaths from natural causes in prison custody (Ministry of Justice, 2022).

As part of the Long Term and High Security Prisons Group, one of the prisons studied (referred to in this book as the LTHSE prison) houses long-term prisoners, the vast majority of whom are serving more than 10 years (HMCIP, 2018a), including a large number of sex offenders. It has an average population of 740 men, typically in single occupancy cells, including Category A and High Risk Category A prisoners. It is on a city centre site, in a large, mostly Victorian structure, with an elegant clock tower, and four wings (A–D), each four storeys high, radiating from a central hub. Separate buildings house a healthcare centre, a segregation centre, which includes a Close Supervision Centre, and administrative functions. There are also several workshops where prisoners are employed in tasks such as braille translation, carpentry, recycling and manufacturing clothes. Others work in the prison kitchen or have tasks on the wing. Education classrooms and rehabilitation programmes are provided in centres attached to the main prison. This prison was of particular interest because it had prisoners employed as carers for their peers who were physically frail, terminally or seriously ill. An unannounced inspection by Her Majesty's Chief Inspector of Prisons, conducted during the fieldwork period, found "the prison was calm and had an atmosphere that spoke of good order, safety, security and decency" and described it as "an essentially respectful prison, with many examples of good relationships and interactions between staff and prisoners" (HMCIP, 2018a, p. 5).

By contrast, the second prison was chosen because it was a local prison, with a higher 'turnover' of male prisoners, including many on remand, housing up to 1,212 Category B prisoners. It is also a largely Victorian prison, built in 1847, situated not far from a city centre. It occupies a prominent site and has a foreboding, castellated gatehouse, at the time of the study used as offices. The original building, as with the other prison, had four wings, A–D, but additional residential units have been added to create a total of 667 cells, most of which contain bunk beds and are shared occupancy. Further buildings have been added resulting in a layout which is difficult to navigate. The prison (referred to in this book as the Category B prison) includes a 'first night unit' to accommodate and facilitate the induction of the large numbers of new prisoners arriving each day. It also has a Segregation Centre and a social care wing which includes provision to accommodate 17 prisoners in need of social care. During the period of fieldwork, Her Majesty's Chief Inspector of Prisons published a report on an earlier unannounced inspection which found it to be an unsafe prison where "levels of violence of all kinds were far too high" and to be "one of the most seriously overcrowded in the country" (HMCIP, 2018b, p. 5).

These prisons were also selected because they had experienced a relatively high number of deaths from natural causes amongst prisoners in the five years prior to the research. They both had some provision of health and social care within the prison which enabled the observation of the care of terminally and seriously ill prisoners within the establishment as well as at 'outside' hospitals. It was also of interest that they both occupied Victorian buildings, a common design of prison, identified as presenting particular challenges to the care of elderly (and by extension frail or dying) prisoners (Crawley, 2005b).

The Hospitals

The selection of hospitals within which research was conducted was based on information from the Governing Governors and Safer Custody Managers in each prison about where prisoners would be taken if requiring medical treatment beyond that available in the prisons. Two hospital trusts were identified but at the outset of the research it could not be estimated which hospitals would receive a seriously or terminally ill prisoner who was willing to participate in the fieldwork. In practice, four incidences of prisoners receiving in-patient treatment in public hospitals were observed.

Five Prisoners

Five prisoners feature strongly throughout this book, only one of whom I ever met. The circumstances of their death and dying, their characters, the friendships they had built in the prison, and the links between their family and prison staff meant their names recurred in my conversations with prisoners and prison staff. In this book, as with all other participants, they are referred to be pseudonyms.

Dean was a relatively young man, with a partner and young son, who had died more than three years before this study, whilst serving a short sentence in the Category B prison. He was diagnosed with cancer after he arrived in the prison and had asked to stay on the wing with his friends for as long as possible. He was transferred to the in-patient unit when he needed more pain management, and then to a local hospice, where he died.

Eddie was a well-liked life-sentenced prisoner in the LTHSE prison, whose terminal diagnosis coincided with the start of this study. He was unusual in this prison for being permitted to stay on the prison wing, at his request. He was supported by friends and prisoner-carers, and it was evident that prison staff changed their working practices to try to accommodate his needs. Eddie died during this study.

Iain died in hospital during my time collecting data, although we didn't meet. He was over 60, and had arrived in the Category B prison on remand. He received a terminal diagnosis between being convicted and sentenced. The family liaison officer who supported his wife, and the healthcare staff who cared for him in the prison, spoke about Iain, and he was well-liked by other prisoners in the healthcare centre.

Neil had died in the palliative care suite of the LTHSE prison seven months before I visited. He was serving a long sentence and had been transferred to the prison following a terminal diagnosis, in order to be nearer to his family. He stood out for staff and prisoners in this prison because his wife had been permitted to be with him overnight when his death was imminent.

William was an elderly man who died whilst on remand in the Category B prison. He spent all of his time in the prison on the healthcare wing, and was well-liked by the nursing staff, who were concerned that his dementia made him unaware of where he was.

Data Collection

Data for this book was collected using ethnographic methods, the principle strengths of which are that they can produce the rich data required for a study of this nature, and bring the researcher closer to understanding the social worlds of research participants. Ethnography includes a number of methods, and in this instance, participant observation, ethnographic conversations, document analysis and semi-structured interviews were established as most suitable for the research setting and likely research participants. This selection of methods also offered a degree of triangulation (Tashakkori & Teddlie, 2003) and enhanced the rigour of the data. Collecting data using a range of methods enabled comparisons to be made. For example, interactions and acts could be observed within the prison and then considered in light of other data collected from documentary analysis, or related to the information offered by participants in semi-structured interviews.

A total of 295 hours were spent in the fieldwork sites over 12 months. The degree to which I was a participant or an observer changed with the particular setting and varied over time. Participation was more difficult to achieve in the high security setting, where the ability to move freely on a prison wing was limited because prison officers wanted to be able to see where any visitors were for their own safety, but it was still possible. This is illustrated by a comment from one participant, when asked whether it was alright to stay on the prison wing after a death had occurred:

> To be honest, we don't notice you're here. You're part of the furniture, without wanting to be rude. (Fieldnote, LTHSE)
>
> My prolonged presence on the wing meant I was regarded by participants as part of their world; my presence was no longer noteworthy.

Data was also collected through semi-structured interviews. Fifteen interviews with staff were held, with an average duration of 56 minutes. Permission had been given to interview up to three prisoners employed as carers in the LTHSE prison. In practice, there were significantly fewer than expected prisoners with experience of this role, one of whom participated extensively in ethnographic conversations throughout the data collection. One semi-structured interview, lasting 90 minutes, was recorded with another prisoner-carer.

As Hammersley and Atkinson (2007) point out, many settings are 'self-documenting', especially government departments. Her Majesty's Prison and Probation Service (HMPPS) produces a range of documents prescribing the functioning of prisons as well as reporting on incidents, activities and conditions. There is no single document from HMPPS detailing the 'rules' relating to dying and deaths from natural causes in prison custody. Instead, the needs of prisoners dying of natural causes, the provisions for their care or suitable responses after a prisoner's death from natural causes are referred to across several relevant sources. These were reviewed as part of this research and included several Prison Service Instructions (PSIs) and Prison Service Orders (PSOs) as well as reports by the Prison and Probation Ombudsman (PPO), Her Majesty's Chief Inspector of Prisons and the Independent Monitoring Board for each fieldwork prison. In addition, Prison Rules (1999) and the ruling in R(Graham) vs Secretary of State for Justice (2007) were reviewed. These documents were selected because they direct the responses of prison staff towards terminally ill prisoners and specify the actions to be taken in relevant circumstances, including during treatment in outside hospitals and immediately following a death from natural causes. Collectively the documents demonstrate the underlying approaches taken by Her Majesty's Prison and Probation Service towards prisoners dying of natural causes. They set what Foucault (1991, p. 80) calls the "rational schema" of prisons.

Researching prisoners, who by the very nature of their imprisonment are vulnerable, raises a number of ethical issues, which are further compounded by the sensitivity of the subject matter and the ways death and dying are often regarded as taboo subjects. My own position as an 'insider' working as a chaplain in prisons elsewhere, also presented ethical challenges. These will be discussed in the appendix.

Outline of the Book

This book is structured into eight chapters. This first chapter establishes the need for this book, along with its aims and objectives. The remaining chapters present findings which illustrate what determines responses to dying prisoners, alongside the impact deaths from natural causes have on the prison regimes, culture and relationships. Essentially, what is being considered in these chapters is how prison changes death, and how death changes prison.

Imprisonment is conceptualised as more than being inside prison walls, in an austere indoor setting of locked gates and doors. Imprisonment also has a psychological dimension, the deprivations of imprisonment bringing their own pains at the end of a life in circumstances where experiences are largely governed by the rules of the prison service and by prison personnel. In this regard, prison is both tangible, the place of incarceration, but also intangible, the situation resulting from 'rules' or symbolically embodied by the escort chains or barred windows that serve as reminders of imprisonment. Discussions of the role of prison officers will feature throughout the book, since they "play an influential role in the lives of many inmates because of their direct and prolonged interaction" (Farkas, 2000, p. 431), but the role of other prison personnel will also be seen to be significant. This includes not just healthcare staff who may have direct contact with seriously or terminally ill prisoners but others such as chaplains, education workers or the governors whose authority determines many actions. A number of themes will reoccur, including stigma, autonomy, discretion, discipline and control. The focus throughout is on how participants are constructing their understandings of the situations they are experiencing, influenced by their social contexts, in this case the prison, but also their experiences outside of the prison. Differences arise between the two prisons studied which will be highlighted when relevant. These results are not just from the differing purposes of the two prisons, but also the different experiences of prisoners' deaths from natural causes.

Chapter 2 provides an overview of the carceral geography associated with these deaths. Particular attention will be paid to four locations: the prison wing; the prison healthcare centre; the palliative care suite and hospitals and hospices to which the dying prisoner may be transferred. Considering the four spaces in which dying and death in prison custody occur demonstrates how the spatial context of deaths in prison custody differs from those of other deaths and how they shape the possibilities for care. The 'myth' of compassionate release to die at home will be examined, along with the desire for a better setting. This chapter will conclude by explaining staff and prisoner expectations associated with the carceral geography of dying and the meanings they read into the location of a prisoner.

Chapter 3 explores the governance of mortality and location by analysing the wider influence of prison 'rules'. This chapter explores the determiners of location at the end of life in prison custody and the circumstances in which limited autonomy is afforded to the dying prisoner. It is in this context that the differing constructions of the dying prisoner, to be discussed in the following chapter, start to have practical effects on the experience of dying in prison custody.

Chapter 4 uses ethnographic data to demonstrate how staff and prisoners identify someone as dying. The primary concern of this chapter is to explore the influence of occupational culture on the preferred terminology used to describe the dying incarcerated individual: 'prisoner', 'patient' or 'person'. The impacts of these different constructions on priorities for how the dying individual is treated are analysed and the relevance of stigma, sympathy and the overriding security concerns of the prison are shown to be relevant.

The next chapter explores how care is expressed and experienced in prison at the end of life. Using research findings from the prison studied and existing typologies of care, it shows the importance of the work of prison staff in all roles in making death, as one described, 'as good as it could be'. The practical limitations placed on care in a prison setting are considered, along with the manner in which adjustments to prison regimes and rules are made, through the careful use of discretion. Decency, privacy and the importance of not dying alone will be explored.

In Chapter 6 attention turns to how end of life care is evaluated by those involved or observing its delivery. The contested nature of the principle of 'equivalence of care' is explored and consideration is given to more formal attempts to evaluate care, including investigations after a death in prison custody by the Prison and Probation Ombudsman. As part of understanding how staff evaluate their own performance, the idea of 'heroic care talk' will be introduced, as a means of understanding how experienced prison offices sometimes discuss providing care.

The final analytical chapter builds on understandings of care developed in the preceding chapters to explore how care is received (or not received) after a death from natural causes in prison custody by those affected, including prisoners' families, prison staff and other prisoners. In doing so, this chapter makes connections with the constructions of the dying prisoner considered in Chapter 4, and suggests ways in which the dead prisoner is constructed. The position of death within prison culture is discussed, drawing on research findings from the prisons studied which show the frequency with which deaths from natural causes occur in prison has reduced the taboo around the subject.

Throughout the book, deaths from natural causes in prison custody are shown to soften the usual distinctions, both tangible and intangible, between what is expected or not expected, permitted or not permitted, in the prison. The conclusion will bring these threads together and consider what advances or inhibits these changes, and how deaths from natural causes impact on prison regimes, culture and relationships. Finally, it will consider suitable policy changes in light of the unique research data presented in this book.

References

Aday, R. (2006). Aging prisoners' concerns toward dying in prison. *OMEGA Journal of Death and Dying, 52*(3), 199–216.

Aday, R., & Wahidin, A. (2016). Older prisoners' experiences of death, dying and grief behind bars. *The Howard Journal of Crime and Justice, 55*(3), 312–327. https://doi.org/10.1111/hojo.12172

Ambitions for Palliative and End of Life Care Partnership. (2018). *Dying well in Custody Charter*. Ambitions for Palliative and End of Life Care Partnership, UK. http://endoflifecareambitions.org.uk/tag/prisons

Arnold, H. (2016). The prison officer. In Y. Jewkes, B. Crewe & J. Bennett (Eds.), *Handbook on prisons*. (2nd ed., pp. 265–284). Routledge.

Arnold, H., Liebling, A., & Tait, S. (2007). Prison officers and prison culture. In Y. Jewkes (Ed.), *Handbook on prisons* (pp. 471–495). Willan.

Bolger, M. (2004). Offenders. In D. Oliviere & B. Monroe (Eds.), *Death, dying and social differences* (pp. 133–148). Oxford University Press.

Burles, M. C., Peternelj-Taylor, C. A., & Holtslander, L. (2016). A 'good death' for all?: Examining issues for palliative care in correctional settings. *Mortality, 21*(2), 93–111. https://doi.org/10.1080/13576275.2015.1098602

Carlton, B., & Sim, J. (2018). Death in sites of state confinement: A continuum of routine violence and terror. In S. Read, S. Santatzoglou, & A. Wrigley (Eds.), *Loss, dying and bereavement in the criminal justice system* (pp. 54–63). Routledge.

Clemmer, D. (1958). *The prison community*. Holt, Rinehart & Winston.

Cohen, S. & Taylor, L. (1972). *Psychological survival: the experience of long-term imprisonment* (2nd ed.). Penguin Books.

Coyle, A. (2012). Forward. In B. Crewe & J. Bennett (Eds.), *The prisoner* (pp xiii–xvii). Routledge.

Craig, R. (2002). Easing the passage: The chaplain's view of prison hospice. *Journal of Correctional Healthcare, 9*(2), 159–168. https://doi.org/10.1177/107834580200900207

Crawley, E. (2004). *Doing prison work: the public and private lives of prison officers*. Willan.

Crawley, E. (2005a). Surviving the prison experience: Imprisonment and elderly men. *Prison Service Journal, 160*, 3–8.

Crawley, E. (2005b). Institutional thoughtlessness in prisons and its impacts on the day-to-day prison lives of elderly men. *Journal of Contemporary Criminal Justice, 21*(4), 350–363. https://doi.org/10.1177/1043986205282018

Crawley, E., & Sparks, R. (2005). Older men in prison: Surviving, coping and identity. In A. Liebling & S. Maruna (Eds.), *The effects of imprisonment* (pp. 343–365). Routledge.

Crewe, B. (2009). *The prisoner society: Power, adaption, and social life in an English prison*. Oxford University Press.

Crewe, B. (2011). Soft power in prison: Implications for staff–prisoner relationships, liberty and legitimacy. *European Journal of Criminology, 8*(6), 455–468. https://doi.org/10.1177/1477370811413805

Crighton, D. (2002). Suicide in prisons: A critique of UK research. In G. Towl, L. Snow, & M. McHugh (Eds.), *Suicide in prisons* (pp. 26–47). Blackwell.

Davies, M., Rolewicz, L., Schlepper, L. & Fagunwa, F. (2020). *Locked out? Prisoners' use of hospital care*. Nuffield Trust.

Dawes, J. (2002). Dying with dignity: Prisoners and terminal illness. *Illness, Crisis & Loss, 10*(3), 188–203. https://doi.org/10.1177/105413730201000 3002

Dawes, J. (2009). Ageing prisoners: Issues for social work. *Australian Social Work, 62*(2), 258–271. https://doi.org/10.1080/03124070902803475
Dooley, E. (1990). Unnatural deaths in prison. *British Journal of Criminology, 30*(2), 229–234. https://doi.org/10.1093/oxfordjournals.bjc.a047991
Drake, D. H. (2008). Staff and order in prison. In J. Bennett, B. Crewe, & A. Wahidin (Eds.), *Understanding prison staff* (pp. 153–216). Willan.
Farkas, M. A. (2000). A typology of correctional officers. *International Journal of Offender Therapy and Comparative Criminology, 44*(4), 431–449. https://doi.org/10.1177/0306624X00444003
Fielding, N. (2001). Ethnography. In N. Gilbert (Ed.), *Researching social life* (pp. 145–163). Sage.
Foucault, M. (1991). Questions of Methods. In G. Burchell, C. Gordon, & P. Miller (Eds.), *The Foucault effect: Studies in governmentality* (pp. 73–86). University of Chicago Press.
Garton Grimwood, G. (2015). *Categorisation of prisoners in the UK*. House of Commons Library.
Giallombardo, R. (1966). *Society of women: a study of a women's prison.* John Wiley and sons.
Girling, E., & Seal, L. (2016). Introduction: The deathscapes of incarceration. *The Howard Journal of Crime and Justice, 55*(3), 267–277. https://doi.org/10.1111/hojo.12169
Glamser, F., & Cabana, D. (2003). Dying in a total institution. In C. D. Bryant (Ed.), *Handbook of death and dying* (pp. 495–550). Sage Publications.
Glaser, B. & Strauss, A. (1968). *Time for dying*. Aldine Publishing Company.
Hammersley, M. (2009). Against the ethicists: On the evils of ethical regulation. *International Journal of Social Research Methodology, 12*(3), 211–225. https://doi.org/10.1080/13645570802170288
Hammersley, M., & Atkinson, P. (2007). Ethnography: Principles in practice. (3rd ed.). Routledge.
Handtke, V., & Wangmo, T. (2014). Ageing prisoners' views on death and dying: Contemplating end of life in prison. *Bioethical Inquiry, 11*, 373–386. https://doi.org/10.1007/s11673-014-9548-x
Hay, W., & Sparks, R. (1991). What is a prison officer? *Prison Service Journal, 83*(3), 2–7.
Health and Social Care Committee. (2018). *Prison Health*. (HC 983, Session 2017–19).
Her Majesty's Inspectorate of Prisons. (1993). *Doing time or using time. Report of a review by HM Chief Inspector of Prisons for England and Wales of regimes*

in Prison Service establishments in England and Wales. CM 2128. UK Parliamentary Papers. https://parlipapers.proquest.com/parlipapers/docview/t70.d75.1992-090766?accountid=15181

Hicks, A. M. (2012). Learning to watch out: Prison chaplains as risk managers. *Journal of Contemporary Ethnography, 41*(6), 636–667. https://doi.org/10.1177/0891241612452139

House of Lords, Written answer HL3278. (January 5, 2017).

House of Lords, Written answer HL2097. (October 27, 2017).

House of Lords written question HL10422. (November 17, 2020).

HM Chief Inspector of Prisons. (2018a). *Report on an unannounced inspection of HMP Wakefield by HM Chief Inspector of Prisons.* HM Chief Inspector of Prisons, UK. https://www.justiceinspectorates.gov.uk/hmiprisons/wp-content/uploads/sites/4/2018a/10/Wakefield-Web-2018a.pdf

HM Chief Inspector of Prisons. (2018b). *Report on an unannounced inspection of HMP Leeds by HM Chief Inspector of Prisons.* HM Chief Inspector of Prisons, UK. https://www.justiceinspectorates.gov.uk/hmiprisons/wp-content/uploads/sites/4/2018b/03/HMP-Leeds-Web-2017.pdf

HMSO. (1984). *Managing the long-term prison system: The report of the control review committee*. HMSO.

Irwin, J. (1970). *The Felon*. Prentice-Hall.

Irwin, J., & Cressey, D. (1962). Thieves, convicts and inmate culture. *Social Problems, 10*(2), 142–153.

Jenkins, D. (1993, January). *Doing time or using time: Report of a review by Her Majesty's Chief Inspector of Prisons for England and Wales of regimes in Prison Service establishments in England and Wales*. Presented to Parliament by the Secretary of State for the Home Department by Command of Her Majesty. H.M.S.O.

Leggett, K. (2002). Excellent organisations have strong cultures. *Prison Service Journal, 139*, 22–25.

Liebling, A. (1999). Prison suicide and prisoner coping. *Crime and Justice, 26*, 283–359. https://doi.org/10.1086/449299

Liebling, A. (2008). Why prison staff culture matters. In J. Byrne, D. Hummer, & F. S. Taxman (Eds.), *The culture of prison violence* (pp. 105–122). Allyn and Bacon.

Liebling, A. (2011). Moral performance, inhuman and degrading treatment and prison pain. *Punishment & Society, 13*(5), 530–550. https://doi.org/10.1177/1462474511422159

Liebling, A. (2017). The meaning of ending life in prison. *Journal of Correctional Health Care, 23*(1), 20–31. https://doi.org/10.1177/1078345816685070

Liebling, A., & Ludlow, A. (2016). Suicide, distress and the quality of life. In Y. Jewkes, B. Crewe, & J. Bennett (Eds.), *Handbook on prisons* (pp. 224–245). Routledge.

Liebling, A., Price, D., & Elliot, C. (1999). Appreciative inquiry and relationships in prison. *Punishment and Society, 1*(1), 71–98. https://doi.org/10.1177/14624749922227711

Liebling, A., Price, D. & Shefer, G. (2011). *The prison officer* (2nd ed). Willan.

Ministry of Justice. (2017). *Safety in custody quarterly: Update to December 2017.* Ministry of Justice. https://www.gov.uk/government/statistics/safety-in-custody-quarterly-update-to-december-2017

Ministry of Justice. (2018). *Safety in custody quarterly: Update to December 2018.* Ministry of Justice. https://www.gov.uk/government/statistics/safety-in-custody-quarterly-update-to-december-2018

Ministry of Justice. (2021a). *Prison population projections 2021 to 2026*. Ministry of Justice.

Ministry of Justice. (2021b). *Safety in custody quarterly: Quarterly update to December 2021.* Ministry of Justice. https://www.gov.uk/government/statistics/safety-in-custody-quarterly-update-to-december-2021b

Ministry of Justice. (2022). *Safety in custody quarterly: Update to March 2022.* Ministry of Justice. https://www.gov.uk/government/statistics/safety-in-custody-quarterly-update-to-march-2022

National Palliative and End of Life Care Partnership. (2015). *Ambitions for palliative and end of life care: A national framework for local action 2015–2020.* National Palliative and End of Life Care Partnership. https://endoflifecareambitions.org.uk/wp-content/uploads/2015/09/Ambitions-for-Palliative-and-End-of-Life-Care.pdf

Newell, T. (2002). The prison officer as moral agent. *Prison Service Journal, 139*, 29–36.

Nylander, P. -Å., Lindberg, O., & Bruhn, A. (2011). Emotional labour and emotional strain among Swedish prison officers. *European Journal of Criminology, 8*(6), 469–483. https://doi.org/10.1177/1477370811413806

Prison Reform Trust. (2022). *Bromley briefings prison factfile winter 2022.* Prison Reform Trust

Rodriguez, D. (2006). *Domestic war zones and the extremities of power: Conceptualising the US prison regime.* University of Minnesota Press.

Sattar, G. (2003). The deaths of offenders in England and Wales. *Crisis, 24*(1), 17–23. https://doi.org/10.1027//0227-5910.24.1.17

Schaefer, I., DiGiacomo, M., Heneka, N., Panozzo, S., Luckett, T., & Phillips, J.L. (2022). Palliative care needs and experiences of people in prison: A systematic review and meta-synthesis. *Palliative medicine.*, 36 (3), 443–461. https://doi.org/10.1177/02692163211068278

Scott, D. (2008). Creating ghosts in the penal machine: Prison officer occupational morality and the techniques of denial. In J. Bennett, B. Crewe, & A. Wahidin (Eds.), *Understanding prison staff* (pp. 168–218). Willan.

Sykes, G. M. (1958). *Society of captives: A study of a maximum security prison.* Princeton University Press.

Tashakkori, A. & Teddlie, C. (2003). *Handbook of mixed methods in social & behavioral research.* Sage.

Turner, M., Payne, S., & Barbarachild, Z. (2011). Care or custody? An evaluation of palliative care in prisons in North West England. *Palliative Medicine, 25*(4), 370–377. https://doi.org/10.1177/0269216310393058

Visser, R. C. (2021). Dying in the margins: A literature review on end of life in English prisons. *Religions., 12*(6), 413.

Wood, F. J. (2007). The challenge of providing palliative care to terminally ill prison inmates in the UK. *International Journal of Palliative Nursing,* 13(3), 131–135. https://doi.org/10.12968/ijpn.2007.13.3.23275

2

The Carceral Geography of Death and Dying in Prison Custody

To be in prison is to be in a place apart, separated from community and family, a place which both looks different to other places and is subject to different social and actual rules. Closed prisons are markedly different physical spaces where the architecture and design features are characteristically those of incarceration. Within the prison, dying prisoners may be further segregated. Experiences within prison, including dying, are inevitably heavily marked by the peculiarities of the physical location. Carceral geography, defined as "geographical engagement with the spaces, practices and experiences of confinement" (Royal Geographical Society, 2018), offers new ways to consider the emplaced and embodied experience of imprisonment. Originating as a part of human geography, the concept of carceral geography, as applied by social scientists such as Jewkes and Moran to the punitive turn within Western societies, suggests the physical environments of prisons both reflect policy and mould experiences of incarceration (Baer & Ravneberg, 2008; Jewkes & Moran, 2017; Jewkes et al., 2017; Moran, 2015; Moran et al., 2016).

To understand how prison changes the experience of dying, it is necessary to start by considering the physical environment—the carceral geography—surrounding death. Schaefer et al. (2022), in a systemic

C. Robinson, *Dying in Prison*, Palgrave Studies in Prisons and Penology, https://doi.org/10.1007/978-3-031-27103-8_2

literature review, found that almost every aspect of prisoners' experiences of palliative care was affected by the physical environment of the prison. Staff and prisoners within the prisons in this study associated four locations with death and dying. Each of these locations will be considered in turn: the prison wing, the prison healthcare centre, the palliative care suite within this if there was one (as in the LTHSE prison), and the hospital outside of the prison. In the Category B prison, prisoners might also be located in a hospice, in similar physical circumstances to being in hospital, but again still in prison custody. These are seen to be highly segmented spaces. Carceral geography influences responses to prisoners dying from natural causes and these deaths in turn impact on places and spaces.

The location of a prisoner between these four spaces might change during the course of the dying trajectory, particularly as they passed through what Glaser and Strauss (1968) refer to as 'transitional statuses' and 'critical junctures'. Understandings of a prisoner's place in the 'dying trajectory' (Glaser & Strauss, 1968) will be seen to be derived from their location, with staff and prisoners making assumptions based on changes to a dying prisoner's physical location.

Having discussed the four locations within prison custody relevant to the dying prisoner, a fifth, rarely used 'space', compassionate release, will be considered. As will be seen, although compassionate release remains a possibility within the prison rules, prisoners and prison staff did not expect it to be granted to terminally ill prisoners. As a result, dying prisoners remain imprisoned, separated from the wider community. It is important to explore the reasons why the physical locations associated with compassionate release, of going 'home', or to a hospital, hospice or care home without the trappings of prison custody, were inaccessible to most dying prisoners.

The Physical Environment of the Prison Wing

The vast majority of prisoners in both prisons studied were accommodated in cells on prison wings. Other locations are relevant to some prisoners in certain circumstances, such as illness, for their own protection or when segregated as further punishment or to protect others, but the prison wing is the main unit of accommodation for prisoners and a key component of prison architecture. As Jewkes and Moran (2017) argue, the architecture of prisons is a physical expression of the penal philosophy of their time. Built largely in the Victorian radial style, both the prisons studied are imposing stark buildings full of long landings, narrow stairs, high ceilings, hard surfaces, artificial lighting and small cells. They have inherited their architecture from an earlier time, but it continues to shape life on the prison wing. The two prisons studied are similar in design to HMP Pentonville, described by Jewkes and Moran (2017) as giving "full expression to the Victorian obsession with discipline, certainty, and systematic uniformity" (p. 546) and reflecting the new objectives of imprisonment at the time—deterrence and repression. As city centre prisons, they were built "as looming warnings of the consequences of crime" (Crewe, 2009, p. 1) and although newer buildings have been added on both sites, they retain an aesthetic which reflects their Victorian origins. The LTHSE prison studied, and to a lesser extent the Category B prison, were sites marked by very obvious security features: strong high walls, towering wire fences, barbed wire, patrol dogs and surveillance cameras, which Jewkes and Moran (2017) suggest reflects the emphasis of the new penology on security and containment.

Turner and Peacock (2017) argue that inside the prison, the design, layout and facilities of prisons are intended for younger, healthier prisoners and that this adversely affects what is possible in terms of care for older or frailer prisoners. They identify a number of practical difficulties arising from the prison setting including cells too small for hospital beds. In keeping with this, cells on the Victorian-era wings in each of the prisons studied were small and cramped, with limited facilities. At both prisons there were in-cell toilets, as is normal in prisons in England and Wales, but only communal shower facilities, with small screens to maintain privacy. Thick pipes running under the cell windows provided the heating, and were put to a variety of uses, including drying laundry, but the temperature could not be controlled by the cell occupant and some landings were colder than others. In all cells, there was a call bell by the door to summon help. Bedding was provided by the prison but often regarded as too thin and inadequate to provide warmth (Fieldnotes, LTHSE).

Adaptions were made to the physical environment of the wings in the LTHSE prison to try to meet the needs of prisoners who were unwell, frail or disabled. Lifts had been added to two wings, although they were often out of order for long periods of time (Fieldnotes, LTHSE). As is usual in high security prisons, cells were single occupancy. Some, nearer the Cleaner's Office, had deliberately lowered doorsteps. These cells often accommodated prisoners with mobility issues who would benefit from the lack of a doorstep, as well as those who were vulnerable for other reasons and who staff wanted to be able to watch more closely. The need for these cells often exceeded their supply. Less structural changes were also made to the physical environment. The prisoners who ran the stores and tried to ensure elderly and frail prisoners got extra mattresses and blankets (Fieldnote, LTHSE). In one instance a terminally ill prisoner, Eddie, was accommodated on the wing in the LTHSE prison. A door-bell was placed near his bed, with a receiver in the Cleaner's Office to alert officers, so he would not need to undertake the struggle to reach the normal cell bell to call for assistance. This had little impact on the regime; officers reported that it only rang when a colleague checked it worked each morning (Fieldnote, LTHSE). More significant was the way in which the presence of a terminally ill prisoner on the wing could change usual practices for locking and unlocking cell doors. In the case of Eddie, officers on the wing left his cell door unlocked for lengthy periods, acknowledging this was a result of his diagnosis and because it would facilitate his care. In this way, his condition materially altered his immediate physical environment, although by this time he was too frail to leave his cell unassisted, even when the door was unlocked.

In the Category B prison, the cells were double occupancy. On F wing, where a number of elderly or disabled prisoners were accommodated, the frailer prisoners tended to occupy the lower bunk. This wing was three landings high, with a central corridor and cell doors the length of each landing. The ground floor landing was known as the '3s':

> Most of the practicalities — servery, laundry, PID desk, phones — are on the 3s. The CM who first showed be round said that he was supposed to put prisoners on Basic on the 3s, so they were less likely to jump on the netting —the metal mesh that covers the open spaces between landings. In practice, he needs to put the elderly, wheelchair users on the 3s so they can access what they need. There are two sets of stairs on the wing; one goes straight up from the middle of the landing, the other is at the end of the landing and has a right-angle bend. There is no lift. (Fieldnote, Category B)

Staff on this wing were thus trying to balance the needs of elderly, frail and disabled prisoners with those who were vulnerable in other ways or likely to present other challenges, but their options were limited by the physical environment. On this wing there were regularly three or four prisoners using wheelchairs, and I witnessed two visually impaired prisoners using white canes to get around (Fieldnotes, Category B). One prisoner spoke about his concerns for the wheelchair users, who had to leave their chairs on the landing outside their cells, a practice observed elsewhere by Mann (2012) who suggests it may be a breach of the Disability Discrimination Act. The prisoner said he had asked the officers if the cell doors could be widened, but had been told the walls were load-bearing and no adjustments could be made (Fieldnote, Category B). During the research, F wing in this prison did acquire a lift to allow less mobile prisoners to access the exercise yard, although there was still no lift between landings (Fieldnote, Category B).

The physical environments of the prison wings in both prisons studied thus presented several challenges to the elderly, frail or disabled prisoners accommodated there. Whilst some adaptions were made, such as lowering doorsteps or introducing cell bells nearer to the bed, prison officers and prisoners were aware of the limitations of the physical environment. Whilst often reflecting social care needs, the challenges witnessed are indicative too of the difficulties faced by prisoners who were nearing the end of life on the wings. The limitations of the physical environment of the prison wing resulted from an earlier conception of the purpose and population of a prison which found its manifestation in narrow landings, steep metal stairs, cramped cells and narrow doorsteps.

This was one of the factors contributing to the expectation, discussed below with regard to the spatial ordering of dying prisoners, that people with such needs would be relocated to the prison healthcare centre.

Prison Healthcare Centres

The physical environments of the healthcare centre in the LTHSE prison and of H3 in the Category B prison, used for prisoners with social, physical and mental health needs, reflected many of the characteristics of the wider prison environment. In both areas, as in the prisons where they were located, windows were barred and in the LTHSE prison they were also covered by wire grilles (Fieldnote, LTHSE). There were locked doors and gates throughout the healthcare centres in the same styles as elsewhere in the prison. However, there were some differences. Whilst retaining the characteristics of a prison, both the LTHSE healthcare centre and H3 in the Category B prison were physically and symbolically spaces apart from the other areas where prisoners were accommodated. Cells in these spaces were single occupancy, something very rare on the wings at the Category B prison and slightly bigger (in the case of some rooms in the LTHSE prison, originally built as wards, considerable bigger) (Fieldnote, LTHSE). Whilst on the wings landings were used for association, in contrast, each healthcare centre had a 'dayroom', where some prisoners spent their time. Attempts had been made to enhance these and other communal spaces with pictures on the walls.

In the Category B prison, the apartness of H3 was most noticeable in the way it operated a slightly different regime to the rest of the prison, responding to the perceived needs of the prisoners. It was described by staff as more relaxed and characterised by mutual respect between staff and prisoners (Interview 3, Category B). There were regular games of dominoes, often involving an officer who would patiently remind prisoners when it was their turn or try to catch the eye of the score-keeper if he had forgotten to add on points (Fieldnote, Category B). Nowhere else were staff observed playing games with prisoners. H3 was often conceptualised by staff as apart from the prison. Some of the nursing staff and a prison officer who spent considerable time in H3 referred to the other areas of the prison as 'the jail', or as 'downstairs' (Interviews 2 and 3, Category B). H3 was also the only place in the prison where those convicted of sex offences and other prisoners mixed (Interview 3, Category B). It was significant that one of the officers regularly working in H3 expressed a wish to differentiate the dayroom from a hospital institution, saying the murals had been put on the walls "because it's too clinical for me up here". Whilst he felt the need to avoid H3 feeling like a hospital, he did not seek to make it different from the prison (Interview 3, Category B). It may be he felt this was neither needed nor desirable.

It could be argued H3 was a 'free place' as suggested by Goffman (1961), meaning a geographical location associated with more licence for prisoners. Goffman describes these as places with a notably lower population density, characterised by a sense of peace, as H3 was, "physical spaces in which ordinary levels of surveillance and restriction were markedly reduced" (1961, p. 205). However, Goffman argues staff "did not know of the existence of these places, or knew but either stayed away or tacitly relinquished their authority when they entered them" (1961, p. 205). This was clearly not the case in H3 at the Category B prison and certainly not in the LTHSE prison's healthcare centre, which will be discussed in more detail below. Despite the regime on H3 being described as more relaxed, there were still obvious restrictions on prisoners' movement and access to activities. The physical environment was clearly marked as a prison. In the dayroom itself, there were notices reminding prisoners of their status, including posters for Veterans in Custody and notices to have recorded on C-Nomis (the database of the prison population) if they were a traveller or gypsy (Fieldnote, Category B).

The situation is more complicated than Goffman's outline. Crewe et al. (2013) suggest spaces such as chaplaincy or education classes within a prison can be 'emotion zones' where deviations from the usual 'feeling rules' of a prison can occur and which provide temporary relief from the realities of the wing. They argue these intermediate zones needed to be cultivated, usually be staff, in order to reflect a different construction of the prisoner. This seemed to be the case in H3 in particular. Far from staff being unaware of the differences in these spaces, the physical environment of H3 was marked by attempts by officers and healthcare staff to reduce the restrictions on prisoners. They were responding to the serious or terminal illnesses of prisoners accommodated here, arising from the different requirements and perceived risks of a population with pronounced social care needs. It is useful to think of H3 as a place where the boundary between 'inside' and 'outside' became slightly less distinct (Baer & Ravneberg, 2008). The space retained an institutional feel (Fieldnotes, Category B) but in subtle and sometimes shifting ways differed from other areas of the prison.

At the LTHSE prison, the healthcare centre was also a place apart, but not in the same way. It was physically apart, occupying a separate, more recent building not connected to the main prison, but the regime operating there differed very little from the main prison. This physical distance from the main accommodation wings was equated by prisoners to a social distance (Fieldnote, LTHSE). Being a resident in the healthcare centre was seen as an isolating experience. Because of its location, in order to access the healthcare centre, prisoners had to be accompanied by a member of staff out of the main building, across the yard and through a locked gate in a tall wire fence. Although staff said they would try to get a prisoner's friends over to see him, there were problems with this in practice including inadequate staffing levels, especially if the friends were Category A prisoners and needed additional escorts (Fieldnote, LTHSE). Chaplains explained their daily visits to the building as being because prisoners there were "isolated from the main prison", (Fieldnote, LTHSE) reinforcing the sense that healthcare was a place apart. In contrast to the Category B prison, at the LTHSE prison there was very little interaction between officers and prisoners in the healthcare centre, with the exception of the prisoner who worked as an orderly. The in-patient prisoners rarely acknowledged the presence of anyone else (Fieldnote, LTHSE). Here there was a notice saying "Offenders are not to leave the dayroom without first seeking permission from a member of staff", (Fieldnote, LTHSE) with the underlining seemingly adding emphasis to the status of the individual. At this prison, prisoners who had previously spent time or visited the healthcare centre described it as depressing and unclean (Fieldnote, LTHSE). Healthcare staff were aware of this reputation (Interview 12, LTHSE). The current and historic presence of terminally ill prisoners in the healthcare centre in this prison did not seem to have impacted on the regime, culture or relationships of the centre in the same way as the social care needs of prisoners in H3 in the Category B prison, at least as far as prison officers were concerned.

Prison healthcare centres, the second locations associated with terminally ill prisoners, were thus spaces apart from the main prison, differing in noticeable ways from the prison wings discussed above. The sense of apartness was stronger in the Category B prison than in the LTHSE prison, and illustrated by changes in the décor and differences in the relationships between prison officers and prisoners. At the LTHSE prison, the physical difference between the healthcare centre and the wings was equated to a social distance, but the regime differed only very slightly. Healthcare centres were not 'free places' (Goffman, 1961) but instead more akin to 'emotion zones' (Crewe et al., 2013) where staff cultivated an intermediate zone where different feeling rules could apply, or perhaps in the case of H3, spaces where the boundary between 'inside' and 'outside' the prison could blur very slightly (Baer & Ravneberg, 2008).

Prison Palliative Care Suites

Prison palliative care suites are not common. Turner et al. (2021) found that of eight countries surveyed, only England and Wales had any palliative care suites in prison, and the exact number was not publicly available. Of the two prisons visited, only the LTHSE prison had a designated palliative care suite. Senior healthcare staff at the Category B prison had used a large room at one end of H3 for this purpose and had recently been given permission to adapt it for more permanent use as a palliative care suite. The rooms used as palliative care suites had a very practical advantage over other cells in the healthcare centres. Typically, cells had solid doors, with flaps on the outside at approximately chest height that could be opened either downwards or sidewards in order to see the prisoner inside. At times during the day and night, the prison regime required these doors would be locked, but where there was also a metal gate across the door, as in the rooms selected for the palliative care suites, the gate could be locked instead and the door left open. This made it easier for nursing staff to do visual checks on the occupant and enabled them to hand over medication without the considerable inconvenience of getting a door unlocked whilst the prison was in patrol state. In both prisons, there was a willingness to leave the door of the palliative care suite open when death was closed, even overnight, in marked contrast to what was normal in the prison environment.

Healthcare staff in the Category B prison felt the room they had available was unsuitable without further development. They had had to make their case to prison governors since the room was also in demand for use with other groups of prisoners and had emphasised adapting the room would not be expensive. It would not be a luxurious space (Interview 1, Category B). In the LTHSE prison, a project to redecorate the palliative care suite began at about the same time as the fieldwork, with prisoners planning and creating new soft furnishings and artworks intended to improve the appearance of the space. Making the palliative care suite different from the prison environment was an important motivation for the healthcare staff at both prisons. The creation of these new spaces was a significant way in which deaths from natural causes had changed the fabric of the prison. Part of creating and trying to improve the appearance of the palliative care suites was an attempt to make the physical environment around the dying prisoner less symbolic of prison, to make it less 'inside':

> So, I think as well, when we get this suite decorated, there's so many great things happening, that will be so much nicer. You'll forget that you've got these bars around you and it will just be "this is a proper hospice". I'm looking forward to that. (Interview 1, LTHSE)
>
> For this nurse, "a proper hospice" environment was better suited as place to die than the prison, and the redecoration of the palliative care suite provided an opportunity to envision the dying individual in a setting which better matched her professional expectations.

At the LTHSE prison, nursing staff knew prisoners referred to the palliative care suite as 'death's waiting room' or the 'departure lounge' and wanted to counter this reputation (Fieldnote, LTHSE). Prisoners working in the art group within the prison's education department created pictures, installations and soft furnishings for the suite. The group visited the existing palliative care suite, describing it as "cold and dirty", "empty", "clinical" and "ugly". Those who had spent some time there said it was "drab". Reflecting on what they would want for a dying prisoner and his family, the group chose the theme of a Japanese garden, wanting to create somewhere "calm and comfortable", "homely, warm, safe" and "pleasant" (Fieldnote, LTHSE). A fieldnote at the conclusion of the project describes the room, renamed as the 'Lilypad' to bring together the ideas of a garden and a 'pad' or prison cell:

> It feels notably softer and more welcoming that my last visit. The most striking thing is the bed, with a shiny grey and white striped single duvet cover and a cushion with a matching background print overprinted with a colourful lotus flower. Two further cushions also stand out — the bamboo striped one and a plainer grey one — on two blue high-backed chairs. Whilst the chairs look institutional, the cushions look welcoming. There are also curtains — cream and billowing in the wind — at both windows. The soft furnishings stand out. They are unexpected, less institutional than I'd expect. The colours are subtle, but colours all the same. (Fieldnote, LTHSE)
>
> In the Category B prison, soft furnishings were also regarded as important in creating the transformation: At the moment it's a very clinical room, it's just got a bed in, the aerial for the telly is appalling so it's not, it's not how it could be... so we're going to get some nice furnishings stuff like that, and we're going to make hopefully a really good palliative care suite. (Interview 10, Category B)

The redecorated palliative care suite in the LTHSE prison served to highlight the harshness and monotony of the usual prison environment. Baer and Ravneberg (2008) highlight the role furniture can play in indicating 'inside' and 'outside'. Soft furnishings were a rarity in the prison setting and their presence in the palliative care suite was both a surprise and a direct physical response to concerns about prisoners who are dying and their families. They introduced a representational meaning which feels very alien from what is normally experienced in the prison. The effect the cushions had on one of the prisoners involved in the project at the LTHSE prison was striking. He kept picking up a cushion, and squeezing it, the softness seeming to be unusual (Fieldnote, LTHSE).

The same prisoner recounted finding softness on a visit to an outside hospital, placing a value on material softness which points to its rarity in the life of a long-term prisoner:

> And they had these chairs that were so comfortable, you kinda sank back into them and could really chill. That's how he imagines heaven, not the thin prison mattresses. As he talks about the chairs, he leans back and closes his eyes. (Fieldnote, LTHSE)

Burles et al. (2016) suggest prison regimes are at odds with the concept of a good death, which is defined as characterised by comfort, control and closure. Here it is the comfort that is being emphasised, the importance of a physical softness which is antithetical to prison life and to the punitive harshness of prison architecture and design. Some prisoners could find this unsettling. One, having seen the completed palliative care suite in the LTHSE prison said: "luxury items like these are not what someone wants who's dying in the hostile environments of prison" (Fieldnote, LTHSE). Instinctively, he seemed to be aware of the disruptive symbolic role of the soft furnishings which had been added to the palliative care suite, hinting at a more luxurious place, softer than the starkness of prison.

Nursing staff were also affected themselves by the physical environment, with one nurse saying when the suite redecoration was finished: "that will be nice for us, because it will be that proper hospice environment, so we can switch off" (Interview 12, LTHSE). She talked about 'switching' off several times, suggesting this was the technique needed to help her nurse prisoners as she wanted to, not overly aware of the reasons why they were in prison or thinking of them exclusively as prisoners. She identified that her experience of the physical environment in which prisoners are dying, when it is changed to look less like a prison, will assist her in her construction of the prisoner as a patient.

The third location associated with dying and deaths from natural causes in the prison, the palliative care suite, thus demonstrates a deliberate effort to alter the physical environment, to introduce elements symbolically differentiating it from the prison. These efforts are motivated by concerns for the dying prisoner and their family. The differences in the physical environment of the palliative care suites have practical relevance, such as facilitating medical care by leaving doors unlocked. However, what is most striking is the psychological impact of introducing soft furnishings into the space, highlighting the absence of softness from the usual environments of the prison, including the prison wing and the prison healthcare centres more generally.

Hospitals and Hospices

Prisoners could be accommodated on the prison wing, in the prison healthcare centre or in a palliative care suite within the prison, but when seriously or terminally ill prisoners required medical treatment beyond what was available within the prison, they were transferred to outside NHS facilities. In the case of the Category B prison, there were also occasions when a terminally ill prisoner had been transferred to a local hospice as they neared the end of life (Interviews 1, 2, 3 and 10, Category B). However, when medical conditions required prisoners to be taken to a hospital or hospice outside of the prison, they would still not be dying in the same environment as other people. In these circumstances, the prisoner remained in the custody of the prison, and although the hospital or hospice settings were not carceral, visible signs of the prison were transported into the hospital with them. Known by the de-personalising term of a 'bedwatch', the accompaniment of the prisoner by prison officers brought into the hospital the trappings of incarceration, including prison uniforms, prison equipment and often the physical restraints of handcuffs or an escort chain. In this respect, the requirements of their ongoing imprisonment impinged on the physical environment of the hospital bedside and whilst the prisoner was materially outside the prison they were simultaneously representationally inside. This can be understood as another way in which the 'inside' and 'outside' (Baer & Ravneberg, 2008) of prison become entangled.

As part of the fieldwork, four 'bedwatches' were observed. One of these was on a shared ward, with the curtain permanently closed around the bed. The others were in individual side rooms, an arrangement which officers and governors said they preferred (Fieldnote, LTHSE). These spaces were, however, changed in their appearance when accommodating a prisoner. Typically small, the presence of two officers, (usually requiring an extra chair), their personal bags and the escort bag containing equipment required by the prison service 'rules', specifically PSI 33/2015, meant the bedside felt very crowded.

All of the prisoners observed in hospitals during the fieldwork were distinguishable by the escort chain they wore, looped over bed rails or hanging beside the bed before attaching to a prison officer sat in a high-backed chair by the head of the hospital bed (Fieldnotes, LTHSE and Category B). In other parts of the hospital, these chairs would have been used by patients, having a change of position from lying or sitting in bed, but the need for the officer to be within a chain's length of the prisoner removed this possibility. When conversation flagged, the most conspicuous sound was that of the escort chain, banging against the metal hospital bed as the prisoner or officer adjusted position (Fieldnotes, LTHSE and Category B). The use of restraints is discussed further in later chapters.

The close proximity of officers and prisoners for prolonged periods of time might be expected to change their relationships, but there was no indication from observations or from interviews that this was the case. The level of interaction between officers and prisoners seemed to vary, but on all the observed 'bedwatches' the radio or TV was playing if the staff wanted it on. One prisoner complained the officers previously with him had not let him watch programmes he wanted (Fieldnote, LTHSE). Another was seemingly deliberately disengaging himself from the officers present, ignoring their choice of TV (Fieldnote, Category B). Sometimes officers and prisoners spoke to each other, but officers more frequently spoke amongst themselves (Fieldnote, LTHSE). On one of the observed 'bedwatches', officers frequently interrupted the prisoner when he spoke to me, seemingly vying for my attention or perhaps assuming he was of less interest (Fieldnote, LTHSE).

It was the presence of escort officers forming the 'bedwatch' that was key to the hospital or hospice bedside being marked as part of prison custody. By providing surveillance over the occupant of the bed, they introduced into the hospital or hospice a function more readily associated with imprisonment. Foucault (1991) suggests the underlying differences between prisons and the hospitals were less marked than might be expected, perhaps explaining how readily the transformation of the hospital bedside into a place of prison custody could be accomplished. Both are institutions where Foucault (1991) argues disciplinary power is used, where bodies are observed and moulded into the correct forms of behaviour. The similarities in how disciplinary spaces were structured and the shared properties of prisons and hospitals that Foucault identifies perhaps explain the ease with which the hospital bedside became a carceral space.

At the very end of life, it was sometimes possible for the characteristics of prison to be diminished in the physical environment of the outside hospital or hospice. Officers accommodating prisoners going from the Category B prison to the hospice were reported to be usually not in uniform (Interviews 10 and 2, Category B). At the hospice, terminally ill prisoners were accommodated in private rooms, although one prison healthcare professional said they were typically put in the end room, furthest from other patients, because of the stigma associated with having an escort (Interview 10, Category B). Wood (2007) suggests hospices are concerned that their charitable support will be compromised if they are seen by the public to be caring for prisoners.

In the case of Iain, who had received a terminal diagnosis between conviction and sentencing, an officer spoke about accompanying his wife when he was close to death in hospital. With no side room available, he was in the middle of a six-bedded ward, with the curtains pulled around him. As a family liaison officer, the officer was not in uniform and uniformed prison officers had moved away from him out of respect, keeping nearby in case needed. He was therefore less identifiable as a prisoner. Other patients in the ward were very disruptive, including one man who repeatedly and loudly said he wanted to die. Whilst the environment was far from ideal, it was in many ways less marked by prison than other deaths in custody. When his end came, however, his wife had briefly left the ward, and it was two prison officers, one in uniform, who were sat with him (Interview 16, Category B).

The fourth location associated with terminally ill prisoners, hospitals and hospices, whilst physically outside the prison, becomes closely associated with the prison by the presence of prison officers performing a 'bedwatch'. The carceral space moves with them and the prisoner they are accompanying, bringing the symbolic and practical changes that result from the use of restraints, the presence of uniformed prison staff and the interactions between the prisoner and the prison officers originating in their relationships within the prison.

Expectations of Location and Understandings Derived from Location

The belief that prisoners who were unwell should be located in certain places was deep-rooted. Officers at the LTHSE prison accepted disabled prisoners might be on the wing, but "what they try and do here is if they are terminally ill, they move them to healthcare" (Interview 11, LTHSE). There was an assumption here that those at the very end of life would be placed in the palliative care suite. Healthcare staff felt aggrieved that when Eddie was finally taken over to the healthcare centre, the palliative care suite was unavailable, sealed off as part of the investigation following the death of another prisoner (Fieldnote, LTHSE). At the end of his life, they expected him to be located in the palliative care suite.

The spatial ordering of a prisoner was also regarded as indicative of their state of health and stage of life, their place in the 'dying trajectory' (Glaser & Strauss, 1968). Other people read meaning into their location, surmising frailties and life expectancies from where they were located, assuming a deterioration or improvement if this location subsequently changed. Location became important in these speculations because the expectation of medical confidentiality meant reliable information was rarely openly shared beyond healthcare staff and the prison officers directly involved in the prisoner's care. For staff not directly involved in the decision, being moved to an outside hospital or hospice might mean a terminally ill prisoner could be expected to die soon; returning would be taken as a sign of improvement (Interviews 16 and 9, Category B; Fieldnotes LTHSE and Category B). If they were willing to stay in the healthcare centre, it might be interpreted as meaning they were very ill (Interview 9, Category B). The death of a prisoner in one prison came as less of a surprise to a staff member who had worked with him because "everyone knew he was going to die. That's why he was on healthcare" (Interview 4, LTHSE). In the LTHSE prison, the palliative care suite was there for prisoners not expected to last long (Fieldnote, LTHSE) and it could be assumed being located there meant death was imminent, although there were prisoners who had been accommodated there for other reasons when the suite was not needed by someone else. At the Category B prison, where there was the possibility of sending a prisoner to a local hospice, this was often taken as evidence his death was expected, although in reality the prisoner may be moved back to the prison if his condition improved (Interviews 1, 8 and 16, Category B). In this way, physical locations served to inform constructions of the dying prisoner, which will be further discussed in Chapter 4.

Seriously and terminally ill prisoners were themselves assumed to make meaning from where they found themselves placed. In the LTHSE prison, there was a belief that people who went to the healthcare centre didn't come back. It was referred to as the "green mile", (Fieldnote, LTHSE) and the palliative care suite was known to be referred to by prisoners as "the departure lounge" or "death's waiting room" (Interview 4, LTHSE and Fieldnotes, LTHSE). When asked, a nurse said Eddie was aware of this and she thought it was one of his reasons for resisting being located in healthcare (Fieldnote, LTHSE). The physical location thus conveyed a symbolic meaning. Eddie's reluctance to be located in the healthcare centre meant his eventual transfer there was interpreted by other people as meaning he must have known death was imminent, either because he was prepared to be taken there, or because he interpreted his transfer as meaning other people thought he had very little time left (Interview 5, LTHSE).

The Rarity of Release to Die at Home and the Desire for a Better Setting

Prison is seen by most prisoners as the least optimal place to die (Aday & Wahidin, 2016), with prisoners on the whole preferring to die as free men, surrounded by their family (Crawley & Sparks, 2005). Having considered four locations associated with dying and death within prison custody, and the mobility of prisoners between them, it is therefore important to consider a fifth 'space', that created by compassionate release. If a prisoner were to be granted compassionate release on the grounds of terminal illness, they would be removed from prison custody and the experience of dying transferred to a non-custodial location, without the rules or trappings of imprisonment. They would be free, and typically located in a family home, or a hospital or hospice, in a similar manner to other people at the end of life.

High profile cases where compassionate release was granted, such as those of the Lockerbie bomber, Abdelbaset Ali al-Megrahi or the Great Train Robber, Ronnie Biggs, resonate in the public consciousness. In practice, compassionate release is very rare. Statistics on compassionate release are not routinely published by the Ministry of Justice but information from Hansard (HC debate, 10 February 2014) indicates that between 2009 and 2013, only 45 prisoners were granted compassionate release in England and Wales, including Abdelbaset Ali al-Megrahi and Ronnie Biggs, during which time there were 606 deaths from natural causes in prison custody. More broadly, in eight high income countries surveyed, Turner et al. (2021), found only France and the Czech Republic used compassionate release frequently, and in both places this was a temporary system, with people subject to recall to prison if they recovered.

Although staff participants in the prisons studied recounted trying to achieve compassionate release for dying prisoners, both prisoners and staff could identify cases where they felt it was needed but hadn't been possible (Fieldnotes, LTHSE and Category B; Interview 9, Category B and Interviews 6 and 14, LTHSE). An officer with 27 years experience, mostly in the LTHSE prison, could think of only one instance where compassionate release had been granted, for a prisoner who had suffered a stroke and died three weeks after being released to the care of the hospital (Interview 6, LTHSE). Similarly, a member of a senior management team with nearly 30 years experience could think of only one prisoner who had been released to die, and that was described as being via the parole system, not a compassionate release (Interview 13, LTHSE). As a result, in neither prison studied was there an expectation that prisoners would be granted compassionate release, even if it was desired. Unless the end of their sentence was imminent, a terminal diagnosis was expected to lead to a prisoner dying in prison custody rather than at home. This is in keeping with studies of elderly prisoners elsewhere, which similarly report on the difficulties in obtaining compassionate release (Turner & Peacock, 2017; Turner et al., 2021). It was most marked in the LTHSE prison where there were significant numbers of people with indeterminate sentences and whole life tariffs. In the Category B prison, where the population included people on remand, there were examples of remand prisoners, such as William, dying of natural causes. At this prison, participants spoke about a prisoner, Iain, who had received a terminal diagnosis between conviction and sentencing. His sentencing was delayed until he was well enough, a week before his eventual death. Healthcare staff in particular felt it was harsh that even in such circumstances compassionate release was not available (Interview 10, Category B).

A number of difficulties were experienced with regard to obtaining compassionate release. Not all prisoners who might be considered for compassionate release could be 'sent home' and staff recounted difficulties in finding somewhere suitable to take prisoners. They felt hospices were reluctant to take a released prisoner because of the reputational risk of accepting a convicted sex offender (Interview 7, LTHSE). This is consistent with the finding of Burles et al. (2016) that a prisoner's offences may make it difficult to access a hospice placement. Releases had also been prevented by disputes over which part of the NHS would take financial responsibility, especially for prisoners who had been away from their local area for a long time (Interview 13, LTHSE). In one case, the process of getting compassionate release had been made more difficult by the prisoner's family's concerns about paying for the subsequent funeral (Interview 13, LTHSE).

The most significant difficulties in obtaining compassionate release were attributed by staff to the expectations embodied in prison service rules and regulations regarding compassionate release. The Prison Rules (1999) specify the Secretary of State may temporarily release a prisoner on compassionate grounds or in order for them to receive medical treatment. They also state the medical officer of a prison should inform the Governing Governor of any prisoner whose health is likely be adversely affected by continued imprisonment and that the Governing Governor should report this to the Secretary of State immediately. However, it is clear from PSI 03/2016 that early release on compassionate grounds is only justified by exceptional circumstances. PSI 64/2011 takes a slightly different approach, saying that it is important to discuss early compassionate release with prisoners, but emphasising in two separate sections that prisoners may not wish to apply. If an application is to be made, PSO 3050 gives two grounds on which it may be considered:

> a patient is suffering from a terminal illness and death is likely to occur soon. There are no set time limits, but 3 months may be considered an appropriate period
>
> or
>
> a patient is bedridden or severely incapacitated. This might include those confined to wheelchairs, paralysed or severe stroke victims. (PSO 3050 paragraph 7.18e)

Despite giving a time period of three months, PSO 3050 also says applications should be made as early as possible and can be reconsidered if the patient's condition deteriorates (PSO 3050 paragraph 7.18d). The input of healthcare staff as to how the prisoner's medical condition may affect their ability to reoffend is to be sought (PSO 3050 paragraph 7.18) together with a specialist opinion on life expectancy. Whilst the PSO recognises clinicians may not wish to provide an estimate of life expectancy, it persists in this requirement, saying: "personal contact between health care and the specialist to explain the process will often resolve this issue" (PSO 3050 paragraph 7.18e). As Bolger (2005) highlights, this requirement of a prognosis that the prisoner will die within three months contradicts the principles of palliative care, which are opposed to setting such timescales.

In practice, staff in both prisons studied had found the regulations on compassionate release unworkable. The difficulties were summed up by a senior member of staff at the LTHSE prison:

> Usually the blockage on that is the information you'll get from the doctors on that because the two-liner saying "he's going to die in three months of this" really isn't enough to justify the compassionate release and we've fallen sort of foul of that. We've gone through the motions of the process but nobody has got released on compassionate release because we haven't got that medical evidence to support it, and that's really hard because a lot of that is out of our control and you're time bound with getting this so by the time you've got something in, if it takes 3 to 4 weeks, then you get to a point where somebody is deteriorating too much to actually, it's less relevant because they are so near the end they that are probably going to die in prison anyway. (Interview 7, LTHSE)
>
> In one instance, a senior prison officer working as an offender supervisor had tried in vain to use the parole system to get release for a prisoner with a terminal diagnosis. Time was against them:
>
> He'd had a parole hearing but the parole board wanted to find a little bit more information out before, so we were trying to push the information through so we that could have another parole hearing. I think they give us 12 weeks, but we tried to push it through at about 6. I don't think he actually would have reached the 12 weeks period. (Interview 6, LTHSE)

It was widely accepted that it was not good to die in prison (Fieldnotes, LTHSE; Interview 8, Category B) and the environment was part of the reason. In the LTHSE prison, two prisoners who knew they would die in prison spoke about desiring a better setting, agreeing that some sort of secure hospital would be better, somewhere that was still a prison but could more adequately meet the needs they expected to have at the end of life (Fieldnote, LTHSE). An elderly prisoner in the Category B prison shared their view, describing his ideal as a secure hospital with lower security; as a wheelchair user he said he was not going to be able to escape. When asked why he preferred this to compassionate release, something neither of the men at the other prison had considered either, he said:

> "Because justice has to be seen to be done". He says it's human nature to want to see that justice has been served; he doesn't expect compassionate. (Fieldnote, Category B)

His comment is reminiscent of Dawes (2009), writing from an Australian context, who suggested compassionate release "requires an act of 'forgiveness' by government on behalf of the community and may be difficult to achieve in the current climate" (p. 268). Recognising the public has a desire for punishment to be delivered, prisoners saw that for the time being at least, compassionate release was not an option. As a result the physical locations in which terminally ill prisoners will typically be cared for and die becomes more significant to prisoners considering the prospect of dying in prison.

Conclusion

Each of the four spaces associated by staff and prisoners with dying in prison custody had its own characteristics. It was apparent that whilst there is not a single direction of movement through these spaces, there was a continuum of the blurring of 'inside' and 'outside' which reflected assumptions that prisoners closer to the end of life will be located in the prison's healthcare centre, and as death approaches, in a palliative care suite. Away from the starkness and physical limitations of the prison wing, the border between 'inside' and 'outside' softened slightly in the more relaxed regimes such as H3 in the Category B prison. In the palliative care suite of the LTHSE prison, this softening was more marked, embodied in soft furnishings and artworks that demonstrated the attempts of some professionals to recast the individual as primarily a 'patient'. There was a deliberate introduction of features which represented the 'outside', with the intention of lessening the physical signs of imprisonment and creating an environment which healthcare professionals regarded as being appropriate for dying. Despite these efforts, these were still deaths in prison custody and the physical markers of such remained evident.

In the hospital, the boundary between 'inside' and 'outside' became entangled. The accompaniment of the prisoner by prison officers brought into the hospital the trappings of incarceration: prison uniforms, prison equipment and often the physical restraints of handcuffs or an escort chain. In this respect, the requirements of a prisoner's ongoing imprisonment impinged on the physical environment of the hospital bedside and whilst the prisoner was materially outside the prison they were simultaneously representationally inside. The physical environments in which prisoners die were therefore very closely associated with the experience of imprisonment, and very different surroundings from the places where most people expect to die.

The desire to meet the changing needs of dying prisoners impacted on the physical setting of the prison, most notably in the commitment of some staff, especially healthcare professionals, to re-purpose spaces as suitable for palliative care. This was also apparent in small adaptions to the physical environment such as leaving doors unlocked or introducing soft furnishings into a palliative care suite. These served symbolic as well as practical purposes. In the prisons studied, there were changes to the regime resulting from the experience of caring for dying prisoners. A terminal diagnosis was usually seen as indicating a prisoner should move to the healthcare centre or H3, but there were exceptions, as Eddie's case shows. Physical adaptions were made on wings to meet the needs of frailer prisoner, including lowered doorsteps, more convenient cell bells and additional bedding.

With compassionate release being so rare, the physical environment of the prison becomes more important in the experience of dying. It is the aspect of carceral geography, together with the rules associated with imprisonment, which sets dying in prison apart from dying in other places.

References

Aday, R., & Wahidin, A. (2016). Older prisoners' experiences of death, dying and grief behind bars. *The Howard Journal of Crime and Justice, 55*(3), 312–327. https://doi.org/10.1111/hojo.12172

Baer, L. D., & Ravneberg, B. R. (2008). The outside and inside in Norwegian and English prisons. *Geografiska Annaler: Series B, Human Geography, 90*(2), 205–216. https://doi.org/10.1111/j.1468-0467.2008.00287.x

Bolger, M. (2005). Dying in prison: Providing palliative care in challenging environments. *International Journal of Palliative Nursing, 11*(12), 619–621. https://doi.org/10.12968/ijpn.2005.11.12.20227

Burles, M. C., Peternelj-Taylor, C. A., & Holtslander, L. (2016). A 'good death' for all?: Examining issues for palliative care in correctional settings. *Mortality, 21*(2), 93–111. https://doi.org/10.1080/13576275.2015.1098602

Crawley, E., & Sparks, R. (2005). Older men in prison: Surviving, coping and identity. In A. Liebling & S. Maruna (Eds.), *The effects of imprisonment* (pp. 343–365). Routledge.

Crewe, B. (2009). *The prisoner society: Power, adaption, and social life in an English prison.* Oxford University Press.

Crewe, B., Warr, J., Bennett, P., & Smith, A. (2013). The emotional geography of prison life. *Theoretical Criminology, 18*(1), 56–74. https://doi.org/10.1177/1362480613497778

Dawes, J. (2009). Ageing prisoners: Issues for social work. *Australian Social Work, 62*(2), 258–271. https://doi.org/10.1080/03124070902803475

Foucault, M. (1991). *Discipline and punish: The birth of the prison* (A. Sheridan, Trans.). Penguin Books.

Glaser, B., & Strauss, A. (1968). *Time for dying*. Aldine Publishing Company.

Goffman, E. (1961). *Asylums: Essays on the social situation of mental patients and other inmates.* Penguin.

House of Commons Debate, 10 February 2014, c 489W.

Jewkes, Y., & Moran, D. (2017). Prison architecture and design: Perspectives from criminology and carceral geography. In A. Liebling, S. Mann, & L. McAra (Eds.), *The Oxford handbook of criminology* (pp. 541–561). Oxford University Press.

Jewkes, Y., Slee, E., & Moran, D. (2017). The visual retreat of the prison. In M. Brow & E. Carrabine (Eds.), *International handbook of visual criminology* (pp. 293–304). Routledge.

Mann, N. (2012). *Doing harder time: The experiences of an ageing male prison population in England and Wales*. Routledge.
Moran, D. (2015). *Carceral geography: Spaces and practices of incarceration*. Routledge.
Moran, D., Jewkes, Y., & Turner, J. (2016). Prison design and carceral space. In Y. Jewkes, B. Crewe, & J. Bennett (Eds.), *Handbook on prisons* (pp. 114–130). Routledge.
Royal Geographical Society. (2018). *About*. Royal Geographical Society. https://carceralgeography.com/about-3/
Schaefer, I., DiGiacomo, M., Heneka, N., Panozzo, S., Luckett, T., & Phillips, J. L. (2022). Palliative care needs and experiences of people in prison: A systematic review and meta-synthesis. *Palliative M, 36*(3), 443–461. https://doi.org/10.1177/02692163211068278
Turner, M., Chassagne, A., Capelas, M. L., Chambaere, K., Panozzo, S., Teves, C. M., & Riegler, E. (2021). Mapping palliative care provision in European prisons: An EAPC Task Force Survey. *BMJ Supportive & Palliative Care*, bmjspcare–2020–002701. https://doi.org/10.1136/bmjspcare-2020-002701
Turner, M., & Peacock, M. (2017). Palliative care in UK prisons: Practical amd emotional challenges for staff and fellow prisoners. *Journal of Correctional Health Care, 23*(1), 56–65. https://doi.org/10.1177/1078345816684847
Wood, F. J. (2007). The challenge of providing palliative care to terminally ill prison inmates in the UK. *International Journal of Palliative Nursing, 13*(3), 131–135. https://doi.org/10.12968/ijpn.2007.13.3.23275

3

The Governance of Mortality

As already established, dying from natural causes in prison is different from dying in other settings (Aday & Wahidin, 2016; Burles et al., 2016; Dawes, 2002; Handtke & Wangmo, 2014; Turner et al., 2011; Wood, 2007). In England and Wales, with compassionate release unlikely in practice, prisoners are separated from their family, sometimes a long way from home, and typically a resident in a large state institution, redolent with rules, control and power directed at purposes other than palliative care. The fact of imprisonment plays a significant role in the environment surrounding dying prisoners. Turner et al. (2011) remind the reader that whilst the National Health Service (NHS) promotes choices for terminally ill patients about where they die, these options are not available to prisoners.

This chapter shows how the rules, regulations and guidance, which control prison regimes and serve to translate power down the prison hierarchy, also affect the experience of dying in prison custody. Alongside these rules, customs, cultural expectations and the exercise of authority within the prison led to a different experience of dying in a prison setting

C. Robinson, *Dying in Prison*, Palgrave Studies in Prisons and Penology, https://doi.org/10.1007/978-3-031-27103-8_3

as compared to the community. Bolger (2005) suggests prison allows very little personal choice, few opportunities to discuss the dying process or chance to involve the family, all of which are important features of palliative care in the community. This chapter looks at how mortality is 'governed' within prisons by examining the impact prison rules have on the experience of dying in prison custody and by paying attention to how the location of dying prisoners is determined. A terminally ill prisoner might be moved between the locations within prison custody described in Chapter 2 during the course of his illness. However, his mobility between these spaces was not within his control, nor was there a single trajectory through these locations. Instead, the location was imposed upon prisoners in part by their physical condition, but also by other factors. Certain indicators, defined by others, can be seen to inform assumptions about the terminally ill prisoner's mobility between the prison wing, the prison healthcare centre, the palliative care suite where there was one, or outside hospital. Three forces are seen to exert particular influence over how mortality is governed within the prison: the exercise of authority, based on professional or hierarchical divisions; custom and cultural expectation and prison 'rules'. These will be considered in turn, in relation to the physical location of the prisoner and their influence on the experience of dying.

Authority

Part of the discipline associated with the prison regime is achieved by governors and officers determining where any prisoner is located, demonstrating an understanding, as Foucault states, that "discipline proceeds from the distribution of individuals in space" (1991a, p. 141). In the prisons studied, this applied to dying prisoners too, although the fact of their dying meant other staff, especially healthcare professionals, played a role in decisions about their location. By considering how location is governed, we can better understand the impact of the exercise of authority over the prisoner on their experience of dying.

As was shown in the previous chapter, there was an established presumption in both prisons studied that seriously or terminally ill prisoners would be located in the prison's healthcare wing. Prisoners known to be terminally ill might exceptionally be housed on prison wings; the circumstances determining when this would happen are discussed below. This was unusual, and is one of the ways in which the experience of more frequent deaths from natural causes was changing the regime, making new practices acceptable.

The case of Neil, a prisoner who had died in the LTHSE prison seven months before the research began, was discussed by staff and prisoners alike. Unusually, he had arrived at the prison after a terminal diagnosis, transferred to be nearer his family after receiving a prognosis of one year to live. Once at the prison, his progression through the physical spaces of the prison was however typical of the expected trajectory of a terminally ill prisoner. Initially he was accommodated on the prison wing, but was then moved to the healthcare centre as soon as he started to experience weakness on one side and a loss of balance. Four weeks later, he was moved from there to the palliative care suite, where he died eight weeks later (Prison & Probation Ombudsman, 2017). This was regarded within the LTHSE prison as the expected pathway.

There were exceptions, which illustrate the lines of authority applicable to decisions associated with dying prisoners. During the fieldwork, Eddie, also a prisoner in the LTHSE prison with a terminal diagnosis, was accommodated on one of the wings. He had initially been moved to the healthcare centre but was returned to the wings after expressing a strong wish to be with his friends and remained there even when he had very limited mobility. His case illustrates several factors in the governance of spatial arrangement of dying prisoners. On one occasion, an officer on his wing told me they were moving another prisoner so Eddie could be accommodated in a cell closer to the officers' base and other facilities in the prison. I asked if Eddie was accepting of this move, knowing how much location mattered to him, and was told he would have to be (Fieldnote, LTHSE). There was an assumption that as a prisoner, he had no choice. The powers of officers in this respect were, however, not total. Overhearing the prison officer say this to me, another officer challenged him, saying that the Senior Officer had spoken with Eddie and this was not going to happen, encouraging the first officer to check the records. The officer's response was that it could wait until the SO was back (Fieldnote, LTHSE); the SO was therefore seen as having the crucial say, but significantly, not the prisoner. The final authority on a prisoner's location was given to the Governing Governor. In the LTHSE prison, the Governing Governor was perceived as previously having been opposed to prisoners staying on the wing if they were ill, to the extent that when an SO returned from leave to find Eddie on the wing, he checked the Governing Governor had approved the arrangement (Fieldnote, LTHSE). The Governing Governor was similarly crucial in decisions about the location of dying prisoners at the Category B prison, although healthcare staff there said the prisoner might be then given options (Interview 1, Category B).

Healthcare professionals within both prisons determined when needs were too complex for the medical services available in the prison. At the Category B prison, prison officers regarded decisions about when to send a prisoner to outside hospital or hospice as resting with healthcare staff (Interview 9, Category B). Healthcare staff in this prison did sometimes feel under pressure not to send someone to outside hospital because of the cost implications of a 'bedwatch' (Interview 12, Category B). They had used concerns about costs to persuade the prison authorities to let them move a prisoner to the room intended as a future palliative care suite, arguing that if he wasn't in a room without the usual cell door, he would have to go to hospital with a costly 'bedwatch' ensuing (Interview 10, Category B).

Terminally ill prisoners in general had very little say about where they were located, to the extent that when they expressed a desire with regard to location which was respected, this was noteworthy. Eddie was not historically unique in this regard, but he was unusual, such that the fact he was "being allowed" to stay on the wing was raised regularly by both staff and prisoners (Fieldnote, LTHSE; Interviews 15, 5, 6 and 12, LTHSE) and often attributed to his perceived stubbornness (Fieldnote, LTHSE). Arguably, he only succeeded in exercising limited autonomy over his location in the prison because he was also liked. Staff described him as a "decent" prisoner and wanted to meet his wishes (Fieldnote, LTHSE). They saw the arrangement as working well because he was popular and had friends willing to provide care (Fieldnotes, LTHSE). Eddie's placement on the wing did however, come with an assumption that at some point his wishes would be overturned. Prison officers, SOs, healthcare staff and the governor involved in his case all said that at some point he would have to be moved (Fieldnotes, LTHSE). One of the nurses thought they would not be able to persuade him, but still saw it as inevitable he would be taken to the healthcare centre to die (Fieldnote, LTHSE). Only so much disruption of the expected norms of location for a dying prisoner could be tolerated, even if the prisoner was well-liked and respected.

Custom and Cultural Expectations

Having established where authority lay for deciding the mobility of a seriously or terminally ill prisoner between the locations associated with dying and death, it is important to consider how these decisions were made by prison staff, including the Governing Governor, healthcare staff and senior officers. Different staff had different indicators of when a move would be needed: signs and symptoms they expected to see that would assist in making the decision about when to move a prisoner, especially someone such as Eddie who had expressed a wish to stay on the wing. Identifying indicators for when the time was right to override his wishes seemed to be part of rationalising to themselves a decision they did not really want to make. Prison officers were frequently heard to ask nursing staff how long they thought Eddie would be on the wing (Fieldnote, LTHSE). One officer said he thought Eddie could stay until he couldn't think straight (Fieldnote, LTHSE) and another until it became "unethical", defined as the point at which respecting his wishes meant Eddie was receiving worse care (Fieldnote, LTHSE). For another officer, once Eddie needed to have 24-hour medical monitoring, he had to be in the healthcare centre because this wasn't possible on the wing. One of the nursing staff was clear a fall indicated Eddie needed to be moved to a cell with a bell near the bed (Fieldnote, LTHSE), something which had been rejected by officers a fortnight earlier when Eddie had said he didn't want the disruption (Fieldnote, LTHSE). Prisoners speculated about this too, with one suggesting Eddie would be moved if he became incontinent (Fieldnote, LTHSE). In essence, staff were trying to identify the 'crucial junctures' that would indicate Eddie had entered a new status in dying (Glaser & Strauss, 1968). It is striking that many of these were closely linked to the physical limitations of spaces within the prison, to when opening doors on the wing would be too disruptive to the established regime or to when the physical environment of the cell would be inadequate to meet his needs.

The Category B prison also had experience of a terminally ill prisoner, Dean, being adamant he wanted to stay on the wing with his friends. In this case, they attributed his eventual decision to accept a move to H3 to his own growing awareness that he was extremely unwell and needed more help (Interview 1, Category B). As his condition deteriorated, officers felt Dean needed to be in H3 for medical reasons (Interview 3, Category B) and nursing staff argued that he could have more input from them on H3; there were not enough nurses to care for him on the wing (Interview 1, Category B). It is noticeable that in a lower security prison, Dean was granted more autonomy, but there were other differences between this prison and the LTHSE establishment which did not reflect the prison's security status as might be expected.

One of the key indicators for when a move from the wings to healthcare would be required was an escalation in the type and amount of pain relief and care required. In the LTHSE prison, there was an assumption Eddie would eventually need pain relief administered through a syringe driver, and therefore for perceived security reasons associated with the syringe, he would be moved the healthcare centre. At the Category B prison, despite being a lower security category prison, a prisoner who had needed a syringe driver had been required to be sent to outside hospital because the prison authorities were not willing for healthcare staff to use syringe drivers anywhere within the prison, stating security considerations as the reason. Decisions about where to locate a dying prisoner were therefore associated with this form of pain relief, but based on custom and expectation, rather than medical or security needs. Other medical reasons could be cited for the move from the wings to the healthcare centre. At the Category B prison, the enhanced ratio of staff to prisoners was a factor (Interview 9, Category B), as was the greater ability to prevent and control infections (Interview 3, Category B).

Spatial location also indicated who was 'in charge' of the prisoner, specifically whether he was regarded primarily as a medical case or a discipline case. This was closely related to the perceived needs of a dying prisoner, and how much emphasis was placed on medical needs as opposed to social, psychological or spiritual needs. It also reflected the perceived risk posed by the prisoner. As one officer at the Category B prison said, in relation to how he saw staff attitudes concerning the location of prisoners as one of the barriers to good care: "they may think that 'someone is dying, they should go to hospital anyway, and we're here for fighting prisoners" (Interview 2, Category B). For some of his colleagues in the LTHSE prison, once a prisoner would not need "fighting", this was an indicator of the stage at which nursing staff would take over and a move to the healthcare centre would be appropriate (Interview 15, LTHSE).

Other reasons were given for why a move was beneficial. This included the impact on other people. With Eddie, there was a growing concern amongst prison officers about finding him dead (Interview 13, LTHSE) and an expectation that healthcare staff would see the signs and take over responsibility for him as this became more likely (Fieldnote, LTHSE). There was also a concern for the well-being of the prisoners caring for him, with his eventual move in part being attributed after his death to concerns about how caring was affecting them, as well as an awareness that because of the wing regime, prisoner-carers could not provide as much care as he was needing (Fieldnote, LTHSE). His deteriorating health also meant keeping him on the wing was seen as unfair to other prisoners, because, as one custodial manager said: "your resources are having to be taken away from dealing with the normal day to day issues" (Interview 6, LTHSE).

Prison 'Rules'

Whilst the exercise of authority, custom and cultural expectations guided many of the decisions made about dying prisoners, particularly in terms of their location within the prison, one of the main influences on the experience of dying in prison custody was the large number of rules, regulations and guidance which control prison regimes and serve to translate power down the prison hierarchy. Prisons are institutions controlled by a large number of very detailed 'rules', some defined in statute, others codified by Ministry of Justice documentation, most reinforced by training and monitoring. The amount of rules and regulations governing prison life leads Liebling and Maruna (2005) to observe that "it is difficult to know all the rules, much less comply with them" (p.105). Difficulties in comprehending what is required in a given situation are not unusual within the prison service, as Loucks (2000, p. 6) indicates:

> Regulations governing the minutiae of prison life often represent an impenetrable bureaucracy. In order to uncover management policy, one has to unravel layers of rules upon rules.
>
> The need to impose order and maintain security is embodied in the rules, regulations and guidance which govern the management of all prisoners, and which continued to be relevant in the treatment of dying prisoners. The two prisons in the study housed Category A prisoners, (LTHSE) and Category B prisoners (LTHSE and Category B prison). As such, security matters dominated all other considerations.

A range of publicly available documents relate to the needs of prisoners dying of natural causes or the provisions for their care but there are also omissions. The statutory instrument, the Prison Rules (1999), is comparatively brief and generic, but forms the basis of the regulations governing the functioning of all aspects of prisons. The brevity of the Prison Rules requires additional regulations and guidance to be issued and leaves scope for discretion for prison authorities (Loucks, 2000). Prison Service Orders (PSOs) and Prison Service Instructions (PSIs) further inform prison 'rules' and a number relate to circumstances likely to be relevant to dying prisoners. Case law is also relevant in establishing what is required.

PSOs are the mandatory instructions intended to be permanent, until replaced by a Prison Service Instruction (PSI) or cancelled, and take precedence over other mandatory manuals (Loucks, 2000). As such, they have no expiry date, although at the time of this study none have been issued since 2009. From PSO 0200, which is the Standard Manual, Section 20 relates to handling a death in custody, and was updated in November 2005. PSO 3050, the 'Continuity of Healthcare for Prisoners', which was issued in February 2006, was also included in this review. PSIs are the rules, regulations and guidelines according to which prisons operate. They can be regarded as short-term directives (Loucks, 2000). Some of their provisions are mandatory; others are not. One of the key recommendations of the Woodcock inquiry (1994) into escapes from the Special Security Unit at HMP Whitemoor was that prison service manuals and instructions should make it clear which provisions are mandatory, advisory or purely informative. In the PSIs and PSOs this is done by italicising text referring to mandatory actions. Five PSIs were reviewed, as follows:

- PSI 64/2011 Management of prisoners at risk of harm to self, to others and from others (Safer Custody), updated April 2012 and still in use at the time of the study, notwithstanding an expiry date of 31 January 2016. Despite its title, this PSI is relevant since it also includes the management of prisoners who are terminally or seriously ill, and actions to be taken, such as liaison with families, following a death in custody from any cause.
- PSI 17/2015 Prisoners Assisting Other Prisoners, effective from April 2015, which formalises the support and care prisoners in need of physical assistance can receive from their peers.
- PSI 33/2015 External Escorts, effective from December 2015, which is part 7.1 of the National Security Framework and details arrangements for when a prisoner is taken outside of the prison, including to attend hospital.
- PSI 03/2016 Adult Social Care, updated April 2016 and largely concerned with the implementation of the Care Act 2014 and the

provision of local authority social care to prisoners. Whilst not all terminally ill prisoners will require social care, this PSI also refers to palliative care for prisoners and compassionate release.

- PSI 05/2016 Faith and Pastoral Care for Prisoners, updated June 2016 and included in the review because it details expectations regarding the role of chaplains in providing pastoral care for terminally or seriously ill prisoners, liaising with their families and supporting staff affected by a prisoners' death.

The review of relevant documents also included the ruling by Judge Mitting in the High Court in 2007 in R (on the application of Graham and another) v Secretary of State for Justice, which provides case law precedent for the use of restraints on prisoners receiving medical treatment. This judgement includes consideration of the application of Article three of the European Convention on Human Rights and is reflected in PSIs concerned with external escorts of prisoners and the use of restraints.

As would be expected, Prison Service Instructions and Prison Service Orders which prescribed the operation of the prison service at the time of the study, focus on the functioning of the prison, what is to be done, and how. There is considerable emphasis placed on where responsibility lies and on joint working between the prison and a range of organisations including other statutory bodies. In the context of dying prisoners, these include the Coroner, the Health and Safety Executive, the police, local hospitals and the Prison and Probation Ombudsman, reflecting a bureaucratisation of death in prison and an emphasis on accountability and investigation.

The documents reviewed share a number of common aims, including attempting to provide guidance and regulation on specific issues. A number of key principles are repeated with regard to seriously ill prisoners. These include the risk to the public and to prisoners being managed and minimised (Graham v Secretary of State, 2007; PSI 03/2016, PSI 33/2005, PSI 64/2011), prisoners entitlement to the same standard of healthcare as the general public (PSI 33/2015) and establishing and maintaining partnerships with other bodies (PSI 03/2016, PSI 33/2015, PSI 64/2011, PSO 3050, PSO 0200). Boundaries are also defined within the PSIs, for example in PSI 17/2015 which defines the limits of intimate and personal care prisoners are permitted to provide to other prisoners. PSIs also designate powers and attribute responsibilities, such as to governors or to the prison officers fulfilling specific roles, and include lists of tasks for example with regard to the duties of prison officer in charge of a prisoner's escort or despatching escorts (PSI 33/2015). At times, the documents are overtly updating and changing existing practice, for example in PSI 33/2015, which explicitly states it is changing policy and ending single officer escorts (PSI 33/2015, 1.4). These changes usually have the end goal of improving outcomes for prisoners and staff. For example PSO 3050 aims "to improve the continuity of healthcare received by prisoners" and PSI 64/2011 aims, amongst other goals, to reduce deaths in custody and "ensure staff, prisoners and visitors affected by incidents of harm are supported appropriately" (PSI 64/2011, p. 4).

Whilst rarely explicitly addressing the circumstances of a dying prisoner, the PSIs, PSOs and Prison Rules emphasise security as the primary concern in a number of situations relevant to the treatment of a dying prisoner. Most of the relevant attention of the 'rules' with regard to dying prisoners is on escorting prisoners to hospitals outside the prison, either to out-patient appointments, for in-patient treatment or as emergency cases. These situations may occur repeatedly for a prisoner with a terminal diagnosis or at the end of life. By far the highest number of references within the 'rules' with regard to prisoners receiving treatment in outside hospitals relate to managing security risks as opposed to aspects of their care. Identified risks include escape, threats towards healthcare staff or members of the public and media interest (PSI 33/2015, Section 6). Treating prisoners in outside hospital is seen as something that should be minimised since it poses a security risk and causes "considerable operational pressures on the prison" (PSO 3050, 4.1) because of the need to provide escorting prison officers. This echoes the experience of healthcare staff in the Category B prison studied, who felt pressure not to send a prisoner to outside hospital for treatment (Interview 12, Category B).

When treatment in an outside hospital is unavoidable, PSI 33/2015 requires a minimum escort of two officers, possibly more depending on the outcome of a risk assessment (PSO 33/2015, 6.5, 6.6). On all of the so-called 'bedwatches' observed as part of this research project, two prison officers were present (Fieldnotes, Category B and LTHSE). The details of the risk assessment for all prisoners are specified in PSI 33/2015. This should include the prisoner's medical condition, their security category, their offending history and prison record, any available intelligence, their motivation to escape and likelihood of having outside assistance to do so (PSI 33/2015, 6.7). It is stated that factors such as advanced age, infirmity or chronic health conditions should be considered and may reduce the need for restraints (PSI 33/2015, 6.8). When discussing risk assessments for the use of restraints, officers, senior managers and healthcare staff participants all emphasised the prisoner's infirmity, framing this as whether he had sufficient mobility to escape (Fieldnotes, Category B and LTHSE; Interview 1, Category B; Interviews 12 and 13, LTHSE).

The 'rules' specify the particular duties of the officer in charge of the escort, including familiarisation with the route, searching the prisoner and preparing an escort bag which includes suitable restraints (PSI 33/2015, 6.34). PSI 33/2015 specifies the actions of officers once at the hospital, such as escort staff not normally accompanying a prisoner into the operating theatre, unless there is an assessed need for them to do so (PSI 33/2015, 6.15). With regard to hospital admissions ('bedwatches'), there are specific requirements for record keeping (PSI 33/2015, Section 3) and for the equipment (such as plastic cutlery and nightclothes) that the prison should provide for the prisoner (PSI 33/2015, 6.37). There are also regulations covering visits from other prison staff such as chaplains (PSI 05/2016, PSI 33/2015), and any family visits (PSI 33/2015). In the case of a prisoner being escorted to hospital in an emergency, the 'rules' specify the usual risk assessments prior to an escort can be delayed, but must be completed as soon as possible (PSI 33/2015, 5.12). Should emergency treatment such as defibrillation be required, escort staff are mandated to comply with any medical practitioner's request to remove the restraints immediately, and inform the duty governor as soon as possible afterwards (PSI 33/2015, 5.9, 6.14).

A number of references are made to record keeping, often as part of demonstrating the management of risk. A Person Escort Record (PER) is regarded as the:

> key document for ensuring that information about the risks posed by prisoners on external movement from prisons or transferred within the criminal justice system is always available to those responsible for their custody. (PSI 33/2015, 3.2)
>
> It is the duty of the officers accompanying the prisoner to keep the PER updated with information about the prison staff on duty, any visitors, and at least once an hour, check and record that the restraints have not been tampered with. If the restraints are removed, the prison officers should record in the PER the reason, the time and the name of the person authorising their removal (PSI 33/2015, 6.36). Record keeping was observed as part of all the 'bedwatches' attended, with the senior escorting officers usually delegated the task (Fieldnotes, Category B and LTHSE).

The Use of Restraints

Details about the use of restraints were included in several places within PSI 33/2015 but the underlying question of when it is appropriate to use restraints on a terminally or seriously ill prisoner was subject to a high court ruling, the Graham Judgement, which PSI 33/2015 sought to implement. The Graham Judgement, and subsequent frequent criticisms of prisons from the PPO for failing to adhere to this ruling, led to staff placing considerable importance on the appropriate use of restraints. Two interviewees, both prison governors, referred explicitly to the Graham Judgement, and the importance of correctly implementing the 'rules' on the use of restraints (Interviews 7 and 13, LTHSE). A further two interviewees, both experienced officers, also talked about the need to be aware of the 'rules' regarding cuffing arrangements when accompanying a prisoner whilst at outside hospital, and of the importance of contacting the prison to review cuffing arrangements if the prisoner's condition changed (Interviews 11, LTHSE and 2, Category B).

In this ruling in 2007, Judge Mitting found that:

> The unnecessary use of handcuffs on a prisoner who is receiving treatment, whether as an in-patient or an out-patient, at a civilian hospital is capable of infringing art[icle] 3 [of the European Convention on Human Rights] in two respects: either because it is inhuman or because it is degrading, or both. The use of handcuffs to guard against an adequately founded risk of escape or of harm to the public in the event of escape does not infringe art[icle] 3. (Item 27)

As a result, the use of restraints without an adequate individual risk assessment which considered the risk of the prisoner escaping, or of harm to the public occurring if they did escape, was found likely to be unlawful. With regard to situations where it would be impossible for the prisoner to escape, the judge found handcuffing him would be unlawful and a breach of Article 3 of the ECHR:

> A dying prisoner, properly assessed as posing a risk of escape when fit, and a risk of violence to the public were he to escape, could properly contend that handcuffing him during his dying hours was nonetheless an infringement of his right not to be treated inhumanely or in a degrading manner. (Item 27)

In the LTHSE prison, a pro forma had been created to assist with decisions about using restraints (Interview 14, LTHSE). The Graham Judgement served as an encouragement to ensure legal requirements were met, reinforced by an awareness that the prison would be criticised by the PPO after a death if restraints were found to have been incorrectly used. The effects of PPO investigations will be discussed further in Chapter 6.

These Prison Rules, PSOs, PSIs and Graham Judgement which form the prison 'rules' as relevant to dying prisoners go some way to explain how responses to dying prisoners are determined. They also show the limitations and possibilities that exist if prison regimes and personnel seek to follow the requirements and guidance set out. They illustrate the "rational schema" of prisons (Foucault, 1991b, p. 80) but also form part of the prevalent discourse about dying in prison, to be discussed in the next chapter.

Tellingly, the 'rules' illustrate a number of assumptions with regard to prisoners and deaths in custody that are apparent through where attention is directed. For example, there are assumptions revealed about the likely causes of deaths in custody. PSI 64/2011 focusses on deaths from suicide and violence more than those from natural causes, despite the dominance of natural causes in the statistics for deaths in prison custody. In doing so, it is implied that prison authorities erroneously see deaths as typically unnatural, unexpected and preventable. This is more marked in the PSO 0200, where the assumption is that deaths will be unexpected, occur in the cell and that first aid interventions will be appropriate. These assumptions are not borne out by the published statistics on deaths in custody, nor by the experiences of many of the prison staff involved in this study. What becomes clear is that the rules, regulations and guidance directing the achievement of prison and shaping discourses about prisoners have not been updated to reflect the impacts of an increasing number of prisoners dying from natural causes.

Discretion and Dealing with 'Rule-Failure'

The inadequacies in the official guidance when it comes to governing dying prisoners inevitably lead to greater emphasis on individual decision-making, custom and cultural expectation. In this context, discretion becomes important, although it is arguably present in all aspects of the prison service. There is considerable consensus about why discretion is needed: because rules cannot exist for every occasion (Hawkins, 1992; Hay & Sparks, 1991) and because where they do exist, they will at times be inadequate for the real situation, as illustrated in relation to dying prisoners. As Liebling and Arnold (2004) argue, "there is a tension between any detached application of the rules and the resolution of real, complex moral and social problems" (p. 266). Discretion is needed because, Liebling (2000) suggests, 'particular' situations cannot be adequately resolved by 'general' rules. In this way, 'rule-failure' discretion (Schneider, 1992) is prominent in prisons. Whilst the literature does not explicitly address the use of discretion in relation to the prison regime experienced by dying prisoners, Crawley (2005) does consider how it is used in work with elderly and frail prisoners. She is critical of the lack of use of discretion, and particularly of the "sameness principle" (p. 356) by which prison officers find moral justification for treating all prisoners the same, regardless of their needs. As part of her study, Crawley (2005) found discretion was sometimes used to assist elderly prisoners, but that these instances ran counter to the prison's tendency to flatten difference.

Whilst some (Bennett, 2016; Cheliotis, 2008; Crewe, 2008) argue increasing managerialism within the prison service has reduced the room for discretion, it is still, according to Liebling (2000) and Bryans and Jones (2001), used a great deal by prison officers and essential to prison managers (Bennett, 2016). Everyday examples include the speed at which prison officers chose to answer cell bells and how they address prisoners (Bryans & Jones, 2001), which rules they ignore or enforce (Bryans & Jones, 2001; Liebling & Arnold, 2004) or what they include or omit in a report which may influence a prisoner's sentence (Bryans & Jones, 2001; Crewe, 2011). Discretion can also be used by governors to achieve moral outcomes, sometimes at the expense of performance targets (Crewe et al., 2015). There is a link between the use of discretion and staff–prisoner relationships, with Liebling (2008) suggesting the rules are relied on when relationships are not working; discretion is used when relationships are good. The use of discretion grants a prisoner such as Eddie some autonomy over his location within the prison whilst dying, but, as is the risk with discretion, on the basis of him being regarded as a "decent" prisoner and popular with both staff and prisoners.

Conclusion

Significant aspects of the care of a dying prisoner are governed by prison rules, the custom and cultural expectations of the prison establishment and by prison authorities, especially the Governing Governor. The locations of prisoners such as Neil, Eddie and Dean during their terminal illnesses and at the point of death serve to illustrate many of the characteristics of how the spatial arrangement of the dying within prison was governed, and the assumptions and expectations that informed the spatial ordering of dying prisoners within the physical environments available.

What is striking is that whilst the prison authorities had great power, they did not have much certainty and the guidance available to them from prison 'rules' was of limited use. Furthermore, the prison 'rules' in place at the time of this study were seen to be inadequate to the changing circumstances arising from increased deaths from natural causes. The prison 'rules' reflected a strong concern to record and demonstrate agreed practices. The focus of these documents was on risk assessments, the appropriate use of restraints, the practicalities of prison officers escorting terminally ill prisoners to hospital for treatment and ensuring that family members have been contacted by a nominated member of the prison's staff. None of these documents, however, was intended specifically to address the circumstances of a prisoner dying of natural causes. Prison 'rules' did however have a particular influence on the experiences of prisoners dying of natural causes with regard to the use of restraints when requiring treatment in hospital, which will be considered further in chapter four. Moreover, prison 'rules' were in stark contrast to the usual concerns of good end of life care. Instead, they demonstrated a different set of priorities which informed the responses of prison regimes and personnel to dying prisoners.

Where rules are inadequate, as in this case, 'rule-failure' discretion (Schneider, 1992) becomes significant. However, discretion, discussed further in Chapter 5, is part of an assemblage, alongside prison rules and the use of authority, but also custom and cultural expectations, all of which contribute to the governance of mortality in prisons. These factors also demonstrate how the differing constructions of the dying prisoner, to be discussed in the next chapter, start to have practical effects on the experience of dying in prison custody. Only by dint of being a prisoner does the dying individual find themselves subject to these forms of the governance of mortality.

References

Bryans, S., & Jones, R. (Eds.). (2001). Prisons and the prisoner : An introduction to the work of Her Majesty's Prison Service. The Stationery Office.

Aday, R., & Wahidin, A. (2016). Older prisoners' experiences of death, dying and grief behind bars. *The Howard Journal of Crime and Justice, 55*(3), 312–327. https://doi.org/10.1111/hojo.12172

Bennett, J. (2016). *The working lives of prison managers: Global change, local culture and individual agency in the late modern prison.* Palgrave Macmillan.

Bolger, M. (2005). Dying in prison: Providing palliative care in challenging environments. *International Journal of Palliative Nursing, 11*(12), 619–621. https://doi.org/10.12968/ijpn.2005.11.12.20227

Burles, M. C., Peternelj-Taylor, C. A., & Holtslander, L. (2016). A 'good death' for all?: Examining issues for palliative care in correctional settings. *Mortality, 21*(2), 93–111. https://doi.org/10.1080/13576275.2015.1098602

Cheliotis, L. K. (2008). Resisting the scourge of managerialism: On the uses of discretion in later-modern prisons. In J. Bennett, B. Crewe, & A. Wahidin (Eds.), *Understanding prison staff* (pp. 247–258). Willan.

Crawley, E. (2005). Institutional thoughtlessness in prisons and its impacts on the day-to-day prison lives of elderly men. *Journal of Contemporary Criminal Justice, 21*(4), 350–363. https://doi.org/10.1177/1043986205282018

Crewe, B. (2008). Concluding comments on the social world of prison staff. In J. Bennett, B. Crewe, & A. Wahidin (Eds.), *Understanding prison staff* (pp. 421–433). Willan.

Crewe, B. (2011). Soft power in prison: Implications for staff–prisoner relationships, liberty and legitimacy. *European Journal of Criminology, 8*(6), 455–468. https://doi.org/10.1177/1477370811413805

Crewe, B., Liebling, A., & Hulley, S. (2015). Staff-prisoner relationships, staff professionalism, and the use of authority in public- and private-sector prisons. *Law and Social Inquiry, 40*(2), 309–344. https://doi.org/10.1111/lsi.12093

Dawes, J. (2002). Dying with dignity: Prisoners and terminal illness. *Illness, Crisis and Loss, 10*(3), 188–203. https://doi.org/10.1177/1054137302010003002

Foucault, M. (1991a). *Discipline and punish: The birth of the prison.* (A. Sheridan, Trans.). Penguin Books.

Foucault, M. (1991b). Questions of methods. In G. Burchell, C. Gordon, & P. Miller (Eds.), *The Foucault effect: Studies in governmentality* (pp. 73–86). The University of Chicago Press.

Handtke, V., & Wangmo, T. (2014). Ageing prisoners' views on death and dying: Contemplating end of life in prison. *Bioethical Inquiry, 11*, 373–386. https://doi.org/10.1007/s11673-014-9548-x

Hawkins, K. (1992). The use of legal discretion: Perspectives from law and social sciences. In K. Hawkins (Ed.), *The uses of discretion* (pp. 11–46). Oxford University Press.

Hay, W., & Sparks, R. (1991). What is a prison officer? *Prison Service Journal, 83*(3), 2–7.

Liebling, A. (2000). Prison officers, policing and the use of discretion. *Theoretical Criminology, 4*(3), 333–357. https://doi.org/10.1177/1362480600004003005

Liebling, A. (2008). Why prison staff culture matters. In J. Byrne, D. Hummer, & F. S. Taxman (Eds.), *The culture of prison violence* (pp. 105–122). Allyn and Bacon.

Liebling, A., & Arnold, H. (2004). *Prisons and their moral performance: A study of values, quality and prison life*. Oxford Univeristy Press.

Liebling, A., & Maruna. S. (2005). *The effects of imprisonment*. Willan.

Loucks, N. (2000). *Prison rules: A working guide*. Prison Reform Trust.

Prison and Probation Ombudsman, (2017). *Independent investigation into the death of (name) a prisoner at HMP Wakefield on (date).* Prison and Probation Ombudsman. https://www.ppo.gov.uk/document/fii-report/

Schneider, C. (1992). Discretion and rules: A lawyers view. In K. Hawkins (Ed.), *The uses of discretion* (pp. 47–89). Oxford University Press.

Turner, M., Payne, S., & Barbarachild, Z. (2011). Care or custody? An evaluation of palliative care in prisons in North West England. *Palliative Medicine, 25*(4), 370–377. https://doi.org/10.1177/0269216310393058

Wood, F. J. (2007). The challenge of providing palliative care to terminally ill prison inmates in the UK. *International Journal of Palliative Nursing, 13*(3), 131–135. https://doi.org/10.12968/ijpn.2007.13.3.23275

Woodcock, J. (1994). *The escape from Whitemoor prison on Friday 9 September 1994*. Home Office. https://assets.publishing.service.gov.uk/government/uploads/system/uploads/attachment_data/file/272031/2741.pdf

4

Constructing the Dying Prisoner

When a death is anticipated, the construction of the individual relies on understandings of dying which are themselves culturally influenced, as Seale (1998, p. 1) argues:

> our own constructions of death, dying and bereavement… are in fact specific to the conditions of late modernity and, indeed, are dominated by the conceptions of particular social groups.

The construction by staff of an individual dying prisoner was influenced both by a perception they were dying and by the implications of their situation as a prisoner. For the prisoner, many aspects of their lives in prison were shaped by the attitudes of staff. The attitudes of prison officers were particularly salient, since as Hay and Sparks (1991) argue, "uniformed staff are the people who have the most contact with prisoners, often in the most difficult circumstances" (p. 415). Staff understandings of the figure of the dying prisoner could arguably be closely related to a more general construction of the prisoner. This chapter will explore how staff, particularly those working with dying prisoners, and other prisoners construct the figure of the dying prisoner and how this differs from the understandings of other prisoners. It will pay particular attention to how prison officers construct dying prisoners and what underlies

C. Robinson, *Dying in Prison*, Palgrave Studies in Prisons and Penology, https://doi.org/10.1007/978-3-031-27103-8_4

these constructions. It will also highlight where there is divergence in the figuring of the dying prisoner by staff in differing occupational roles. It is suggested here that how individuals who are dying are constructed by the staff working around them can potentially determine the responses of prison regimes and personnel to their situation.

The chapter is arranged into four parts. It will begin by exploring how dying was defined by prison staff and prisoners, including examining how prisoners self-defined as expecting to die in prison and the close link made by participants between ageing and dying. Secondly, the chapter will consider how different groups of people within the prison applied differing dominant statuses to the figure of the dying prisoner. In particular, attention will be paid to the clear tension between the figuring of the individual by healthcare staff as a 'patient' and by prison officers as a 'prisoner', terms which evoke different levels of humanity. These constructions will be seen to sit alongside the rarer construction of the individual as a 'person'. Examples will be provided of how the different dominant statuses given to dying individuals affected the interactions staff had with them and therefore influenced the care received at the end of life. The importance of occupational culture will be considered here, alongside the extent to which matching the expectations of occupational culture is achievable when prisoners are especially stigmatised.

The third section of this chapter considers three implications of constructing the dying individual's dominant status as 'prisoner'. It examines how by figuring the individual as a 'prisoner' they become someone who is stigmatised, who is seen as posing a risk to others and who is denied autonomy. How this influenced the experience of the dying prisoner is explored particularly with reference to the experience of hospital escorts, the use of restraints and the limited scope for agency available to prisoners receiving palliative care.

The next section of this chapter will consider the effects of seeing the prisoner as a 'patient' or 'person', and the extent to which this was an achieved priority within the two prisons studied. The effects of imprisonment were in some circumstances lessened by the new constructions of the individual resulting from a terminal diagnosis, allowing prisoners to be afforded more humanity by staff, including prison officers.

The mechanisms for this will be explored, including the importance of constructing the prisoner as part of a family. The circumstances and limitations of sympathy in restoring a prisoner's humanity in the eyes of staff will also be considered.

Defining Expectations of Death and Dying in Prison Custody

As Glaser and Strauss (1968) state: "Dying must be defined in order to be reacted to as dying" (p. 242). Both staff and prisoners demonstrated ways in which they constructed a personal understanding that a prisoner was dying. In part, as discussed above, this was influenced by physical location, with the location of the prisoner being used to construct understandings of his condition and the likely progression of his illness. Often it was based on the prisoner's physical condition, with weight loss, pale or yellowing skin colour and an increased dependence on pain relief regarded as indicative of the approaching end of life (Interviews 4 and 15, LTHSE; Fieldnotes, LTHSE). Sometimes, participants knew of other people, including their own family members, who had died of the same condition and when they were aware of a prisoner's diagnosis, assumed they were therefore dying (Fieldnotes, LTHSE). More generally, death was regarded as something that happened to the elderly and associated with an ageing prison population. For example, one staff member said:

> I think especially with the population of [LTHSE prison], it's an ageing population and with older people you tend to get a lot more terminal illnesses or people who they are going to die aren't they? (Interview 4, LTHSE)

Staff at the LTHSE prison in particular encouraged me to watch the regular movement of prisoners across the 'centre' at the beginning and end of every session. They wanted me to see for myself the age and physical infirmities of the prison population, equating this to a demonstration of the extent of the tasks they would face in the future in responding to prisoners dying in prison custody. Similarly, in the Category B prison, senior officers assumed I would spend much of my time on F wing, where the population was noticeably more elderly, based on the perceived link between ageing and dying. For some very old prisoners, it seemed to be accepted that because of their age there was no other option than death in prison custody. One prisoner in the Category B prison spoke of helping a peer put his affairs in order. He:

> tells me about a new arrival on H3, aged 92. He says he's been helping him sell his house and change his will. The assumption that the man will die in prison is unspoken. (Fieldnote, Category B)
>
> A number of prisoners in the LTHSE prison with long sentences anticipated dying in prison and spoke to staff about this. One governor there recounted talking to a prisoner who regularly said he would die in prison and spoke about a conversation with another, not terminally ill, but already planning his funeral "because he doesn't think he'll finish serving his time out". (Interview 13, LTHSE)

In both prisons studied, there was a generalised acceptance that deaths from natural causes in prison custody were to be expected. There was also an individual expectation of death, seen mostly in elderly prisoners but also in prisoners with long sentences, particularly in the LTHSE prison. Age, particular medical conditions, physical location and physical appearance were all associated by participants as indicating a prisoner was nearer death.

Dominant Status: 'Prisoner', 'Patient' or 'Person'?

Studies of prison staff working with dying or frail prisoners commonly find they do not differentiate in their treatment of them from other prisoners (Crawley, 2005; HMCIP, 2004). Crawley (2005) finds that this "flattening of different needs" (p. 357) means elderly prisoners are required to fit in with existing routines and practices and struggle as a result. Similarly, Aday and Wahidin (2016), writing about the difficulties of reconciling the values of prison hospices with the security concerns of a prison, find:

> Prisons, as a rule, have promoted conformity rather than individuality and frequently dehumanised criminals who are perceived to have little worth. (p. 320)

Although prison officers have the most contact with prisoners (Hay & Sparks, 1991), other prison staff with different occupational cultures also have close involvement with terminally ill prisoners. This is especially the case when a prisoner is transferred to the prison's healthcare centre, and deemed, in the eyes of some staff, to have become a 'medical' rather than a 'discipline' case. Even amongst prison officers, there are different ways of categorising prisoners and even then, in their study of another high security prison, HMP Whitemoor, Liebling et al. (2011) found some officers resisted their colleagues' efforts to categorise prisoners, preferring to see prisoners just as human beings. Sykes (1958) suggests "in the eyes of the custodian, the inmate tends to become a man in prison, rather than a criminal in prison" (p. 55) but the situation in the prisons studied was more complicated.

In both prisons studied there was a tension over whether the dominant status of someone dying in prison was regarded by staff as being that of a 'prisoner', 'patient' or 'person', which was reflected in the use of terminology. The three prison chaplains interviewed used 'person' more readily than the term 'prisoner', referring to individuals by the term 'person' 39 times, as a 'prisoner' 21 times (four times echoing a phrase from the interviewer) and only once as a 'patient'. The use of language did not seem to be a contested issue for them. Instead, the division was typically characterised as officers seeing the individual primarily as a 'prisoner' and healthcare staff thinking of them primarily as their 'patient'. Prisoners were aware of this dichotomy, as were officers (Fieldnote, LTHSE) but it was healthcare staff who raised it most frequently and felt most passionately about the use of language. Officers routinely described the individuals they worked with as 'prisoners', or 'them', this latter term also being used by prisoners to refer to officers. It was noticeable that 'prisoner' was consistently used by officers in preference to 'inmate' or 'resident'. As discussed in chapter one, during the fieldwork, prisoners in the LTHSE prison were being consulted on which term they preferred and chose 'prisoner'. The terms 'offender' or 'criminal', which would have foregrounded the offence, were not used, with the exception of a poster in the healthcare centre at the LTHSE prison. Instead, 'prisoner' described someone incarcerated and placed in the care of prison personnel.

In keeping with Liebling et al. (2011), some staff, including officers, emphasised prisoners should be seen as human beings. (Interview 13, LTHSE; Interviews 12 and 9, Category B; Fieldnotes, LTHSE). Seeing someone as a 'normal person' or 'human' was regarded by many of the prisoners who participated in the study as the gold standard. They expressed appreciation for when this had happened (Fieldnote, Category B) and regarded it as indicative of a lack of care when it did not (Fieldnote, LTHSE). Nursing staff also regarded this as the ideal, perhaps reflecting a different occupational culture from prison officers (Thomson & Parrish, 2002), but maintained a preference for the term 'patient' rather than 'person' for someone who was unwell. In interviews with three nurses, the individuals they cared for were referred to by the term 'patient' 33 times, as a 'person' 9 times and only 2 times as a 'prisoner'.

An account given by a healthcare professional in the Category B prison of trying to co-opt officers on a wing to assist with the care of Dean is illustrative of the attitudes associated by healthcare staff with the different occupation roles of officers and nursing staff. The nurse recounted saying:

> "I need you to be supportive of this because he's staying on the wing and I need everyone involved." And one of them went "Oh, I'll help you. I'll carry his coffin" And I went, I said "Do you know what, that's why you're a prison officer and I'm healthcare, because of that disgusting attitude". And I went and reported it. (*Interview 10, Category B*)

Officers were aware of the reputation they could have in this regard. Prisoners regarded officers as typically seeing them as 'a number', a statistic, with a death equating to just 'one off the roll' (Fieldnotes,

> LTHSE). They also contested the extent to which healthcare professionals did view them as 'patients', both in the prison's healthcare centre and when receiving treatment in outside hospitals, believing instead they were seen by healthcare staff primarily as 'prisoners' (Fieldnote, LTHSE).

Whilst healthcare staff in both prisons spoke about having to defend their construction of the individual as a 'patient' against officers who insisted they were 'prisoners' (Interviews 1 and 10, Category B; Fieldnote, LTHSE), it was noticeable officers almost never mentioned these disagreements. In the one case where the differing constructions of seriously or terminally ill individuals were raised by an officer, the balance of statuses between 'patient' and 'prisoner' was attributed to his location. He described individuals accommodated in the healthcare centre as "patients before they are prisoners", whereas the focus of their treatment on the wing was about discipline (Fieldnote, LTHSE).

In defending their figuring of the individual as a 'patient', little distinction was made by healthcare staff with regard to the severity of any medical diagnosis. Instead there was an emphasis on the relationship between the individual and the healthcare staff: "they're my patients" or "our patients" (Interview 1, Category B). The construction of the individual as a 'patient' was heavily influenced by the position of the person doing the figuring, with one nurse saying: "It doesn't matter what they've done, they are my patient because I'm a nurse" (Interview 10, Category B).

Which status was regarded as dominant did have some effect on the care received by a dying prisoner. Nursing staff spoke about trying to undo behaviours associated with being figured as 'prisoner'. They reported needing to persuade people who had been moved to the healthcare centre that they would be treated differently, including encouraging them to press their cell bell when needed, in contrast to the approach taken by officers on the wing (Interview 12, LTHSE). One nurse spoke about a nursing colleague having held the hand of a dying prisoner, and officers disapproving, although for the nursing staff this was a normal part of nursing (Fieldnote, LTHSE). Savage (1999) says modern nursing care expects at least a theoretical involvement with the patient, and that medical outcomes will be achieved through emotionally close relations.

In the prison context, other studies (Burles et al., 2016; Thomson & Parrish, 2002) suggest nursing staff have to be careful that compassionate behaviour such as this is not misunderstood by prison officers: "healthcare providers face the ongoing challenge of providing care and comfort to ailing patients amidst an atmosphere of animosity towards the individuals for whom they care" (Burles et al., 2016, p.101).

In the LTHSE prison, nurses were cautious in this regard, consciously adapting their nursing techniques to the prison and aware they would still face disapproval:

> because when you're nursing people on the ward you're very touchy feely and you're cuddling and touchy, whereas here you've just to be that little bit more careful, but sometimes you can be a good judge and think yeah I can hold his hand, or 'hmm'. Then again, officers: "what are you doing that for?" (Interview 12, LTHSE)

This is in keeping with Aday and Wahidin (2016) who suggest in prison "even simple, platonic gestures such as touching a patient's hand or shoulder during an assessment, are often discouraged" (p.320). In the Category B prison, touch was observed being used by nurses more naturally (Fieldnote, Category B), but the construction of the individual by officers as primarily a 'prisoner' was still regarded by nurses as adversely affecting their social care. Laughter was seen by healthcare staff as important to mental well-being, but one senior nurse felt some officers saw it as inappropriate, and akin to 'conditioning', the term used to suggest prisoners are 'grooming' or training staff so they can be corrupted or manipulated (Fieldnote, Category B).

Seeing the 'Prisoner'

The implication of constructing the individual as a 'prisoner' is that it evokes someone who is potentially dangerous, who poses a risk because of their past and potential future behaviour. It is known that a number of factors can influence the nature of staff–prisoner relationships between prison officers and prisoners. Crawley (2004) suggests that whether prison officers can identify with prisoners, in terms of finding shared values and interests, depends on the kind of the prison, the age and background of the prisoner and to a lesser extent the offence, as well as the staff member's prior work experience and the occupational culture of the prison. Newell (2002) shares Tait's (2012) analysis that good relationships between staff and prisoner involve the staff treating the prisoner as morally equivalent to them. He claims relationships are based on the prison officers' understanding, awareness and sensitivity towards the prisoner and rely on respect for the personhood of the prisoner, irrespective of their status, value or behaviour. Without this respect, he argues prison officers cannot provide supervision and care to prisoners. Humour can also serve a function in building relationships. Nielson (2011) suggests its use facilitates social spaces where staff and prisoners can relate as equals and helps avoid and diffuse conflicts and smooth interactions. She suggests humour functions as a "transformative and dynamic device" (p. 520).

With regard to prison healthcare staff, a number of studies suggest one of the most dominant features in nurses' relationships with prisoners is the nurses' need to avoid being manipulated by prisoners in their care. Prisoner–patients' manipulative behaviour is reported as presenting challenges designed to compromise or undermine the essence of nursing care (Choudry et al., 2017; Norman & Parrish, 2002), with Foster et al. (2013), MacDonald and Fallon (2008), Walsh and Freshwater (2009) and Weiskopf (2005) all suggesting prison nurses need to be alert to the danger of being manipulated by prisoners. Consequently, Norman and Parrish, (2002) argue prison nursing is an area where nurse–patient relationships and boundaries are of paramount importance. Studies also acknowledge nurses may struggle to feel compassion in their relationships with prisoners, since prisoners have committed crimes against the society of which nurses are a part (Weiskopf, 2005).

The 'prisoner' is someone inherently stigmatised. Constructing the individual dying in prison as primarily a 'prisoner' brings with it a diminished assessment of their value because of the stigma associated with the status, prioritises security considerations and maintains the deprivation of autonomy associated with imprisonment. Understandings of people dying in prison as primarily 'prisoners' will be seen to direct the ways in which prison regimes and personnel respond to the dying.

Stigmatized Individuals

Goffman (1963) defines stigma as an attribute or characteristic that is discreditable to the self. He illustrates this by identifying prisoners as a stigmatised group. Whilst in prison, efforts are made by prison staff to keep track of and control prisoners' behaviour in a manner that never neglects their inherently stigmatised status. This continues even, as will be seen, in the circumstances of approaching death, although broader cultural attitudes towards death and dying helped some staff, in their minds at least, to partially restore the fuller humanity of dying prisoners.

Outside of the prison, escorted to hospital or hospice appointments, prisoners became more conscious of their stigma because it was physically manifested in the escort chain they might have to wear. The rules, regulations and guidance of the Prison Service discussed in chapter three include provisions for the use of restraints in such cases. Prisoners who had attended appointments or received treatment in outside hospitals had two common responses to the use of restraints; they were unnecessary and they provoked an unwelcome response from members of the public. Once seen to be in restraints, the individual was clearly identifiable to as a prisoner. Four prisoners in particular, on separate occasions, explained how this affected them. One prisoner said people stood aside, fearful of him (Fieldnote, LTHSE). Another reported the same response, but demonstrated bravado in saying he enjoyed having people wonder what he had done (Fieldnote, LTHSE). A third prisoner, a wheelchair user, said attending hospital appointments was 'traumatic' because of the chain:

> He says people are looking at you, indicating what he means by turning his head round to the sides and staring. He says they are wondering what he's done, what awful thing. He goes in his wheelchair, with staff pushing him. Even though the hospital knows he's coming, he has to sit in the waiting room, sensing people are looking at him, for maybe up to an hour and a half. (Fieldnote, Category B)

Another wheelchair user was simply grateful he was only on an escort chain and not additionally double cuffed, wrists cuffed together (Fieldnote, LTHSE). What is striking here is the way in which prisoners experienced being a public spectacle whilst restraints were used.

The Prison Rules (1999) provide the principle that an individual being escorted outside of the prison:

> shall be exposed as little as possible to public observation, and proper care shall be taken to protect him from curiosity and insult. (*SI 1999/728, 40*)

It is significant that in a relatively brief document, this is accorded so much importance. The rules are seeking to protect the prisoner from becoming a public spectacle. The escort chain, whilst keeping the prisoner from the public, undermines this and serves as a stigma, marking the individual as a prisoner and thus attracting public attention. It is one of the examples of stigma given by Goffman (1963). Staff were aware of this stigma, with one member of the prison's nursing staff saying of her hospital colleagues: "it's understandable, if the nursing staff see someone in cuffs, that they think the worst" (Fieldnote, Category B) and relating this to her own experience of working in a hospital, knowing if someone was brought in under escort and restrained they had "done something serious" (Fieldnote, Category B). Officers had to respond to public concerns arising from the stigma embodied by the restraints. An officer observed on a 'bedwatch' reported a nurse in the hospital had asked whether the man posed any risk to children visiting other people on the ward (Fieldnote, LTHSE). The use of restraints thus directly led to the construction of the dying prisoner by those outside of the prison as someone who posed a risk or who was responsible for potentially abhorrent crimes.

Within the prison, some prisoners could be singled out for additional stigma. In the LTHSE prison this included indicating if a prisoner was Category A by the use of red card for ID badges and cell labels. Others would have to be unmasked, in this case to the researcher, as 'no-one-to-one', meaning they were judged to pose a heightened risk if with someone by themselves. Some offences, particularly those against children or of a sexual nature, carried an additional stigma. In the Category B prison, where vulnerable prisoners were accommodated separately, those convicted of sexual offences were more readily identifiable by staff and other prisoners because of their location. This was less possible in the LTHSE prison, where there was no such separation. However, any attempts by prisoners to conceal additionally discreditable convictions were unlikely to succeed with prison staff who had access to the prisoner's record.

Spencer and Ricciardelli (2016) argue in their study of correctional officers' attitudes towards sex offenders that: "While officers are primarily attuned to their occupational culture, they are also embedded in broader society and affected by their interactions with prisoners" (p. 382). This was the case in the prisons studied. Whilst some officers and staff in other roles tried not to think about a prisoner's offences, others were very aware of their crimes, and when these were of a sexual nature, this awareness could impact on how they felt about working with them. In some circumstances the additional stigma of conviction for certain offences made sympathy less likely to be extended to some dying prisoners, even when officers felt, as discussed below, their occupational culture expected them to feel sympathetic.

An officer spoke about working with a prisoner who was dying during the fieldwork period as:

> harder than some of the others I've done, mainly because he'd just got a 36 year sentence, er, for sex offences against children. ... Er, so trying to keep professional but having that at the back of your mind's been really difficult. (Interview 16, Category B)

Another officer spoke frankly about her feelings towards prisoners who had harmed children, saying:

> Because a lot of people see it as erm, "they've done a crime, they're here, that's it, that's the end of it". As I see it as more of "they've caused suffering to someone else, so if God's given them this path to go down, then that's just the way it is". Sometimes it's an eye for an eye. So I kind of [two second pause] see it as justice in my eyes... You're working with these, and we're all about rehabilitation and once they come in here "they've done the crime, however, they're still a normal person and de de de de". But unfortunately, someone's killed a child or raped a child, when they are dying, I'm not really feeling <u>any</u> kind of empathy for them...I find it hard, if I'm being honest, to feel sorry for someone when they've caused probably a lot worse to someone else. (Interview 15, LTHSE)

The revulsion she felt towards prisoners who had harmed children was clear; she did not mind they were dying in prison. In both these cases, the officers interviewed felt the expected professional standards required them to not think differently about a prisoner because of the nature of his offences, but they found this difficult to achieve. By emphasising what she felt "if I'm being honest" (Interview 15, LTHSE), there is a suggestion such honesty was not always possible. Both of these officers were female and it may have been they were navigating professional norms that intersected with gender norms, struggling not appear "too soft" in an evolving occupational culture traditionally regarded as macho (Cheek & Miller, 1983; Tait, 2011).

Emotional labour is recognised as crucial to the functioning of a prison (Crawley, 2004). Tait (2008) maintains there is a gender difference in what emotional displays are acceptable amongst prison officers, with male officers facing occupational cultural pressure to be 'hard' which female prison officers do not experience to the same extent. The situation suggested by the two female officers quoted here is clearly more complex. Spencer and Ricciardelli (2016) find in a Canadian context that "correctional officers' feelings of disgust towards sex offenders render them less-than-human" (p. 390), but in this research project it was only female officers who expressed such feelings, directed towards prisoners guilty of specific offences, particularly those against children. Working with these men if they were terminally ill meant that for much of the time, they were engaged in emotional labour, performing the necessary 'surface acting' to hide deeper feelings they deemed unacceptable in their working environment. Their male colleagues may have felt the same, but spoke more generically about the nature of the crimes committed and implied less of a conflict in performing the 'deep acting' required to set aside the specifics of the offences for which the prisoner was convicted.

> Regardless what these people here have done, and some of these, the majority of what's in this prison are the worst offences in the country, horrendous, but you're still responsible for the care of what they are about. (Interview 11, LTHSE)

The tension inherent in providing this care whilst regarding the prisoner's offences as "horrendous" required forms of emotional labour and deep acting. One approach to this was described by an officer who regarded some prisoners as "horrid" (Fieldnote, LTHSE) and found knowing the details of their crimes could provoke anger. He suggested he could set aside these feelings if the prisoner was regarded by trusted colleagues as helpful to staff and not a difficult prisoner. For such officers, the prisoner was less stigmatised by his crime, more judged on his behaviour towards prison staff. The dilemma of showing care for someone stigmatised by the horrific things he had done was therefore lessened.

Security Considerations and Prison 'Rules'

Male prisoners are classified as Category A, B, C or D according to how likely they are to try to escape and their risk of causing harm to other prisoners and prison staff. The two prisons in the study housed Category A prisoners, (LTHSE) and Category B prisoners (LTHSE and Category B prison). As such, security matters dominated all other considerations. The need to impose order and maintain security was embodied in the rules, regulations and guidance which govern the management of all prisoners, and which continued to be relevant in the treatment of dying prisoners. However, as Lillie (2018) states, "the propensity to focus on security can lead to an unnecessary diminishment of dignity in dying" (p. 49).

Whilst rarely explicitly addressing the circumstances of a dying prisoner, the PSIs, PSOs and Prison Rules discussed in the previous chapter emphasise security as the primary concern in a number of situations relevant to the treatment of a dying prisoner. However, understanding these regulations has an importance beyond providing insights into how prisoners should be treated or tasks performed. Carrabine (2000) states: "the penal system can be regarded as a composite of diverse forces, techniques, rationalities and devices which seek to regulate the actions and decisions of individuals and groups in relation to certain authoritative criteria". He continues, "these criteria and the ability to act are performed through discourse" (p. 316). It is argued here that prison 'rules' form part of the discourse in prisons about dying prisoners and inform constructions of the dying prisoner. Carrabine (2000) argues discourses structure action, belief and conduct. It therefore follows that the discourses created by the prison rules around dying prisoners, palliative care and responses after a death will shape not just what happens in relation to a specific rule but also attitudes towards dying prisoners more generally. Similarly, the rules applying to the deaths of prisoners are part of a broader framework of beliefs and conduct which are in part shaped by the discourses arising from other regulations. In a setting where "rules may be the anchor in a world of uncertainty" (Liebling & Price, 2003, p.74), it is inevitable they set the tone for how dying prisoners are perceived and treated, although they were "resources upon which to draw, rather than templates to be applied" (Liebling & Price, 2003, p. 74).

All of the meticulous detail of prison rules, explored in Chapter 3, serves to emphasise the prisoner is being constructed as a potential danger, as someone who poses a risk that must be managed at all times. The 'rules', which officers are expected to be familiar with, also form a discourse which shapes the actions of staff, particularly prison officers. In the 'rules', only when they are unconscious, on the operating table or requiring extreme treatment such as defibrillation (itself a risk to any officers attached to the escort chain) can the level of security assessed to be appropriate be relaxed. The dominance of this agenda inevitably influences discourses about dying prisoners.

The use of restraints was the most visible representation of security considerations when a prisoner was escorted to outside hospitals. The appropriate use of restraints in terms of an assessed security risk was an important part of how staff considered their responsibilities to dying prisoners. On occasions, staff were unhappy about the use of restraints, with both officers and nursing staff expressing dissatisfaction with risk assessments resulting in the use of restraints on prisoners felt to be too frail to escape or unlikely to pose a risk (Fieldnote, Category B). Nursing staff reported having to 'fight' the prison over this issue (Interviews 1, Category B; Interview 12, LTHSE). Their unease is reflected in a report from the Prison and Probation Ombudsman for England and Wales (2013) which looks at lessons to be learned from investigations into end of life care in prisons:

> While a prison's first duty is to protect the public, too often restraints are used in a disproportionate, inappropriate and sometimes inhumane way (p. 5).

Key to the Graham Judgement, discussed in chapter three, was the notion that restraints should only be used if the risk of escape, or of harm to the public occurring if the prisoner did escape, had been adequately assessed and was well founded. In this respect, the ruling in this case emphasised the need to regard the prisoner as an individual, not as a member of a stigmatised group. The ruling also encouraged officers to openly reassess the construction of the prisoner as he approached death, to consider it possible he no longer posed the same risk, with two officers (Interview 11, LTHSE; Interview 2, Category B) mentioning the need to review cuffing arrangements if the prisoner's condition changed. For some of the staff in the prisons studied, although risk assessments had been conducted they struggled to accept an outcome which led to someone in their care being treated in restraints. The use of restraints, for both prisoners and staff, embodied the effects of constructing the dying individual as a 'prisoner' rather than a 'patient' or 'person'. Having restraints applied was part of being a prisoner; it was not something typically associated with the experience of dying for someone not imprisoned.

The Deprivation of Autonomy

In his seminal study of a 1950s American maximum security prison, Sykes (1958) identifies the deprivation of autonomy as one of the five pains of imprisonment. For him, this is defined as resulting from the prisoner's subjugation to a "vast body of rules and commands which are designed to control his behaviour in minute detail" (p.73). He suggests that whilst the matters controlled may be trivial, prisoners feel intense hostility at being dependent on the unexplained decisions of people with very different objectives to their own. He argues this lack of autonomy presents a psychological challenge to the prisoner, undermining their self-image by reducing them to "the weak, helpless, dependent status of childhood" (p. 75). Sykes suggests the prison custodians in his study avoided giving explanations in order to prevent prisoners from being able to present an alternative viewpoint and challenge the rules, which is echoed by Goffman's (1961) claim that "characteristically the inmate is excluded from knowledge of the decisions taken regarding his fate.... Such exclusion gives staff a special basis of distance from and control over inmates" (pp. 19–20). With regard to prisoners dying of natural causes, Aday (2006) states that "in an institution such as a prison, which controls living as well as dying, a sense of helplessness is almost unavoidable" (p. 201). A lack of autonomy is also characteristic of the healthcare available to prisoners, with Bolger (2005), Turner et al. (2011) and Condon et al. (2007) all suggesting prisons allow prisoners very little personal choice regarding healthcare. This lack of autonomy is inextricably linked to the individual's status as a prisoner.

When some limited autonomy was available to a dying prisoner, it was noteworthy. In the LTHSE prison, staff in a variety of roles repeatedly referenced Eddie as a prisoner whose wishes had been respected (Fieldnotes, LTHSE; Interviews 13 and 15, LTHSE). During the last few months of his life, he had expressed a wish to be accommodated on the wing rather than in the healthcare centre as was expected. A number of staff, nurses and officers reported they wouldn't force him to move cells (Fieldnotes, LTHSE) and expressed satisfaction that the wing was the best place for him because it was what he wanted (Fieldnote, LTHSE). The exercise of autonomy by a dying prisoner was however, not without contest or concern. When asked if they could compel Eddie to move to healthcare, another senior officer was clearly reluctant to do so, but would not rule out the possibility (Fieldnote, LTHSE). As he grew more obviously frail, staff concerns about Eddie's location intensified and the commitment to facilitating his wishes diminished. Even before this, Eddie's options were limited. When a fall in his cell resulted in staff wanting him to be in a cell with a bell by the bed, he was consulted, but his options framed as moving cell on the wing or going to healthcare. Staff knew he was aware he was not being given a choice (Fieldnote, LTHSE). Interestingly, no other cases in this prison were offered as examples of prisoners being granted such autonomy. It was not clear whether this was because it had not occurred, or had happened but subsequently been forgotten. One officer who was interviewed talked about being sensitive to the needs of another prisoner accommodated in the healthcare centre towards the end of life, albeit on a less significant issue:

> Y'know some days he'd come and sit and eat a little bit at table, er, and some days he didn't even want his tea. So it were just, we kind of let him lead, if you know what I mean, and we just worked round him. (Interview 15, LTHSE)
>
> Other prisoners recounted narrow choices being offered to their peers, with one saying the withdrawal of medication was used as a 'threat' to get unwell prisoners to move to the healthcare centre (Fieldnote, LTHSE). Location in the healthcare centre was recognised to make the administering of medication easier for a variety of reasons, but prisoners clearly saw this 'threat' as another way of minimising their agency.

The construction of dying prisoners in relation to their entitlement to autonomy was slightly different at the Category B prison, where there were more examples of granting autonomy, including to Dean, who had similarly had his wish to stay in the wing after a terminal diagnosis respected and was only relocated to H3 when he said he wanted to move (Interviews 1 and 3, Category B). Furthermore, a nurse at the Category B prison talked about meeting a dying prisoner's wishes in other ways, saying they would ensure his friends were present even though it was late at night, or arrange for him to see a particular film if he wanted (Interview 2, Category B). Small concessions were seen as significant. An officer here spoke about the importance of giving prisoners the choice as to whether to have their cell door open or closed during unlock periods, a means of them controlling which prisoners came into their cell (Interview 3, Category B).

With Eddie, the source of the decision to move him was less clear to many people, but the agency for the action was attributed to staff, not him. One interviewee said that they 'got him over', meaning moved him to the healthcare centre regardless (Interview 13, LTHSE). Another knew of Eddie's case, but wasn't sure whether he'd died in hospital. When I told him what I knew, the interviewee said 'So they did eventually move him', again attributing the agency for this to someone other than Eddie (Interview 11, LTHSE). Although Eddie was well-liked and much sympathy was expressed for him, he could still be talked of as an object to be managed.

Eddie's case also illustrates the limited means by which prisoners could exercise their autonomy at the end of life. Irwin and Owen (2011) regard loss of agency as one of the forms of psychological damage which result from imprisonment and which erode a prisoner's ability to cope with life outside. They point out that with few opportunities to make decisions or exert choice in their daily routine:

> prisoners steadily lose their capacity to exert power and control their destiny as they serve time in prison. Prison life is completely routinized and restricted (p. 98).

Eddie's ability to control, to small extent, his location within the prison was attributed by staff and prisoners who knew him to his stubbornness (Interview 13, LTHSE; Fieldnote, LTHSE), a characteristic that other prisoners associated with a number of their older colleagues (Interview 14, LTHSE; Fieldnote, LTHSE). His tools to exert his will were however limited; he was reported to have refused to eat until transferred from the healthcare centre to the wing (Interview 5, LTHSE) and then to have lied about his condition, in the opinion of healthcare staff, to avoid being moved back off the wing (Fieldnote, LTHSE). Although he had clearly not, as Irwin and Owen (2011) suggest, lost the habit of agency, he had few resources to use in a situation where the power relationships were stacked against him. What seemed more significant in explaining why he was afforded some autonomy was the fact he was liked and respected by officers, who expressed sympathy for him.

Seeing the 'Patient' or 'Person'

A terminal diagnosis and the approach of the end of life made it more likely for a prisoner to be constructed as 'patient' or 'person' by staff in all roles. Although these terms were used predominately by healthcare professionals and chaplains, in the face of a terminal diagnosis officers also described a softening of the usual distinctions between their position and that of the prisoner, and a greater awareness of the individual as a fellow human being. Key to this experience were feelings of sympathy towards the individual provoked by their failing health, although not in all circumstances. An impending death also brought prison officers and other staff into unexpected contact with the prisoner's family, potentially leading to new constructions of the individual as part of a family, emphasising they were someone with links beyond the prison wall, rather than solely a prisoner. Again, these constructions influenced the care prisoners received, and impacted on the regime and the relationships and culture within the prison.

Sympathy

The fact of imprisonment when dying was for some staff, especially those not working as prison officers, itself a reason for sympathy and a softening of attitudes. One of the healthcare team in the Category B prison felt if other staff were more conscious that dying in prison was unpleasant, and more aware of the restrictions placed on the individual even though he was dying, they would be more understanding. Prison was seen as a hard place to be, even if not ill, and so much harder for the dying (Interview 1, Category B). A prison chaplain in this prison keenly felt the loneliness of dying in prison:

> When a person passes, if they've got the family around them, erm, or if they've died with the support of the family around them, erm, you get, you get a sense, of feeling that that person died knowing that they were well loved, y'know? But when a person dies in prison, even though, obviously, it's not the prison's fault that they're here in the first place, I think as a human being, there is this thought in my head that that person has died on their own, y'know, there was no one there. (Interview 8, Category B)

For this chaplain, one of the main regrets about someone dying in custody was the lack of family support they would receive. They may in practice be accompanied by officers or nursing staff at the moment they died, but without his family, the prisoner was in the eyes of the chaplain 'alone'. His comment highlights the lack of love that a dying prisoner would experience, and a deep compassion for them stemming from the awareness they would probably die without their family. For many healthcare staff and for other chaplains, concerns that a prisoner would die alone contributed to generating sympathy for their situation (Fieldnotes,

LTHSE; Interviews 5 and 12, LTHSE). As one nurse said, equating prisoners to people in general, "nobody wants to die alone" (Interview 12, LTHSE).

In terms of the relationships between prison officers and prisoners, Arnold (2016) suggests prison officers are trained to see these relationships as procedural and instrumental, achieving something in line with the prison officer's and prison service's agenda. In contrast, Liebling et al. (1999) find: "the sort of relationships staff tried to cultivate with prisoners were—at their best—fair, honest and good humoured" (p. 84). For them, good staff–prisoner relationships do not involve the prison officer 'giving in' to prisoners, but instead illustrate the complexity involved, with staff needed to demonstrate both consistency and a degree of flexibility. Crawley (2004) suggests that: "the 'trick' was to develop a relationship whereby staff and prisoners could recognise each other's predicament and 'rub along' on a day to day basis with minimal friction" (p. 108). In keeping with her suggestion that prisoners and officers may find they have things in common over long periods of knowing each other, in these prisons, when a prisoner was known to be dying, the relationships between them and many staff, including some prison officers, were marked by sympathy towards the prisoner. Prison officers undertook considerable emotional labour and expressed a seemingly genuine sympathy for the prisoner at being in the situation of dying in prison, especially if the prisoner was young or liked and respected for behaviour transcending the usual expectations of staff. Any instrumental nature to the relationship was less apparent. Additionally, far from the retributive culture sometimes attributed to prison officers (Crawley, 2004), officers often felt that when a prisoner was dying they were expected to feel forgiveness and sympathy. This was particularly striking in the instance quoted earlier in this chapter, where a female officer's repulsion for prisoners who had harmed children meant she felt unable to experience the sympathy she regarded as required by her occupational culture. The officer was clear she needed to hide from her colleagues her lack of sympathy and performed the necessary 'surface acting' to demonstrate the expected 'feeling rules' of her role (Interview 15, LTHSE).

One of the recognised difficulties faced by staff is that of establishing the 'boundary' in their relationships with prisoners. Liebling et al. (2011) suggest prison officers experience a lack of clarity about the 'right' relationship with prisoners. Liebling et al. (2011) and Crawley (2004) find that officers talk about the 'boundary' or 'drawing a line' but that there are discrepancies and difficulties in defining where this should be. In this study, many officers reported maintaining a distinction between themselves and a prisoner as part of being professional but, if a prisoner was terminally ill, experienced a softening of this difference. They were aware their officer colleagues could struggle to feel the sympathy now regarded by them as an expected part of their professionalism. Prison officers could feel required to perform the deep acting of allowing a terminal diagnosis to provoke a sympathetic response in themselves:

> Me, me personally I would do it in a professional way that he's still a prisoner, I'm still an officer, but there's an element of you've got to feel sorry for them because they are dying. So, but not everyone can do that because of the nature of what they have done. (Interview 11, LTHSE)

Such comments show an awareness of the complexity experienced by officers in feeling sympathy for a prisoner. They illuminate the tension inherent in recognising the prisoner's humanity whilst maintaining the dynamic expected to exist between an officer and a prisoner. The 'feeling rules' of the prison officer's role required professionalism, including sympathy, which for some was 'surface acting'. Significantly, the humanity of a prisoner became more apparent to a prison officer when there was a terminal diagnosis:

> It becomes more of a human nature than an officer-prisoner and you maybe do things, not wrong, not, not legally wrong, but for support of the person who is going to pass away. (Interview 11, LTHSE)
>
> There were several examples of how knowledge that a prisoner was dying did seem to subtly change their relationship with staff, encouraging sympathy and making it easier for officers to see a 'person' rather than just a 'prisoner' (Fieldnote, LTHSE). One senior officer said:
>
> That's where the decency part comes in I think. You've still got to maintain the fact that yes it's a prisoner and you know the fact that you've

> got to keep that prisoner within this environment, but you know that you make it as easy as possible for them, because you know that that is the last part of his life. Y'know. You will make it as comfortable for them as you possibly could, or possibly can. (Interview 6, LTHSE)

This was not universal. Two officers were observed passing the time during a 'bedwatch' in a conversation, overheard by the prisoner, in which they both emphasised not caring about prisoners, not thinking about them after work and in which one of them in particular spoke about prisoners he found unpleasant and even about being impatient for a prisoner to die during a previous 'bedwatch'. Nevertheless, the officer expressed sympathy for a prisoner he had escorted to a hospital appointment where he had been given a terminal diagnosis:

> He says it felt like the man had been "given a kick in the balls", and then apologises for swearing. He says this time he did talk about it at home. (Fieldnote, LTHSE)

Crawley (2004) is thus correct in suggesting there are organisational norms for prison staff expressing sympathy but the fieldwork in this study does not support her claim prison officer culture forbids expressions of sympathy for prisoners, or that sympathy is not likely to be expressed in the hearing of other officers. In this study, a terminal diagnosis often resulted in an expectation amongst prison officers that sympathy would be shown to a prisoner. What is significant is how some officers struggled to meet this expectation when the prisoner was doubly stigmatised by having committed sexual offences or crimes against children.

The nature of a prisoner's offence could also positively influence attitudes towards them at the end of life and make it more likely they would be viewed sympathetically. An example was given in the Category B prison as an illustration, with the suggestion that a shoplifter, first time in prison, would probably be released on the licence to the hospice (Interview 1, Category B). A more sympathetic treatment could be afforded to him because his crimes were regarded as minor. Remand prisoners, typically only accommodated at the Category B prison, provoked further sympathy. One of the healthcare staff in this prison spoke of her anger after the death of William, an elderly remand prisoner whose dementia meant he was in her opinion unaware even that he was in prison. He died before being convicted of any crime, in her eyes therefore an innocent man, and she was furious when:

> the actual vicar in the service made comments of "Well it's a shame really, because this congregation would have been really full had it not been for his crimes". (Interview 10, Category B)
>
> She felt an injustice was being done to the deceased prisoner and that, because he had not been convicted, a stigma had been incorrectly applied to him.

Age could also invoke sympathy, with staff displaying more regret at atypically early deaths. This reflects the assumption, discussed earlier, that deaths from natural causes would be associated with ageing. Dean, who had stayed on the wing in the Category B prison after his terminal diagnosis, stood out for interviewees because of his age (Interviews 1 and 10, Category B). The behaviour and demeanour of the prisoner, both before and after a terminal diagnosis could also dramatically influence the extent to which sympathy was expressed to them, and indeed how care was performed. The healthcare worker at the Category B prison who spoke about William said: "I liked him. Regardless of what crime he'd done, he was lovely man" (Interview 10, Category B). His putative crimes were not an obstacle to her favourable opinion.

Eddie was another good example of this. Officers in the LTHSE prison were clear "he's no trouble, doesn't make extra demands on staff, isn't on his bell" and that he was a "decent prisoner" (Fieldnote, LTHSE). There was a slight hesitation and awkwardness about the use of this latter term in front of me, an awareness it was a term used amongst themselves that might not be politically correct to the researcher and that he had earned the epithet of "decent prisoner" because they had not had to do much for him. Crawley (2004) suggests officers more readily feel sympathy for a cooperative rather than a disruptive prisoner, and this was the case with Eddie. Opinions towards him also seemed to be influenced by his attitude towards his terminal illness. He was described as having been "positive", not moaning or playing on his diagnosis for more attention, which garnered respect because it was atypical of many prison officers' expectations of prisoners (Interview 5, LTHSE). He was also popular, liked by his peers on the wing, with friendships in which his previous support for others was now being reciprocated (Fieldnotes, LTHSE). In his uncomplaining approach to his terminal illness, Eddie was seemingly enacting something both convenient and inspiring for staff and peers around him. In a similar way, another prisoner who had had a stroke was spoken of fondly by a peer. The man was regarded highly because he kept cheerful, and although he only had two words, made people laugh (Fieldnote, LTHSE). Liebling et al. (2011) talk about different forms of respect in prison, suggesting that whilst fear and power can gain respect for staff and prisoners alike, respect also derives from the individual stepping out of the limitations and expectations of their role and showing moral strength. It is arguably in these latter regards that Eddie and the stroke survivor earned respect.

Those prisoners who were less popular were less likely to provoke sympathy. A member of staff, when asked about the impact on prisoners in H3 of the Category B prison if one of their number needed to go to outside hospital said that in the case of a man who had been taken out the day before, not expected to live, it had had no effect: he had not been there long and was not liked (Fieldnote, Category B). A prisoner in the LTHSE prison, in contrast to Eddie, but who had been on the same wing, was reported to be disliked because he and his cell were unhygienic, and the prisoner-carers cleaning for him were frustrated by his habits (Fieldnote, LTHSE). His diagnosis did not favourably change the relationships he had with those around him.

Constructing the Family Man: The Influence of a Prisoner's Family

A terminal diagnosis or a death from natural causes frequently brought prison staff into contact with the prisoner's family in ways that would not otherwise have occurred. Central to this was the work of the family liaison officer (FLO), whose role was to be a contact point between the prison and the prisoner's family, providing information and support to the family (Bending & Malone, 2007). The FLOs who participated in this research project all expressed sympathy for the families. They saw their role as helping the family at a difficult time (Interview 15, LTHSE; Interview 16, Category B), and as making things as straightforward as possible for the family (Interview 15, LTHSE). Arguably, this interaction with prisoners' families also influenced the construction of the dying prisoner, situating an individual in relation to a group of people who were not incarcerated, reminding staff of their connections beyond the prison and of identities other than 'prisoner'. This could serve to enhance sympathy for the prisoner. However, it was also noticeable that it was often easier for staff to feel sympathetic towards the prisoner's family than towards the prisoner. This sometimes led to adjustments to the physical environment or to routines to support prisoners' families which also served to better meet the needs of the dying prisoner. Seeing the prisoner as someone's relative could result in adaptions to the regime and changes to relationships within the prison.

Sympathy was extended to the family, by FLOs and other staff, for several reasons. In the LTHSE prison in particular, families were seen as having been negatively affected by the crime. They were described as the "innocent party" and it was recognised that the crime could split families, disrupt lives and place a stigma on the prisoner's family (Interview 15, LTHSE). Deaths could also leave unanswered questions for family members, relating to the original crime, and staff felt sympathetic about this. One governor saw deaths as leaving unanswered questions which they could imagine sharing in similar circumstances:

> There's always those questions, "what did we do wrong, as a family". And that could be any one of us, it could be any one us that are left asking those questions: "If I'd have done so and so, would it have changed". And I've found that quite a bit with the families, when you speak to them … that's the question they want to know. Why? What made them do what they did?... One guy murdered his wife, and his brother actually said, he said, "He was part of the family firm, what went wrong?" He said "We'd been at a family do. He'd gone to bed early. They'd had a fall out. He murdered her". He said "I just don't know what went wrong with my little brother". (Interview 13, LTHSE)

> Accounts such as this served to emphasise the humanity of the prisoner as someone's 'little brother', but also to build an empathetic connection between the staff member and family member. Prison staff could identify with the situation of a prisoner's relative more easily than with that of the prisoner who had committed an appalling crime.

The repulsion felt towards prisoners who had committed sexual offences was mirrored in the tremendous sympathy expressed by staff for victims within the family. The encounters with this side of the prisoner's story resulting from their death could be profoundly affecting:

> when they went, the staff went down, all the daughter wanted to know was "was there anything that could have been passed on to her and her daughter from the father?". Was there any illness we could tell them, which we couldn't. Erm, and then she proceeded to tell them of the things the father had done. And I know both FLOs, both female FLOs, had to stop the car on the way back and just sat and sobbed. (Interview 13, LTHSE)

Staff had to attempt to contact a next of kin when a prisoner was dying, with his permission, or after an unexpected death. Given the sexual nature of the offences of many prisoners in the LTHSE prison, staff were understanding when a family chose not to have anything to do with them, although this placed more pressure on the prison in terms of taking responsibility for the practicalities of arranging the funeral (Interview 15, LTHSE). When there was family involvement, there was a concern for the family facing a more complicated bereavement process because of their family member's imprisonment (Interviews 8, 16 and 1, Category B; Interviews 15 and 4, LTHSE). It was recognised that families would not be able to plan the funeral in the usual way because of the investigations following a death and that they would need regular contact in order to get through the process that followed a death (Interview 15, LTHSE; Interview 16, Category B).

FLOs in particular often built close relationships with the prisoner's family, maintaining contact over a number of weeks. They got to know about the family's financial circumstances, helping out with taxi costs (Interview 9, Category B), talked about their employment (Interviews

2 and 16, Category B) or simply chatted in general terms (Interview 7, LTHSE; Interview 9, Category B). This could present difficulties, as in one case where a FLO subsequently needed to contact the police about the prisoner's wife's possible criminal activity (Interview 16, Category B).

Staff expressions of concern for the family of a dying or deceased prisoner seemed to serve a number of purposes. Often, staff felt they could identify with the family more than the prisoner. This was especially the case where the additional stigma associated with certain abhorrent crimes could make identification with the prisoner deeply uncomfortable and sympathy hard to generate. Most significantly, by foregrounding the involvement of the family, some prisoners could be seen as 'family men'. For example, in talking about Dean, a young prisoner in the Category B prison, nursing staff emphasised he had a wife and child, and expressed concern that the nature of his death had been distressing for them. They recounted having had considerable contact with his family during his illness because they had visited him in H3. Dean was constructed as a family man who wanted to fulfil the responsibilities of this role:

> his little son, erm, he was a little superstar, he was so brave, so brave, and all he wanted was a new bike. And all Dean ever talked about was "I wish I wasn't in here so I could get him a bike" (Interview 10, Category B).
>
> After his death, prisoners from Dean's wing raised money to buy his son a bicycle (Interviews 1 and 10, Category B).

How dying prisoners were constructed in relation to their family had an impact on the sympathy afforded to them and arguably introduced a different construction of the individual as part of a family, not solely a 'prisoner'. It also resulted in some adjustments being made to their care. Most commonly this led to family visits in areas of the prison not normally accessed by visitors, especially the healthcare centres, when the prisoner lacked the mobility to access the Visits hall. In both prisons studied, visits were facilitated in locations other than the Visits hall when deemed necessary, even though this caused some practical difficulties (Interviews 1, 2, 3, 10, 9, 16, Category B; Interview 13, LTHSE). Sympathy for families was also a significant motivation for prisoners, healthcare professionals and other staff in seeking to create pleasant palliative care suites in both of the prisons something which also benefitted prisoners.

One of the more significant adjustments resulting from constructing the prisoner as a family man occurred in the LTHSE prison. The wife of a prisoner, Neil, had been permitted to stay overnight with him in the healthcare centre when his death was imminent. Staff in all roles regarded it as a highly unusual move, especially in a high security prison, and it was not without controversy. There was also considerable pride amongst staff that it had been possible to do this, and a conviction it would happen again in future cases (Interviews 7, 12 and 12, LTHSE).

> It was such a huge thing for her to be able to spend the night there with her husband, y'know the staff tried to make it as comfortable as possible for her and she got to be there while her husband passed away. So it were really, she were so grateful for that. (Interview 15, LTHSE)

It had only been considered because Neil's wife was liked by staff and not seen as likely to cause any problems. Despite that, staff were still present, and their presence attributed to a need to make sure she didn't hasten his death (Fieldnote, LTHSE; Interviews 7 and 13, LTHSE). Neil's status as a dying prisoner had been established before his arrival in the prison. He had been transferred to the prison to be nearer his family because he was known to be dying. As such, his wife was already prefigured as his widow when he arrived, and the sympathy extended to her doubtless reflected this. Extending sympathy to the family, or displacing it to the family if the prisoner was beyond sympathy, led to other new tasks for prison staff, which will be discussed in chapter five in connection with the performance of care.

Conclusion

Dying was closely associated by many participants with ageing, and the ageing prison population, especially in the LTHSE prison, was regarded as presaging more deaths from natural causes in the future. Understanding dying as linked to ageing changed attitudes towards some prisoners, including from their peers. It also changed the attitudes of some prisoners towards their own sentence, increasing an awareness when a death occurred that it would one day be them. Death was linked by participants to certain ailments, to the individual's physical appearance and as discussed in chapter three, to their location within prison custody.

Considering how an individual was constructed as a dying prisoner illuminates both what influences responses to terminally ill prisoners and how the relationships within a prison were affected by deaths from natural causes. Dying individuals were awarded different dominant statuses by prison staff, typically 'prisoner' or 'patient', but sometimes 'person'. These constructions of the dying individual were shaped by differing occupational cultures and staff roles in the prison. Healthcare staff in particular experienced a tension between whether these men were 'patients', their preferred construction, or 'prisoners', the perceived construction of prison officers. Not all staff experienced this in the same way, but these constructions were relevant because of the way they affected care, discussed in the next chapter. The different constructions of the dying prisoner's dominant status were intrinsically linked to the value placed on them as an individual, but also to the relationship between them and the staff member doing the figuring. Prison officers, focussed traditionally on discipline, were more likely to see the 'prisoner', healthcare professionals, with a focus on care, the 'patient'. Arguably it was the chaplain's role in providing pastoral care that led to them constructing the individual as a 'person'. As has been seen, attitudes towards a prisoner could soften in light of a terminal diagnosis or the approaching end of life. The humanity of prisoners often became more apparent to staff when they were aware the individual had a terminal diagnosis, but this was not universal.

Even though sympathy could be extended to some dying prisoners, the fact of their imprisonment remained a strong determinant of their experience of dying. The deprivation of autonomy associated with being a prisoner (Sykes, 1958) continued after a terminal diagnosis, limiting the autonomy and agency available to a prisoner at the end of life. If he is to have his wishes respected, Eddie's case illustrates the importance of a prisoner being liked, having a record of not being problematic to staff and having friends willing to care for him. Nurses, professionally used to building emotionally close relationships to facilitate medical outcomes (Savage, 1999), could find their approaches challenged when surrounded by prison officers with a different occupational culture. For the nurses, constructing the dying individual as a 'patient' led to encouraging them to ask for help, and using physical touch, including hand holding, in ways they felt were disapproved of by officers. For prison officers, more typically constructing the same individuals as 'prisoners', the dying prisoner's dominant status meant their responses to the situation were predicated on maintaining security and discipline and managing risks. Each of these constructions brought its own consequences for the treatment of the dying prisoner, with displays of compassion being more closely associated with the 'patient' status, and security considerations being foregrounded when the individual was regarded as a 'prisoner', stigmatised and posing a risk needing managing.

The typical approach taken by prison officers to the dominant status of the individual as 'prisoner' regardless of a terminal diagnosis was also the one reflected in the prison rules. It permitted a lingering stigmatisation (often visible) of dying prisoners and maintained the loss of autonomy associated with imprisonment, which at the end of life was potentially experienced as less than optimal care. The priorities of the prison rules are security and bureaucracy. When these were connected to the circumstances around the end of life, they become the prevention of prisoners escaping or harming people, the imperative of keeping records, and of producing the documentation that after a death would be essential for the inevitable investigation.

However, staff, including prison officers, did feel sympathy for dying prisoners that led to them amending their construction of these individuals, softening their approaches and making it more possible to see the humanity of the prisoner, to construct them as a 'person'. Several factors influenced how much sympathy was felt towards a dying prisoner. These included their age, the nature of their offence, their behaviour towards staff whilst in prison and their attitude towards their illness. In many cases, building a relationship with the prisoner's family served to increase sympathy for the prisoner, constructing another identity for them as part of a 'normal' family. The most significant factor in how much sympathy a prisoner was afforded was the nature of their offence. Officers in particular were aware they were expected to feel sympathy towards dying prisoners, but struggled to do so when the individual's crimes were of a sexual nature or against children. In this respect, they were arguably influenced by the attitudes of the broader society. Sympathy mattered because it affected constructions of the dying prisoner and informed adjustments to the prison regime (the usual running of the prison) that influenced the provision of care, as discussed in the next chapter.

References

Aday, R. (2006). Aging prisoners' concerns toward dying in prison. *OMEGA Journal of Death and Dying, 52*(3), 199–216.

Aday, R., & Wahidin, A. (2016). Older prisoners' experiences of death, dying and grief behind bars. *The Howard Journal of Crime and Justice, 55*(3), 312–327. https://doi.org/10.1111/hojo.12172

Arnold, H. (2016). The prison officer. In Y. Jewkes, B. Crewe, & J. Bennett (Eds.), *Handbook on prisons* (2nd ed., pp. 265–284). Routledge.

Bending, B., & Malone, T. (2007). The hardest job of all: Family liaison following a death in custody. *Prison Service Journal, 172*, 24–28.

Bolger, M. (2005). Dying in prison: providing palliative care in challenging environments. *International Journal of Palliative Nursing, 11*(12), 619–621. https://doi.org/10.12968/ijpn.2005.11.12.20227

Burles, M. C., Peternelj-Taylor, C. A., & Holtslander, L. (2016). A 'good death' for all?: Examining issues for palliative care in correctional settings. *Mortality, 21*(2), 93–111. https://doi.org/10.1080/13576275.2015.1098602

Carrabine, E. (2000). Discourse, governmentality and translation: Towards a social theory of imprisonment. *Theoretical Criminology, 4*(3), 309–331. https://doi.org/10.1177/1362480600004003004

Cheek, F. E., & Miller, M. D. S. (1983). The experience of stress for correction officers: A double-bind theory of correctional stress. *Journal of Criminal Justice, 11*(2), 105–120. https://doi.org/10.1016/0047-2352(83)90046-6

Choudry, K., Armstrong, D., & Dregan, A. (2017). Prison nursing: Formation of a stable professional identity. *Journal of Forensic Nursing, 13*(1), 20–25.

Condon, L., Hek, G., Harris, F., Powell, J., Kemple, T., & Priscoe, S. (2007). Users' views of prison health services: A qualitative study. *Journal of Advanced Nursing, 58*(3), 216–226. https://doi.org/10.1111/j.1365-2648.2007.04221.x

Crawley, E. (2004). *Doing prison work: The public and private lives of prison officers*. Willan.

Crawley, E. (2005). Institutional thoughtlessness in prisons and its impacts on the day-to-day prison lives of elderly men. *Journal of Contemporary Criminal Justice, 21*(4), 350–363. https://doi.org/10.1177/1043986205282018
Foster, J., Bell, L., & Jayasinge, N. (2013). Care, control and collaborative working in a prison hospital. *Journal of Interprofessional Care, 27*, 184–190. https://doi.org/10.3109/13561820.2012.730073
Glaser, B., & Strauss, A. (1968). *Time for dying*. Aldine Publishing Company.
Goffman, E. (1961). *Asylums: Essays on the social situation of mental patients and other inmates.* Penguin.
Goffman, E. (1963). *Stigma: Notes on the management of spoiled identity.* Penguin.
Hay, W., & Sparks, R. (1991). What is a prison officer? *Prison Service Journal, 83*(3), 2–7.
Her Majesty's Inspectorate of Prisons. (2004). *'No problems—old and quiet': Older prisoners in England and Wales. A thematic review by HM Chief Inspector of Prisons.* HM Chief Inspector of prisons. https://www.justiceinspectorates.gov.uk/hmiprisons/wp-content/uploads/sites/4/2014/08/OlderPrisoners-2004.pdf
Irwin, J., & Owen, B. (2011). Harm and the contemporary prison. In A. Liebling & S. Maruna (Eds.), *The effects of imprisonment* (pp. 94–117). Routledge.
Liebling, A., & Price, D. (2003). Prison officers and the use of discretion. In L. Gelsthorpe & N. Padfield (Eds.), *Exercising discretion: Decision making in the criminal justice system and beyond* (pp. 74–96). Willan.
Liebling, A., Price, D., & Elliot, C. (1999). Appreciative inquiry and relationships in prison. *Punishment and Society, 1*(1), 71–98. https://doi.org/10.1177/14624749922227711
Liebling, A., Price, D., & Shefer, G. (2011). *The prison officer* (2nd ed.). Willan.
Lillie, K. (2018). Loss at the end of life: Palliative care in prisons. In S. Read, S. Santatzoglou, & A. Wrigley (Eds.), *Loss, dying and bereavement in the criminal justice system* (pp. 43–53). Routledge.
MacDonald, M., & Fallon, P. (2008). Health professionals in prison. In J. Bennett, B. Crewe, & A. Wahidin (Eds.), *Understanding prison staff* (pp. 349–366). Willan.
Newell, T. (2002). The prison officer as moral agent. *Prison Service Journal, 139*, 29–36.
Nielsen, M. M. (2011). On humour in prison. *European Journal of Criminology, 8*(6), 500–514. https://doi.org/10.1177/1477370811413818

Norman, A. E., & Parrish, A. (Eds.). (2002). *Prison nursing*. Blackwell Science.
Prison and Probation Ombudsman for England and Wales. (2013). *Learning from PPO investigations: End of life care*. London: Crown copyright.
Savage, J. (1999). Relative stranger: Caring for patients as the expression of nurses' moral/political voice. In T. Kohn & R. McKechnie (Eds.), *Extending the boundaries of care* (pp. 181–201). Berg.
Seale, C. (1998). *Constructing death: The sociology of dying and bereavement*. Cambridge University Press.
Spencer, D., & Ricciardelli, R. (2016). 'They're a very sick group of individuals': Correctional officers, emotions, and sex offenders. *Theoretical Criminology, 21*(3), 380–394. https://doi.org/10.1177/1362480616647590
Sykes, G. M. (1958). *Society of captives: A study of a maximum security prison*. Princeton University Press.
Tait, S. (2008). Prison officers and gender. In J. Bennett, B. Crewe, & A. Wahidin (Eds.), *Understanding prison staff* (pp. 65–91). Willan.
Tait, S. (2011). A typology of prison officer approaches to care. *European Journal of Criminology, 8*(6), 440–454. https://doi.org/10.1177/1477370811413804
Tait, S. (2012). Custody, care and staff-prisoner relationships. In B. Crewe & J. Bennett (Eds.), *The prisoner* (pp. 13–26). Routledge.
The Prison Rules. (1999). no. 728.
Thomson, S., & Parrish, A. (2002). Understanding and changing the dynamics of the prison culture. In A. Norman & A. Parrish (Eds.), *Prison nursing* (pp. 45–57). Blackwell Science.
Turner, M., Payne, S., & Barbarachild, Z. (2011). Care or custody? An evaluation of palliative care in prisons in North West England. *Palliative Medicine, 25*(4), 370–377. https://doi.org/10.1177/0269216310393058
Walsh, E., & Freshwater, D. (2009). The mental well-being of prison nurses in England and Wales. *Journal of Research in Nursing, 14*(6), 553–564. https://doi.org/10.1177/1744987109346762
Weiskopf, C. S. (2005). Nurses' experience of caring for inmate patients. *Journal of Advanced Nursing, 49*(4), 336–343. https://doi.org/10.1111/j.1365-2648.2004.03297.x

5

Caring at the End of Life in Prison Custody

The World Health Organisation (2019) defines palliative care as:

> An approach that improves the quality of life of patients and their families facing the problems associated with life-threatening illness, through the prevention and relief of suffering by means of early identification and impeccable assessment and treatment of pain and other problems, physical, psychosocial and spiritual.
>
> Good quality care for people who are dying therefore needs to integrate psychological, social and spiritual aspects, alongside the medical management of symptoms, and include their families. Delivering quality end of life care in prisons does not rely solely on the medical expertise of the healthcare team. Nurses, prison officers, chaplains, governors and others, including prisoner-carers and family liaison officers, all potentially have a role in meeting the holistic needs of a dying prisoner.

This chapter considers the caring culture and caring relationships within the prison. It will apply typologies of care (Fisher & Tronto, 1990; Kohn & McKechnie, 1999) to the caring actions apparent in the prisons studied, in order to illuminate the breadth of how care was conceptualised and performed. Looking at relationships between prisoners, the

C. Robinson, *Dying in Prison*, Palgrave Studies in Prisons and Penology, https://doi.org/10.1007/978-3-031-27103-8_5

importance of the role of the prisoner-carer in meeting the dying prisoner's social and psychological needs becomes apparent. It is argued the care found in the community of prisoners can positively impact the experience of dying. However, as a result of bullying and victimisation, the community around the dying prisoner may also have a negative impact. As part of considering how care was conceptualised, this chapter introduces the idea of 'heroic' care talk, a phenomenon associated with older male prison officers making sense of their caring roles in the context of the assumptions of hegemonic masculinity and their need to develop caring masculinities in order to address the work required of them with dying prisoners.

The understanding of care held by prison staff was essential in determining responses to the dying prisoner and influenced the extent to which deaths from natural causes impacted on the prison regime. One particular discourse for shaping constructions of end of life care in prison is discussed below. Whilst loosely defined, unsystematic, and often highly personal, a sense of what makes for a good death, amended to recognise the limitations of the prison setting, is summarised by one participant as making death 'as good as it could be'. The importance of personal values and experience, particularly understandings of 'decency', are very relevant to this objective.

It is also important to consider the practical impacts on care resulting from the dying prisoner's incarceration and the extent to which these could be ameliorated. The implications of security considerations on the delivery of palliative care are considered in this chapter, together with the mechanisms by which adjustments were made to meet the needs of dying prisoners within the demands of the prison regime. The use of discretion and the role of authority are of significance and it will be suggested that 'rule-failure' discretion (Schneider, 1992) is prominent because of the lack of rules, regulations or guidance to inform the broader palliative care of dying prisoners. Lastly, in this chapter, the challenges of providing care which respects the medical confidentiality of prisoners are considered, in particular, regarding any wish for resuscitation not to be attempted.

The Caring Culture

Prisons could be assumed to be places where care is absent. Laws and Lieber (2022) suggest that care in prison can be hard to investigate because it is "often hidden behind scripts of denial, suppression and a general environment that tends to diminish open displays of emotion" (p. 484). However, they and others acknowledge care is present in prisons, although when it is discussed in the existing literature this is in a more general context than the care of terminally or seriously ill prisoners. Laws and Lieber (2022) mobilise Moore and Gillette's 1990 work on masculine archetypes to argue "care is a fundamental feature of prison life that takes on a wide range of forms including: including: paternal roles, intellectual expertise, information sharing and close physical bonds" (p. 469). Tait (2011) argues there is a lack of understanding of what 'care' means in prison. In her research, she interviewed prisoners about their definition of care, based on their experiences of prison officers they regarded as showing a caring attitude towards them. In this context, caring interactions were those grounded in respect, fairness and sociability, where prison officers demonstrated their care for prisoners by taking time to listen and by providing practical help. Tait uses her definition of care to provide a typology of five prison officers' approaches to care. Tait's *true carer* is confident, secure and highly engaged in their caring role and identified by prisoners as caring. The prison officer who is a *limited carer* has sympathy for the prisoner, but follows bureaucratic rules in how they care. The *'old school' prison officer* provides limited emotional support, regards 'care' as a loaded term, but is paternal and protective. The *conflicted carer* conflates care with control and offers conditional care to 'deserving' prisoners. Lastly, the *damaged carer* used to care, but no longer does, often as the result of a traumatic incident or a lack of management support. Key to this, Tait (2011) argues, is how prison officers view prisoners. She later suggests that care is found in staff–prisoner relationships, describing how prisoners interviewed in her study experienced care as part of their relationship with staff, both as an isolated experience and as something that was unexceptional and part of day-to-day life. Such relationships had a particular quality: "Caring officers treated prisoners as if they were of equal moral worth. They spoke to prisoners with respect and empathised with prisoners' situations" (Tait, 2012, p. 19).

This day-to-day care is very different from the caring Crawley (2005) describes as needed by elderly prisoners. Caring for prisoners is discussed by Crawley (2004) in the context of expressing sympathy. Whilst prison officer culture does not forbid expressions of sympathy, they are expected to fit within organisational norms. Kindness to prisoners can be seen as weakness, especially in the context of a perceived conflict between discipline and care (Crawley, 2004). In contrast, for Arnold (2016), there is a close link in prison officers' minds between security and care, with the provision of a safe environment being associated with meeting a duty of care.

In both prisons studied, there were many examples of care attempting to meet the needs of seriously and terminally ill prisoners. This care was apparent with regard to other prisoners too. Arnold (2016), discussing how prison officers understand their 'duty of care', suggests officers interpret this as needing to care for prisoners, not care *about* them. However, in the prisons studied, the care shown by some officers extended beyond this. Fisher and Tronto (1990) suggest care in its broadest meaning has four components: caring about, taking care of, caregiving and care receiving, and all were observed in the prisons studied. Care could be seen in small actions, such as an officer taking a few moments to quietly watch a prisoner walk away from him, a look of tenderness on his face as he tried to assess how the prisoner was doing that day (Fieldnote, LTHSE). It was apparent in a nurse carefully checking the temperature of a drink she was taking to a prisoner no longer able to feed himself (Fieldnote, LTHSE). It was present when a chaplain spontaneously placed his hands under a prisoner's armpit, talking him through the manoeuvre from wheelchair to armchair to improve his comfort (Fieldnote, Category B) or when one of his colleagues made a point of spending more time with someone who had just received a terminal diagnosis (Interview 8, Category B). Care was evident in another chaplain's account of helping a prisoner prepare for death (Interview 5, LTHSE). It was shown on a regular basis by one of the prisoners helping Eddie, where the tenderness of the activity described below is redolent with care and respect, supporting psychological as well as physical needs.

> He goes back into Eddie's cell and comes out with a pillow, in a prison-issue green pillowslip, which he sets squarely on the wheelchair. Then he's back into Eddie's cell, for longer this time. When he comes out, he's walking backwards, slowly, helping Eddie out and down the step. He's holding Eddie's left hand with his left hand and has his right hand under Eddie's bent left arm. It's done with care, but strength. Once Eddie is lowered into the wheelchair, they set off. ...On their return, he helps Eddie out of the wheelchair. He stands behind him as Eddie climbs up the step back into the cell, his hand on Eddie's left side, guiding him in, poised in case he falls back. Again, it's done with gentleness and calmly, but with assurance. (Fieldnote, LTHSE)

Discourses and examples of providing care were very apparent. Care permeated the prison culture, especially in the LTHSE prison, to an unexpected extent. Care was a source of pride for those who cared about, took care of or gave care. Officers on Eddie's wing were proud of comments from the nurses that he was doing better than expected because of the care he was getting there (Fieldnote, LTHSE). The concerns expressed by the officers on Eddie's wing suggested a more holistic view of palliative care than that which some of the healthcare team held. The officers were anxious to keep him on the wing so he didn't feel isolated and because that would ensure contact with his friends (Fieldnote, LTHSE). There were several ongoing conversations where officers checked with each other, and the researcher, what they understood to be the course of action most likely to meet not only his physical but also his psychosocial needs (Fieldnotes, LTHSE).

Kohn and McKechnie (1999) suggest care can be conceptualised in a variety of ways: as a duty, as a responsibility, a professional task or as a labour of love. Examples of each of these motivations in terms of the care of the dying were present in both prisons. Prisoners often regarded staff as having a duty to care, to the extent they expressed anger if this duty was not met and relief when it was. Officers, nurses, chaplains, governors and prisoners' friends all expressed a sense of responsibility to care. For nurses, in particular, it was part of their professional identity. For prison officers, care could be a professional task, part of a security-driven imperative, the professional commitment to 'know your prisoners', adapted to knowing when care might be needed:

> It's like the lad, the lad we've got here now, er he went out for chemotherapy yesterday, and he's always poorly two days after because the hospital want to keep him in but he won't stay in. So he has his chemo, he comes back. So the trigger with him is two days after he's had his chemo, so we know to keep an eye on him. (Interview 3, Category B)

Officers who regularly worked with the same prisoners could notice small changes in their behaviour indicating something was wrong, and which led to them contacting nursing staff. But care could also be a labour of love between prisoners. Those caring for Eddie said they were "doing it for him" and 'it's not an obligation, it's a devotion' (Fieldnotes, LTHSE).

'Heroic' Care Talk

Kohn and McKechnie (1999) framework is useful for conceptualised care and illuminates much of the care observed in this study. How care was talked about by some prison officers, however, demonstrates a particular approach to caring which echoes earlier findings by Crawley (2004). These narratives, whilst not contradicting Kohn and McKechnie's (1999) framing of care, provide nuance to some prison officers approach to caring for the dying prisoner, and suggest how the task of caring might be operationalised and understood, by older male officers in particular, when providing care.

Crawley (2004) shows that much of the work of a prison officer is mundane and domestic in nature, comprising of cleaning, serving meals, and doing laundry—tasks traditionally regarded as 'women's work'. She says this work is downplayed by prison officers in their accounts of the jobs: "the contrast between officers 'war stories' and the mundane realities of their everyday lives on the landing is marked" (p. 130). This echoes Liebling et al. (2011) finding, discussed above in the context of defining prison regimes: "much of their daily work involves the accomplishment of routines: unlocking, delivering meals, counting, moving, receiving, discharging, observing and locking up" (p. 78).

Furthermore, much of how prison officers undertake their role is, Crawley (2004) argues, based on performance. She finds it takes time for a new prison officer to acquire "the walk, the talk, the posture, jargon, mindset, values and beliefs" (p. 84) that constitute their working identity. Some tasks challenge how prison officers manage their performance and control the impression they give to both colleagues and prisoners. Crawley (2004) suggests "officers who chose to work with elderly prisoners are seen as not doing 'proper' prison work because it is seen as too quiet, too predictable and too safe" (p. 221). Working with elderly prisoners has implications for their self-identity, their relationships with 'mainstream' colleagues and their interactions with prisoners. When the officers choosing to do this are themselves older, they can, Crawley claims, achieve a strong sense of job satisfaction and may also be excused compliance with organisational norms because of their age and experience. However, Crawley argues, prison officer choosing to work in specialists regimes risk spoiled work identities either from working with despised prisoner groups or from being part of regimes with values which are counter to traditional prison work norms. In these circumstances, officers risk ridicule from their peers and will need to renegotiate their working identities to demonstrate the positive values of their roles. Whilst none of the literature on prison officers discusses their work with dying prisoners, Crawley's (2004) finding illuminates the challenges faced by prison officers choosing to work in specialist roles, which could include palliative care.

What was observed in the prison's studies was the use of a discourse about caring which implies an approach that could be termed 'heroic care talk'. It is noticeable in the way some older, male, prison officers talked about delivering care. Their accounts of caring for seriously ill and dying prisoners echoed the 'war stories' identified by Crawley (2004) in her ethnography of prison officers. In this study, 'war stories' of dealing with violent and dangerous criminals and of physical bravery and heroics, were replaced by stories of providing care that required a certain form of masculinity. A small number of male prison officers, including one who had worked under a previous system where officers were trained to offer some nursing care, recounted providing care in a way that emphasised their own strength and masculinity through stories of dealing with difficult prisoners at the end of life. They gave accounts of dealing with things that other people found too distressing and of a 'competitive' caring in which they cared better than anyone else. In doing so, they arguably retrieved some of the spoilings of work identity precipitated by undertaking caring work traditionally regarded as 'unmasculine'. Their approach however is very different from Crawley's suggestion that older male officers are granted some freedom from conforming to occupational norms, suggesting that they at least felt the need to construct a narrative which aligned their work with expectations of a 'macho' prison officer type.

In their accounts of caring for dying prisoners, these male officers foregrounded tales of bodily fluids, gruesome bedsores, wounds or corpses, told with dramatic effect to reinforce the idea of their own bravery. A prison officer who had started work with the prison service as a healthcare officer, a prison officer with some nursing training, spoke about providing nursing care to a prisoner using stomach-churning imagery:

> And when an ulcer appears, you've to get the slough out (mimes scoping). There was one lad, I had to put my hand right in upto my thumb, into his groin, to get the slough out. (Interview 3, Category B)

Another officer talked about seeing unpleasant scenes when escorting prisoners for treatment at an outside hospital.

> You get in situations out on escorts, and daily escorts, hospital bedwatches and procedures that take place that are intrusive to the prisoner. You could be, erm, sat in a room with a person having an endoscopy and you're sat literally like that (*mimes being close to something).* And whichever way you look there are TV screens with their internal what's going on. You can't get away from that situation. I've been in a room where they've had surgery and I've been in the room, where they've had the surgery. I've been in the rooms where they are having X-rays, where they are having MRIs, where they are having endoscopies, where they are having, erm, their arm stitched back on. (Interview 11, LTHSE)

A further account of dealing with the body of a prisoner after death highlights the emotional challenge of providing care that involves confronting bodily decay:

> There was one in the healthcare that passed away when I was Oscar 1 on nights, he was absolutely riddled with cancer and D (*first name*), the nurse that were on at the time, we went to go in and we had to get him ready prior to morticians and everybody coming and police and

> everything, er and she asked me to help turn him over because his skin and everything were that thin because, erm were that thin, but were all bloated up. You could virtually see through the skin. And it were, that were quite intense and er in-depth. (Interview 6, LTHSE)

Stories about 'heroic' care often emphasised the teller's special skills or abilities, contrasted with other peoples' inability to perform the tasks being undertaken, that served to strengthen the heroism and courage of the teller. The former healthcare officers said "there were jobs as well that other people wouldn't like to do, and I tended to do it". He gave as an example his ability to deal calmly with "big, hard men" responding violently to the frustrations of living with a colostomy. Another, talking about an incident that was not related to a prisoner dying, reported that a prisoner who had boiling water poured over his head and naked body had no scars: "now the actions of that was my first aid skills and background, first aid instructor, knew what to do, knew what to do straightaway. New member of staff wouldn't have a clue" (Interview 11, LTHSE).

'Heroic' care stories had little room for modesty and set high standards of care, which only the 'hero' could fulfil. The former healthcare officer said:

> I once went mad when I found some bedsores on one of my patients. I'd had a four day weekend off and you'd think you, you could trust your colleagues. And I come back and he'd not been in bath and he'd got bedsores. And he was saying to me 'I think there's an elastic band on me bum' (mimes reaching for own right bottom cheek). … 'Turnover; ah it's a pressure sore.' Y'know. And then everybody got a bollocking from the charge nurse then about them being preventable, that you should be checking the skin, heels and back and things like that. (Interview 3, Category B)

In many of these accounts of 'heroic' care, someone else was reported to have been less able to provide care or less able to cope with the situation. Often, the colleagues reported to be struggling in 'heroic' care talk were women. One officer spoke of having to restrain a dying prisoner, described as suffering from cancer that had 'gone into the brain' and was causing him to be violent. He spoke about restraining the man as gently as possible, with two male colleagues working with him to hold the prisoner in the bed, saying "It got a bit distressing for some of the women that worked upstairs, although they had seen it before, but they let the men do the restraining" (Interview 3, Category B). Restraining the prisoner in these circumstances work was clearly seen by him as 'men's work' and too upsetting for female colleagues. Another officer talked about a female officer, with him on a bedwatch when a prisoner's life support machine was turned off, being upset. He had previous work experience in the NHS which he felt had hardened him to such events (Fieldnote, LTHSE). There was also a gendered dimension to how much some prison officers felt they could show they had been affected by a prisoner's death. An older male officer spoke of being on a 'bedwatch' with a female colleague when the prisoner they were escorting died. The female officer took a week's sick leave as a consequence, but he said this was not something a man "would have got away with" (Fieldnote, LTHSE). Instead, he and a younger male colleague agreed, despite any expressions of sympathy extended to them, there was an expectation that they would just get on with things.

Providing care was not without consequences for male colleagues. A number of prison staff expressed concerns about how colleagues, especially those who had not seen a body before, would be effected by death from natural causes. An experienced governor worried about how staff on Eddie's wing who had experienced recent bereavements in their personal life would cope with his death and was also concerned about young staff who might never have witnessed a death. The former healthcare officer quoted above said he had seen lots of staff go off sick having been at the scene of a death. There was an implication, however, when 'heroic' care talk was enacted, that 'heroes' would cope, or at least bottle up their reactions:

> But both me and N (first name) are long in tooth now. I wouldn't say look after usselves, but we're blokes, and I think with blokes you tend not to ask for help until it's too late and you've gone passed that point of no return. (Interview 9, Category B)

Accounts of how other people had been affected could serve to highlight the strength of the 'heroic' carer. An experienced CM talked about arriving at a hospital with a prisoner who had died in the ambulance on the way from the prison. The ambulance, with the two escorting prison officers, was directed round to the mortuary, where the officers had to wait until the mortician returned from lunch. The interviewee said:

> The ambulance staff put *(prisoner's name…)* I think it was, er, on the, what we would call the slab and just left him there. And we was there with all the other bodies around in the fr.. And B (*prison officer's first name*) he couldn't cope with that he: "I need to get out" "We can't go anywhere B (*first name*)" And it effected B (*first name*) for quite a while did that…. (Interview 6, LTHSE)

It is striking that the stories told about 'heroic' care were limited to a small group of male officers aged 46–55. Hanlon (2012) suggests that because care is seen as traditionally feminine, and involving emotions and actions, such as intimacy, sensitivity and touch, often associated with women, this can present obstacles to men who feel they cannot care in this way. In the accounts of 'heroic' care provided, there is nothing soft or 'feminised'. If these officers had tales of bodily fluids, gruesome bedsores, anything likely to turn my stomach, then they obviously enjoyed recounting them in ways that foregrounded their unique abilities and skills. Alongside emphasising the challenge of the tasks faced, these stories included recognition of the costs of heroic caring, but highlighted the care-giver's special skills, physical and emotional toughness and comparative strength as opposed to other colleagues, especially women.

Understanding how prison officers conceptualise care and what motivates them to provide it is important. Kohn and McKechnie's (1999) framing of care as a duty, as a responsibility, as a professional task or as a labour of love is helpful in this regard, but in the specific circumstances of prison officers, it is worth considering other studies in order to better understating how care fits within existing prison officer' cultures. Prison officers are the largest group of employees within the prison service

(Arnold, 2005) and the main providers of care and supervision to prisoners (Newell, 2002). Their importance in operationalising the prison regime is not disputed. Prison officers have the most contact with prisoners (Hay & Sparks, 1991). As Chief Inspector of Prisons, Ann Owers regarded them as key to the delivery of Her Majesty's Chief Inspector of Prisons' four 'tests of a healthy prison' (Owers, 2006). Prison officers make the paramount contribution to the prisoner's experience of imprisonment: "it is in the hands of staff to either aggravate or alleviate the inherent pains of imprisonment" (Hay & Sparks, 1991, p. 6). As Crawley (2004) argues, how prison officers regard their work, the prisoners they work with and their colleagues, has implications for the prison regime and relationships within the prison system. Whilst most studies recognise the motivations of prison officers for joining the service are mixed (Arnold, 2016; Arnold et al., 2007; Bryans & Jones, 2001; Crawley, 2004; Liebling et al., 2011), Arnold et al. (2007) also say good officers "reconstruct their sense of 'meaningfulness' in the job and their concept of what it means to 'make a difference'" (p. 478).

In the telling of 'heroic' care stories, the male prison officers interviewed seem to be reconstructing what is meaningful in their roles, creating discourses that align the nature of the care they are providing with other, more traditionally masculine, values. Caring is gendered and marked by cultural and social values (Tronto, 2013). Tronto claims that whilst men do care about, care for, give care and receive care, "the image persists that what it means to be a man is not to care, or at least, not to care well" (2013, p. 68). The pride taken by these male officers in caring well, and in their eyes caring better than anyone else, suggests this is not the case. Elliott (2016) provides a more nuanced understanding of masculinities and caring, suggesting caring masculinities recast traditional masculine values such as protection and providing (both of which Tronto [2013] suggests are socially acceptable masculine approaches to care, delivered to subordinate others) into care-orientated, relational values. In the prison officer's stories of 'heroic' care, however, there was little to suggest a foregrounding of relational values or an overturning of the dominance and relationships of inequality that Elliot claims are core to caring masculinities. In Tait's (2011) typology, these men could be classified as 'old school' prison officers, paternal and protective in their approach, but something more was being enacted. Instead, narratives about delivering care to prisoners emphasised the 'heroic' and even the competitive. These officers found meaning in their work by focussing on the strength, skill and endurance needed to overcome the difficulties of caring which required considerable 'dirty work' and unpleasantness. Contrasting themselves with others who were unable to do this work, emphasising their own high standards, and the toll such work could take, helped them make sense of their work within the culture of the prison and their own assumptions of masculine values. It was also arguably a form of self-motivation in challenging circumstances.

The Community Around the Dying: Caring Relationships?

Whilst in prison, the prisoner has very little say over who is near him. Sykes (1958) suggests one of the pains of imprisonment is the deprivation of security arising from being forced to associate with men with violent and aggressive pasts who cannot be expected to abide by the rules of society. However, it was clear in both prisons that prisoners who were terminally ill could also expect to be part of a community of prisoners who in Fisher and Tronto's (1990) terms cared about them and took care of them.

Despite the existence in many UK prisons of prisoners employed as carers for their peers, very little academic research within the UK has considered their motivations, training or tasks, or looked at the impact their work with frail and dying prisoners has on them. A small number of studies do exist of prisoner-carers in the US, including those working as inmate-volunteers in prison hospices (Cloyes et al., 2013; Loeb et al., 2013; Supiano et al., 2014). The usefulness of these studies is limited by the significant differences between the roles of prisoners working as carers in the US and the UK. Within US prison hospices, inmate-volunteers provide a variety of services to dying prisoners, including assisting with personal care such as toileting and skin care, providing companionship and offering religious fellowship. Prisoners employed as carers in the UK are not permitted to provide intimate care (PSI 17/2015, Annex A).

In a study in the UK, peer support for frail prisoners at HMP Wakefield, HMP Leyhill, HMP Hull, HMP Isle of Wight and HMP Whatton instead involved wheelchair pushing, cell cleaning and collecting meals and laundry (Moll, 2013).

In the prisons studied, prisoner-carers were seen to both care about and take care of other prisoners, but friendships were also significant in providing care for seriously and terminally ill prisoners. In the close-knit community of H3 in the Category B prison, a healthcare professional reported that when Iain had been admitted to the hospital, she had found two of the prisoners "sat crying in their rooms" (Interview 10, Category B). These prisoners had got everyone to sign one of his T-shirts, which Iain kept as an indication of their esteem for him:

> It's his most prized possession now. He actually has it up in the wall of his room. He loves it. And he said when he got it, it was such a pick me up because he was like "they all care about me". (Interview 10, Category B)
> Likewise, in the LTHSE prison, the healthcare centre formed a small unit in which prisoners got to know each other well. As one officer said:
> They all eat their dinner at the same table. You don't have that on wings. So they get like a tight little unit. And when people are old and frail on there, you'll find the other guys will look after them, y'know. They'll fill their flasks up for them, they'll push their chair for them. So it's sad for them because they obviously realise that he's very ill. (Interview 15, LTHSE)
> Crewe et al. (2013) suggest that although prisoners often dispute their relationships with other prisoners are substantial, in their daily practices they are quite intimate. The examples they give from their research are domestic in nature, including waking each other up with cups of tea. Similar practices were found in the LTHSE prison. In general though, prisoners made a distinction between 'prison acquaintances' of which there were many, and 'prison friends', of which there were very few (Fieldnote, LTHSE).

Crewe et al. (2013) report that the prisoners they interviewed found it difficult if they could not show their 'caring side' whilst in prison. It was noticeable in the LTHSE prison how much prisoners employed as carers for their peers appreciated being able to express care. Those caring for Eddie were enacting a labour of love (Fieldnotes, LTHSE). How effective prisoners could be as carers for their peers was sometimes doubted. One prisoner felt there was not much Eddie's friends could do for him, suggesting their care was limited to fetching him water and clean bedding. Whilst Moll's (2013) description of peer support for frail prisoners being limited to pushing wheelchairs, cleaning cells and collecting meals and laundry accurately describes the tasks undertaken by some prisoner-carers (Interview 14, LTHSE), in practice, Eddie's friends and carers did much more. Two prisoners in particular were observed checking with officers when to take Eddie for his medication, helping him into his wheelchair and pushing him across to the medicine hatch (Fieldnote, LTHSE). Officers knew they and others were cooking for Eddie (Fieldnote, LTHSE). His main carer gave officers a daily report on him, raising any issues and especially reporting on how he was eating (Fieldnote, LTHSE). This carer outlined a daily routine based on taking Eddie for his medication, getting him drinks and helping with his meals. Each day started at morning unlock by checking Eddie was awake and getting him a drink. Once he knew Eddie was alright, he went back up to the other landings to let his friends know and reassure them Eddie had made it through another night (Fieldnote, LTHSE). Caring for Eddie therefore extended to his friends caring for each other. One of them, conscious of the burden carried by Eddie's main carer, tried to take care of him, making sure they watched the football together and took time out to have a laugh (Fieldnote, LTHSE).

Prisoner-carers in the UK are not permitted to assist with washing, dressing or undressing areas of the body "usually clothed for privacy and dignity" (PSI 17/2015, Annex A). In practice, the distinction between appropriate and inappropriate care became blurred. Eddie's main carer reported helping him into the shower, taking the cubicle opposite him for himself, but then helping him dry himself. He was quick to assert there was nothing untoward going on. He told me on three occasions about helping Eddie shower, but when an officer was nearby, the account was adjusted to not mention drying Eddie (Fieldnotes, LTHSE). He was also concerned about how Eddie felt about this, fearing he was ashamed to need the help, but stressing he should not be. The approach of the prisoners caring for Eddie aimed to meet his physical needs but was very much informed by a concern for his psychological well-being. They knew Eddie liked to be on his own and worked to maintain his independence as far as possible, knowing Eddie valued it (Fieldnote, LTHSE). Eddie thus found himself in a community prepared to help which was instinctively trying to address the physical and psychosocial needs prioritised by the WHO definition of palliative care.

However, not all of the community surrounding a dying prisoner is caring. The deprivation of security that Sykes (1958) associates with imprisonment was also present in both prisons studied with regard to seriously and terminally ill prisoners. Dawes (2009), writing about ageing in prison, suggests some elderly prisoners were fearful of younger ones and avoided participation in activities in order to prevent victimisation. Accordingly, staff in H3 in the Category B prison worried the older men accommodated on the wing with physical and age-related infirmities needed protection from the younger, mentally unwell prisoners also placed there:

> You've got vulnerable, very vulnerable prisoners up here. Old, on historic charges, you know from 70s and what have you, which means they are old men now, in their 70s, some in their 80s, wheelchair bound, very vulnerable, to unpredictable prisoners, which some of these are, under the mental health. And that's been my argument; you can't mix 'em. (Interview 3, Category B)

In responding to the behaviour of disruptive prisoners, staff often had to think of the needs of the more vulnerable prisoners in their care, including the dying. When a disgruntled prisoner in the LTHSE prison protested by flooding his cell, staff were concerned about whether this was affecting Eddie, whose cell was two landings below. Whilst both prisons had anti-bullying activities, bullying was reported and prisoners recognised that terminally ill prisoners on the wing were vulnerable (Fieldnote, LTHSE). This is in keeping with a point made by Lillie (2018): the bodily losses such as the loss of mobility, continence and cognitive function experienced by prisoners at the end of life make them vulnerable. Staff in the Category B prison, where Dean had asked to stay on the wing with his friends, reported that the same 'friends' stole from him, targeting his medication (Interview 10, Category B). One prisoner in the LTHSE prison gave as an example someone having been bullied for their morphine patch and commented on the lack of morality in such an action saying, "if they can do that, bullies can do anything" (Fieldnote, LTHSE). Another prisoner, expecting to die in prison, said he saw younger prisoners bullying older ones, and worried how he would cope in 20 years' time (Fieldnote, LTHSE).

Staff as well as prisoners were aware some prisoners would behave disrespectfully towards the dying. The concept of decency, discussed below, was important, so it is not surprising that officers and others worked hard to try to maintain standards of decency around terminally or seriously ill prisoners, protecting them from the curiosity of their neighbours. One officer said:

> I don't think they should be a side show. Do you know what I mean? Because, they are. We've had it before where people have never spoke to this guy before in their life and just go for, a look. So no, it's not a peep show, it's not a side show. The lad's dying, he needs his privacy. (Fieldnote, LTHSE)
> Similarly, the prisoners working as part of the art group to enhance the palliative care suite in the LTHSE prison (discussed above in relation to the carceral geography of dying) emphasised the importance of providing a screen to shield the dying prisoner and his family from prying eyes (Fieldnote, LTHSE). They felt that privacy was lacking on the wing and they wanted to restore it at the end of life.

The community around the dying prisoner could thus positively affect his circumstances, developing and enacting relationships based on care. The circumstances of a dying prisoner could also negatively impact their relationships with their peers, making them vulnerable to bullying, depriving them of respect and thus adversely affecting their psychosocial well-being.

Trying to Make Death "as Good as It Could Be"

For staff and prisoners alike, the principle aim of the care shown to dying prisoners was summarised by one senior member of staff as making death "as good as it could be" (Interview 13, LTHSE). This was based on assessments of what was desirable for prisoners at the end of life, but lacked clear or shared standards against which to form assessments. It was nebulous, but encompassed all aspects of the WHO definition of palliative care, cited at the start of this chapter, and was often informed by personal values or personal experiences of bereavement. Implicit in making death 'as good as it could be' was a recognition that dying in prison is far from ideal. It could be argued, as Lillie (2018) does, that a good death is not easy to achieve in any setting, and many staff and prisoners were aware of this. However, most of the participants who were actively trying to make death 'as good as it could be' saw dying in prison as a deeply unattractive prospect, regardless of the care available. Setting an ambition of making a death 'as good as it could be' was often pragmatic but tinged with sadness. Ultimately, dying in prison was not a good ending. An exchange with an experienced senior officer sums this up:

> Participant: I think that I'd try to do the best for anybody to make their last few days as, er, best possible for them.
> Interviewer: Right. And prison's not that?
> Participant: Course it isn't. (Interview 6, LTHSE)

Studies regarding the provision of palliative care in prison often highlight the contradictions between the aims of palliative care and the purpose of imprisonment. Wrigley (2018) summarises this:

> The goals, aims and means of providing good end-of-life care are precisely those that are difficult or impossible to secure in a prison environment. (p. 22)
> Similarly, for Burles et al. (2016), prison regimes are at odds with the concept of a good death, which is characterised by comfort, control and closure. However, those staff and prisoners overtly trying to make death as 'good as it could be' were seen to be prioritising both psychological and physical needs. Providing comfort, control and closure were all part of their efforts. Chaplains also attended to the spiritual needs of the

prisoners, and on occasions of their families too (Interview 5, LTHSE). This led to a broad understanding of palliative care which looked beyond physical needs and medical treatment.

Certain core human values underpinned understandings of what a death 'as good as it could be' would involve. In the prisons studied, the concept of decency in death was given great importance, even if it was rarely defined or definable. One nurse said:

> So for me it's about people dying with dignity, respect and comfortable. And if I've done that, then I'm happy. We all die, don't we? And it's all about dying the right way. (Interview 10, Category B)

Decency involved meeting the individual's psychosocial needs and was very much shaped by culturally specific constructions. Decency was particularly important when it came to prisoners dying outside of the prison who could be subject to the use of restraints. Officers who had been on 'bedwatches' spoke about decency as the motivating force for removing restraints when a prisoner was close to death (Interview 6, LTHSE). This was another example of how an approaching death could lead to a softening of the prison regime. Notions of decency played a significant part in decisions about the application of restraints and whilst senior managers were conscious of potential criticism from the Prison and Probation Ombudsman, they were also aware of how inappropriate cuffing could look to the public:

> So you've got the decency element, y'know. And your walk into a hospital, local hospital, if he's in a yellow and green suit, an SO and three staff or SO and 2, and he's walking with two sticks and he's on an escort chain, I don't think that portrays us particularly well if I'm honest. (Interview 13, LTHSE)

Whilst the prison setting changed how 'dying the right way' could be achieved, it also explained some of the importance placed on decency as death approached. Decency is a term that resonates with the prison service. 'Decent' prisons are one of the aims of HMPPS (HMPPS, 2017), treating people with "decency and respect" is one of the values expressed in the HMPPS annual review (2019, p. 5). Ensuring decency was part of trying to make death 'as good as it could be' in prison. It was closely linked to dignity and privacy, a concept usually hard to find in prison but highly valued around death, for example in the provision of a screen in the palliative care suite (Fieldnote, LTHSE) and the expectation that the body would be shielded from view (Fieldnote, LTHSE). For prison staff and prisoners alike, a good death meant making the dying prisoner as comfortable as possible. Physical comfort, the tangible softening of an often harsh environment, was important, with the officers on Eddie's wing seeking to get a more comfortable mattress for him (Fieldnote, LTHSE), and concerned about noise near his cell (Fieldnote, LTHSE). It was also regarded as important to ensure someone died peacefully (Fieldnotes, LTHSE; Interview 10, Category B). One of the significant concerns associated with dying in prison was the fear that someone would die alone. After Eddie's death, nursing staff felt upset he had been alone when he died (Fieldnote, LTHSE).

Similarly, as mentioned in Chapter Four, a chaplain in the Category B prison reported being saddened when he thought someone had died alone. In the LTHSE prison, a nurse reported:

> I know L, one of our other nurses, she once sat with a gentleman all night, just so that he wasn't on his own. It don't go down well with officers, but you have to. Nobody wants to die alone. (Interview 12, LTHSE)
> The importance of ensuring the prisoner did not die alone was a strong enough motivation to overcome the practical difficulties and criticism from those officers who did not share the same construction of quality care. Seale (1995) suggests when people die alone, it is regarded by others as indicative of their failure to provide emotional accompaniment. It is striking that it was nurses and a chaplain, people in occupational roles associated with caring for the dying, who most keenly felt the need for the dying not to be alone. Caswell and O'Connor (2019) similarly find nurses working with the dying believe no one should die alone, although they also found that in their study, older people found the prospect of dying alone less problematic.

In these regards, trying to make death 'as good as it could be' resulted in a broader understanding of palliative care. Staff recognised the wing could become someone's 'home', and that when people in the community expressed a wish to die at home, for some prisoners the equivalent was being on the wing, in the surroundings that had become normal to them, and with their friends close by (Interview 15, LTHSE). For some staff, the goal was to provide for a dying prisoner the care they would like for their parent (Fieldnote, LTHSE) and comparisons with the death of a loved one could be used to inform the desired standard of care for the dying prisoner (Interviews 15 and 5, LTHSE).

The Practical Limitations of Care

A number of studies highlight the tension between the values and aims of palliative care and prisons and find prison regimes at odds with the concept of a good death (Burles et al., 2016; Lillie, 2018; Wrigley, 2018). In this section, security considerations will be shown to have implications for end of life care in prison, including for the delivery of medical care. However, prison regimes are not inflexible. Small adjustments are possible in certain circumstances. How these adjustments happen, including the role of discretion and the relevance of authority will be discussed below. In some regards, however, prison staff struggled to negotiate the challenges of providing palliative care. This reflects the very different values of health care and prison settings, as illustrated by the discussion of problems around maintaining medical confidentiality, which closes this chapter. As will be seen, when the usual expectations of the prison and of palliative care are in conflict, finding a resolution is not easy.

The Implications of Security Considerations

In the prisons studied, care for dying prisoners was frequently subject to the overarching security agenda inherent in prisons. Security considerations influenced the physical, psychosocial and spiritual care of prisoners in often unexpected ways and made some adjustments impossible. As

Lillie (2018) suggests, "the propensity to focus on security can lead to unnecessary diminishment of dignity in dying" (p. 49).

For example, the appropriate use of syringe drivers to administer pain relief was of deep concern to staff. This was a contested subject and an area where the cultures of prison officers and prison management teams could clash with that of healthcare staff. The issue of access to drugs, including for pain release, is highlighted by a number of studies (Burles et al., 2016; Condon et al., 2007; Turner et al., 2011). These studies find a reluctance to administer drugs to relieve pain because of their potential misuse in the prison and a concern that vulnerable prisoners will be bullied if they have medication in their possession. In the prisons studied, syringe drivers were seen to present a risk because it was thought by some that they could be used to kill the prisoner (Fieldnote, LTHSE). At the very least, their use on the wing was considered to be too risky. In the LTHSE prison it was expected that when a prisoner needed pain relief administered via a syringe driver, he would have to move to the healthcare centre (Fieldnote, LTHSE). In the Category B prison, despite accommodating lower risk prisoners, healthcare staff were prevented from using syringe drivers at all, even though other prisons did, and they felt this prohibition arose from prison governors' fears of the unknown (Interview 10, Category B). Similarly, they were not allowed to provide terminally ill prisoners with doses of Oramorph (an oral solution of Morphine Sulfate), although they knew other prisons provided three doses in a locked cabinet in the prisoner's cell for them to use as needed (Interview 10, Category B). The security agenda of the prison thus directly influenced how terminally ill prisoners were administered with pain relief.

The provision of equipment for the terminally ill prisoner was also affected by security concerns. When Eddie needed an air mattress, there was a concern about how long it would take the Security department to approve it, but no question of it being allocated without their approval (Fieldnote, LTHSE). Similarly, the group of prisoners redecorating the palliative care suite in the LTHSE prison had so internalised the expectations of the Security department that although they wanted a screen in place to protect the privacy of dying prisoners, they designed it so staff could see over it (Fieldnote, LTHSE). The impact of security considerations was also present in other situations. In the LTHSE prison, the quality of the spiritual care one of the chaplains could provide for Eddie was in their view impaired because they felt unable to enter Eddie's cell without approval from the Security department (Fieldnote, LTHSE). In the Category B prison, taxis were used to transport prisoners and the officers escorting them to local hospitals. The taxi needed to enter the prison to pick up and drop off the group, but only taxi drivers with appropriate security clearances could do this. One officer recounted, without criticism, having waited five hours for a suitable driver to be available to return an elderly, frail prisoner to the prison after he was discharged from the hospital.

The use of restraints on prisoners receiving treatment in outside hospitals, discussed earlier with regard to prison rules and constructing the individual as a stigmatised security risk, had a number of immediate practical effects on the provision of care. Firstly, the prisoner and prison officer had to stay within a few feet of each other. When the prisoner was in bed, this meant the officer was by the bedhead, which impeded medical confidentiality. Escort chains were also observed to limit movement for eating (Fieldnote, Category B) and although not tight, to leave temporary marks on the prisoner's wrist where the weight of the cuff rested (Fieldnote, Category B).

Prisoners spoke about the psychological effects of being restrained. One, from the LTHSE prison, was distressed about being handcuffed whilst unconscious. He was later restrained using an escort chain, including when going to the toilet or for a shower in a room with no windows and only one, shut, door. He spoke about another man on the ward, from the Category B prison, who had no legs but was also restrained with an escort chain (Fieldnote, LTHSE). Another prisoner, who had been on an escort chain for seven weeks in hospital following a major operation described having a:

> stent in his side, a catheter, and a feeding tube in his arm. He holds his left arm out to one side as he says this, and then holds his right arm out, saying he was cuffed. He indicates that he was pinned down by the

> equipment and the chain, 'couldn't move; literally crucified'. (Fieldnote, LTHSE)

Being restrained was experienced by prisoners as unnecessary and uncaring. It had a negative practical and psychological impact on seriously and terminally ill prisoners. Ironically, it only happened because the prisoner was seriously ill. In stark contrast to the other ways in which tangible and intangible aspects of the prison experience potentially softened as death approached, if a prisoner needed medical treatment outside of the prison, they were likely to experience an intensification of the harshness of prison in the form of the use of restraints.

There were occasions in the Category B prison, although not in the higher-security LTHSE prison, in which individual understandings of care overrode security concerns, even if the result was that staff would be reprimanded. For example, officers on one of the 'bedwatches' observed were reprimanded by a senior colleague for allowing the prisoner to be in his own clothes, not in hospital pyjamas as the PSI stated (Fieldnote, Category B). Another member of staff reported having had his 'wrist slapped' after phoning the wife of a prisoner who was in an outside hospital and thought not to have long to live. Both the staff member and his line manager thought he had done the right thing and that security had been unnecessarily strict (Fieldnote, Category B). In these circumstances, staff were often placing notions of decency or care above the idea of security, using their own experiences to make decisions about the appropriate course of action. However, such incidences were rare, and not simply about providing care. With regard to the prisoner wearing his own clothes, officers were also making a pragmatic decision. They knew the prisoner would not be out of the prison long and, given the short-staffing in the prison, judged it an ineffective use of resources to ask for an officer to collect the prisoner's day clothes.

Adjusting the Regime

In order to achieve a standard of care perceived by staff to be acceptable, to make death 'as good as it could be', staff in the prisons studied considered adjustments needed to be made to the prison regime. A number of changes which softened the usual prison regime were apparent, at least in the immediate vicinity of a terminally ill prisoner, and were discussed by participants. This was especially the case in the LTHSE prison, where arguably as a high-security prison, the usual regime imposed more restrictions on prisoners. The changes made were often small but were usually intended to improve the physical or psychosocial care of the dying prisoner. Some adjustments were possible at the discretion of the individual officer, but at both prisons, there was a reliance on the authority of the Governing Governor to permit some of the changes regarded as necessary to improve palliative care.

In some instances, providing care meant changes were needed to staffing levels or to the tasks undertaken by staff. In the LTHSE prison, additional staff had to be on duty to facilitate cell doors being kept open overnight, such as when Neil's wife was permitted to stay with him when his death was imminent (Interview 7, LTHSE). Similarly, when an FLO was spending time supporting the family of a prisoner who was close to death or who had died, another officer was needed to cover their usual tasks (Interview 7, LTHSE). Prison officers helped out healthcare staff in informal ways. One recounted helping nurses turn a very large prisoner in bed, aware the nurses could not do it without his help. He also reported officers helping nurses get a prisoner to the bathroom, again recognising they were going beyond the expectations of their role but saying: "it becomes a situation where you don't like to see someone that is going to die, suffer" (Interview 11, LTHSE).

This reinforces the argument that an impending death results in officers sometimes feeling and expressing sympathy towards prisoners. It shows the importance of such sympathy in generating a willingness to make adaptions and soften usual practices. Other officers were critical of their colleagues who didn't help in this way, especially when it came to refusing to push a wheelchair (Fieldnote, LTHSE). Sometimes officers were conscious this was not their job, but they did it because nobody else was available (Interview 11, LTHSE). Healthcare staff made adjustments to their working practices too, with the presence of prisoners such as Eddie or Dean on the wing requiring them to visit areas outside of the healthcare centre more regularly (Interview 12, LTHSE).

There were also changes to the equipment, food or visits that prisoners received, aimed at providing them with more appropriate care but granting them something to which other prisoners were not entitled. Some of the adaptions made for Eddie included installing a doorbell near his bed. When he was first ill, the prisoner responsible for allocating bedding made sure he got an extra mattress, arranging this himself rather than discussing it with staff (Fieldnote, LTHSE). A few months later, as Eddie's condition deteriorated, handrails were fitted in his cell and later the doctor was reported to be trying to get an air mattress for him (Fieldnotes, LTHSE). Adjustments were also made to the meals served to Eddie, including to the timing, which was otherwise incompatible with his medication:

> He has to have his meds at five, and then can't eat at five [as with the regime], so they've sorted out for him to have eggs, and dried potato and soup, but with bits of chicken in it. (Fieldnote, LTHSE)

There were some concerns that he wasn't getting good enough food, that the portions were too small, and that a man in Eddie's circumstances should have whatever food he wanted (Fieldnote, LTHSE). At the Category B prison, this concern had in the past led to officers sometimes cooking for prisoners themselves, recognising the prisoner may not then be able to eat much because of his frailty, but concerned to provide him with whatever food he wanted as part of providing palliative care (Interview 2, Category B). Adjustments were also made to visiting arrangements, with family members being permitted to enter parts of the prison not usually accessible to them, such as the healthcare centres. There were also small adaptions such as cell doors being left open.

The adjustments were made because the prisoner was thought to be dying and because this provoked sympathy amongst officers. Rules were less enforceable around terminally ill prisoners because their impending death often made officers more aware of a prisoner's humanity. As one officer said:

> They tend to get a bit more grace. Er, staff tend not to be so robust with them, there's a bit of lee-way. A bit of. Most staff are very black and white, no grey areas. But yet with someone who's terminally ill, you let grey areas slip in. (Interview 9, Category B)

The danger in this use of discretion, based as it was on a sense of sympathy and notions of decency, was that it could become arbitrary. One prisoner, speaking about how to get what was needed as an elderly prisoner or a wheelchair user, said: "if you're lucky your face fits and you know which officers to ask" (Fieldnote, Category B). Here the construction of individual prisoners became relevant. Those for whom staff were more able to feel sympathy were arguably more likely to experience the small adjustments to the regime that facilitated good palliative care.

For more significant adjustments and deviations from the 'rules', there was a reliance on the authority of the Governing Governor. The Governing Governor had a key role in determining the location of a dying prisoner and thus could determine the extent to which the psychosocial needs of the prisoner were met. If he was content for a prisoner to stay on the wing, even though this was not usual practice, senior officers would accept it. Staff in all roles placed considerable weight on following the rules and constructed some rules as requiring permission from someone higher in the hierarchy before they could be overturned. How much discretion they had depended on their own place in the hierarchy. One officer spoke about always checking with the prison authorities before changing a prisoner's restraints at the request of a hospital consultant (Interview 11, LTHSE). In contrast, a custodial manager at the same prison felt comfortable making that judgement himself, but still immediately contacted the duty governor to get agreement to the decision (Interview 6, LTHSE). A governor, who had worked with the then Governing Governor for a number of years, felt confident they knew what he would think about a subject, and so might act first, but would still contact him to explain what had been done and why (Interview 7, LTHSE). In other cases, such as when Neil's wife had stayed with him overnight immediately prior to his death, when one senior member of staff had challenged another about what was planned, it was sufficient for her to respond: "I said it had all gone passed the Number One "Oh, it's going to happen then". "Yes, it is". In other words, wind your neck in and get on with it" (Interview 13, LTHSE). Likewise, in the Category B prison, when there was insufficient staff available to facilitate a prisoner receiving a visit in H3 rather than the Visits hall, if the instruction had come from higher up in the hierarchy, it had to be done regardless (Interviews 9 and 16, Category B).

In the context of a more general prison population, Liebling and Maruna (2005) argue the rules, regulations and guidelines in place within the prison service require subjective interpretation. They find the use of staff discretion leads to inconsistencies and arbitrariness in how rules are implemented. In the prisons studied in this instance, for prison officers working with dying prisoners, there was a concern that the rules and guidelines in place did not cover the situation in which they found themselves. As previously discussed, the PSIs, PSO and Prison Rules did not directly address the likely needs of dying prisoners, relating to arguably tangential matters such as the arrangements for hospital escorts and the use of restraints. They did not embody the principles of palliative care many prison staff were instinctively trying to implement when a death was expected. One CM said that most of the time he and his colleagues were guessing what to do (Fieldnote, LTHSE). Schneider's (1992) suggestion that 'rule-failure' discretion is prominent in prisons was apparent when it came to the care of dying prisoners. In the very hierarchical and rules-based environment of the prison, discretion has become an intrinsic part of a prison officer's role (Liebling et al., 2011). In the context of dying prisoners, discretion is even more important because the gaps in the 'rules' left prison officers feeling they are guessing what to do.

Ultimately, however, the need to keep the routines of the prison running, to maintain the prison regime, meant that in the prisons studied any adjustments were limited, noticeable to perhaps only a few people. As one officer said: "the wing will carry on as normal regardless of their ailments and regardless of their condition" (Interview 11, LTHSE). Practical changes might be made, informed by use of discretion that was often hierarchical in nature, but the desire to provide what was perceived as the quality end of life care would not significantly disrupt the prison regime.

Medical Confidentiality and Dealing with DNR

Medical confidentiality in prison is a contentious issue. For example, Condon et al. (2007) find a lack of privacy in accessing medical services was an issue for prisoners in all twelve prisons they studied, with prisoners feeling nurses were careless about medical confidentiality. This was not an issue raised by prisoners in this research project. Instead, the tension was between the professional expectations of healthcare staff and those of prison officers, not between prisoners and staff. Prison officers working on the wings complained that despite having the most contact with terminally and seriously ill prisoners, they were not informed about prisoners' conditions. Some saw this as adversely affecting their ability to care for prisoners (Fieldnotes, LTHSE). Nursing staff understood that officers might struggle to know what was needed:

> Obviously as a nurse, information governance comes at the top of the tree and you don't disclose any confidential information to anybody that's not medical. But there's cert… you have to keep them in the loop about certain things that are going on because they are with them sometimes more than the nursing staff. (Interview 1, Category B)
> Nursing staff said there was a fine line between letting an officer know a prisoner was unwell and telling them too many details in a manner that would breach the expectations of medical confidentiality. For them, the important thing was ensuring officers knew there was a reason why the prisoner may need a nurse and would therefore fetch one in a timely manner (Interview 1, Category B). The issue for both groups of staff was ensuring palliative care was coordinated and there was a strong sense amongst officers that practices related to medical confidentiality were a barrier to this.

The fact of imprisonment did significantly change the standard of medical confidentiality available for the prisoner. In part, this resulted from practical considerations. Hospital escorts were particularly difficult times to maintain medical confidentiality. Although medical information was not recorded in the Person Escort Record (PSI 33/2015, 6.4), confidentiality was often impossible to maintain and even officers could find the situation difficult, as one acknowledged:

> They can't leave when medical information is being discussed and often hear things they don't want to. He says medical people are often not comfortable with this, and sometimes officers aren't. (Fieldnote, LTHSE)

Some officers reported that prisoners willingly shared medically confidential information with them (Interview 15, LTHSE; Interview 3, Category B). One FLO spoke about checking with prisoners if it was alright to remain with them when nursing staff were present and found prisoners usually felt it was useful for the FLO to know about their condition:

> I'll just be saying to the prisoner, "Are you happy that I sit here and obviously I'm your FLO" and they are normally just fine with that, y'know. They know that obviously, they are not in a good way so there's no point really keeping it private. But I would ask them if they minded me sitting there. (Interview 15, LTHSE)
> This was indicative of the quality of relationship within the prison but also of the dependant nature of prisoners.

Some of the challenges of providing quality care that respected the prisoner's wishes whilst maintaining appropriate medical confidentiality were highlighted by the difficulties presented by a prisoner's request for resuscitation not to be attempted. Dealing correctly with a 'Do Not Resuscitate' (DNR) request was a source of concern for staff, but also a way in which care was shown. Officers and healthcare staff demonstrated care through their commitment to respect a dying prisoner's wishes (Fieldnote, LTHSE). This was part of the value set informing the motivation to make dying in prison 'as good as it could be'. Dealing correctly with a DNR request was also a way of caring for colleagues, closely linked to the expectation of an investigation and concerns that staff could be criticised for not attempting resuscitation (Fieldnote, LTHSE). Or for attempting resuscitation on a prisoner who had a DNR request in place (Interview 3, Category B).

The importance of a DNR as a means of granting dying prisoners some autonomy was reflected in its inclusion in PSI 64/2011, where as part of a brief section on the "Management of prisoners who are terminally or seriously ill" it was stated:

> Prisoners are able to be involved in the decisions made about the care they receive and in some cases make a decision not to be resuscitated. (PSI 64/2011, Chapter 11)
>
> PSI 64/2011 also states that:
>
> It is key that information is recorded and that if a DNR is in place this information is shared with staff in order that the prisoner's wishes not to receive treatment are respected. (PSI 64/2011, Chapter 11)

Senior officers in particular worried about how to communicate the existence of a DNR request to other officers whilst not breaking the expectations of medical confidentiality. The two prisons took very different approaches. In the Category B prison, there was an established practice of storing the DNR somewhere visible in the prisoner's cell, including when they were accommodated on a wing (Fieldnote; Interviews 1 and 9, Category B) and of taking a copy with the prisoner if he was taken to outside hospital (Interview 9, Category B). Prisoners mostly accepted this (Fieldnote, Category B), although one did ask for it to be moved so he could not see it from his bed (Interview 2, Category B). In H3, where terminally ill prisoners were most likely to be accommodated, the information would also be recorded on a white board in the staff office which listed each cell occupant and was included in staff handovers between shifts (Interview 2, Category B). There could still be problems with communicating this information. One officer reported a recent incident when a night nurse had spotted a prisoner with a DNR in place who was having a heart attack and had started resuscitation (Interview 2, Category B).

In the LTHSE prison, there was some confusion amongst prison officers and healthcare staff about what information could be or needed to be shared. Senior officers on Eddie's wing were concerned about how to ensure their junior colleagues knew he did not wish resuscitation to be attempted. Nursing staff advised that the officers involved would have to have a copy of Eddie's signed request before not doing or stopping resuscitation (Fieldnote, LTHSE). This was kept in the Primary Care Centre in the centre of the prison, but inaccessible overnight. The senior officer had seen the original with Eddie present, talked it over with him, and then told his staff, but was concerned this was not legally sufficient. He thought it would be best to have a copy in Eddie's cell, but had been told by healthcare professionals this would breach rules on medical confidentiality and could be stolen or tampered with by other prisoners (Fieldnote, LTHSE). What was common practice in one prison in this regard was not considered possible in the other.

Conclusion

Prisons are places in which care is expressed, especially towards prisoners at the end of life. The four components of Fisher and Tronto's (1990) typology of care in its broadest meaning (caring about, taking care of, caregiving and care receiving), could all be observed with regard to prisoners dying of natural causes in the prisons studied. Expressions of care were not limited to healthcare professionals, but found in prison officers, chaplains, governors, family liaison officers and fellow prisoners. All of these people potentially had a role in meeting the holistic needs of a dying prisoner as set out in the WHO definition of palliative care. For some, especially older male prison officers, narratives of 'heroic' care were constructed to lessen the effects of a spoiled work identity.

In many cases, staff and prisoners were instinctively seeking to care about and take care of dying prisoners in ways that met their physical and psychosocial and, to a lesser extent, spiritual needs. These efforts were informed by often very personal assessments about what constituted quality care, based for some staff on experiences of loved ones dying, or on the care they imagined appropriate for their parents. Efforts to make dying in prison 'as good as it could be' served to highlight decency, a value treasured in other contexts within the prison service. Hard to define, closely linked to privacy, comfort and respect, it was a value that prison service employees were familiar with, enshrined as it is in the service's value statements and the broader aims. Nevertheless, they often felt they were guessing what to do, in part due to gaps in the 'rules' and the guidance provided. Discretion was so important because there was 'rule-failure' (Schneider, 1992); the prison 'rules' had not been changed to reflect the new tasks of caring for dying prisoners.

Constructing quality palliative care as something that was regarded as important was linked to seeing the prisoner as someone deserving of sympathy because they were dying. It often led to a willingness to adjust the prison regime, change normal practices and find space within the rules in ways that softened the usual experience of the harsh prison setting and subtly changed prison regimes. Some adaptions, particularly those concerning the location of a prisoner or security considerations such as the removal of restraints, needed approval from senior managers or Governing Governors. However, many changes might be scarcely noticed by most people. These changes did not necessarily have a significant impact on the prison regime but they happened nevertheless, quietly adjusting normal practice by flexing timings, altering routines, deploying additional staff and providing additional goods to meet the needs of a dying prisoner. Deaths from natural causes thus generated new tasks and changed the normal practices of the prison. Studies of prison officers (Liebling, 2016; Tait, 2011) suggest some officers have always cared for prisoners, but now they found themselves helping nurses provide physical care, pushing wheelchairs and negotiating for better food for a dying prisoner. The differences between the two prisons in how they dealt with DNR requests perhaps captures a moment where one prison was trying to catch up with new circumstances. In one prison, there was an accepted method for communicating DNR requests. In the other, the unusualness of accommodating on a wing a prisoner so close to death was presenting staff with challenges that at the time of the fieldwork still needed resolving.

The relatively small adaptions made were more significant in changing the culture of the prison. Discretion has always been part of how prison officers achieve their tasks but meeting the needs of dying prisoners pushed the use of discretion further. Prisoner culture softened too, with the circumstances of dying prisoners providing opportunities to display a caring nature and to embody feelings towards fellow prisoners in practical actions. Relationships between prisoners became more intimate, as between Eddie and his main carer, because this was essential to providing good palliative care.

There were limitations. The security imperative, dominant in both prisons, negatively affected palliative care, limiting options for receiving pain relief or requiring the use of restraints that affected both physical and psychosocial care. Medical confidentiality was often hard to maintain, reflecting the low importance often placed on it because of the prisoner's status. Seriously and terminally ill prisoners were surrounded by criminogenic neighbours and, for some, the vulnerability associated with their bodily losses could make them prone to bullying from their peers. However, in contrast with other studies (Burles et al., 2016; Wood, 2007) which identify only difficulties arising from the prison regime for the provision of palliative care, the normal expectations of the prison regime, embodied in the standard practices within the prison, could also assist efforts to provide palliative care. Care at the end of life in prison custody happened, despite all the challenges.

References

Arnold, H. (2005). The effects of prison work. In A. Liebling & S. Maruna (Eds.), *The effects of imprisonment* (pp. 391–420). Routledge.

Arnold, H. (2016). The prison officer. In Y. Jewkes, B. Crewe, & J. Bennett (Eds.), *Handbook on prisons* (2nd ed., pp. 265–284). Routledge.

Arnold, H., Liebling, A., & Tait, S. (2007). Prison officers and prison culture. In Y. Jewkes (Ed.), *Handbook on prisons* (pp. 471–495). Willan.

Bryans, S., & Jones, R. (Eds.). (2001). *Prisons and the prisoner : An introduction to the work of Her Majesty's prison service*. The Stationery Office.

Burles, M. C., Peternelj-Taylor, C. A., & Holtslander, L. (2016). A 'good death' for all? Examining issues for palliative care in correctional settings. *Mortality, 21*(2), 93–111. https://doi.org/10.1080/13576275.2015.1098602

Caswell, G., & O'Connor, M. (2019). 'I've no fear of dying alone': Exploring perspectives on living and dying alone. *Mortality, 24*(1), 17–31. https://doi.org/10.1080/13576275.2017.1413542

Cloyes, K. G., Rosenkranz, S. J., Wold, D., Berry, P. H., & Supiano, K. P. (2013). To be truly alive: Motivation among prison inmate hospice volunteers and the transformative process of end-of-life peer care service. *American Journal of Hospice and Palliative Medicine, 31*(7), 735–748. https://doi.org/10.1177/1049909113506035

Condon, L., Hek, G., Harris, F., Powell, J., Kemple, T., & Priscoe, S. (2007). Users' views of prison health services: A qualitative study. *Journal of Advanced Nursing, 58*(3), 216–226. https://doi.org/10.1111/j.1365-2648.2007.04221.x

Crawley, E. (2004). *Doing prison work: The public and private lives of prison officers*. Willan.

Crawley, E. (2005). Institutional thoughtlessness in prisons and its impacts on the day-to-day prison lives of elderly men. *Journal of Contemporary Criminal Justice, 21*(4), 350–363. https://doi.org/10.1177/1043986205282018

Crewe, B., Warr, J., Bennett, P., & Smith, A. (2013). The emotional geography of prison life. *Theoretical Criminology, 18*(1), 56–74. https://doi.org/10.1177/1362480613497778

Dawes, J. (2009). Ageing prisoners: Issues for social work. *Australian Social Work, 62*(2), 258–271. https://doi.org/10.1080/03124070902803475

Elliott, K. (2016). Caring masculinities: Theorizing an emerging concept. *Men and Masculinities, 19*(3), 240–259. https://doi.org/10.1177/1097184X15576203

Fisher, B., & Tronto, J. (1990). Towards a feminist theory of caring. In E. Abel & M. Nelson (Eds.), *Circles of care: Work and identity in women's lives* (pp. 35–62). State University of New York.

Hanlon, N. (2012). *Masculinities, care and equality*. Palgrave Macmillan.

Hay, W., & Sparks, R. (1991). What is a prison officer? *Prison Service Journal, 83*(3), 2–7.

Her Majesty's Prison and Probation Service. (2017). *HMPPS business plan, 2017–18*. Her Majesty's Prison and Probation Service, UK. https://assets.publishing.service.gov.uk/government/uploads/system/uploads/attachment_data/file/668256/HMPPS_Business_Plan_2017_to_2018.pdf

Her Majesty's Prison and Probation Service. (2019). *Annual report and accounts 2018–19. HC 2291*. London: The Stationery Office.

Kohn, T., & McKechnie, R. (Eds.). (1999). *Extending the boundaries of care*. Berg.

Laws, B., & Lieber, E. (2022). 'King, warrior, magician, lover': Understanding expressions of care among male prisoners. *European Journal of Criminology, 19*(4), 469–487. https://doi.org/10.1177/1477370819896207

Liebling, A. (2016). High security prisons in England and Wales. In Y. Jewkes, B. Crewe, & J. Bennett (Eds.), *Handbook on prisons*. Abingdon.
Liebling, A., & Maruna, S. (2005). *The effects of imprisonment*. Willan.
Liebling, A., Price, D., & Shefer, G. (2011). *The prison officer* (2nd ed.). Willan.
Lillie, K. (2018). Loss at the end of life: Palliative care in prisons. In S. Read, S. Santatzoglou, & A. Wrigley (Eds.), *Loss, dying and bereavement in the criminal justice system* (pp. 43–53). Routledge.
Loeb, S. J., Hollenbeak, C. S., Penrod, J., Smith, C. A., Kitt-Lewis, E., & Crouse, S. B. (2013). Care and companionship in an isolating environment: Inmates attending to dying peers. *Journal of Forensic Nursing, 9*(1), 35–44.
Moll, A. (2013). *Losing track of time: Dementia and the ageing prison population—Treatment challenges and examples of good practice.* Mental Health Foundation. https://www.mentalhealth.org.uk/content/assets/PDF/publications/losing-track-of-time-2013.pdf
Moore, R. L., & Gillette, D. (1990). *King, warrior, magician, lover: Rediscovering the archetypes of the mature masculine*. Harper.
Newell, T. (2002). The prison officer as moral agent. *Prison Service Journal, 139*, 29–36.
Owers, A. (2006). Turnkeys or role models. *Prison Service Journal, 168*, 20–26.
Schneider, C. (1992). Discretion and rules: A lawyers view. In K. Hawkins (Ed.), *The uses of discretion* (pp. 47–89). Oxford University Press.
Seale, C. (1995). Dying alone. *Sociology of Health and Illness, 17*(3), 376–392. https://doi.org/10.1111/1467-9566.ep10933327
Supiano, K. P., Cloyes, K. G., & Berry, P. H. (2014). The grief experience of prison inmate hospice volunteer caregivers. *Journal of Social Work in End-of-Life & Palliative Care, 10*(1), 80–94. https://doi.org/10.1080/15524256.2013.877866
Sykes, G. M. (1958). *Society of captives: A study of a maximum security prison.* Princeton University Press.
Tait, S. (2011). A typology of prison officer approaches to care. *European Journal of Criminology, 8*(6), 440–454. https://doi.org/10.1177/1477370811413804
Tait, S. (2012). Custody, care and staff-prisoner relationships. In B. Crewe & J. Bennett (Eds.), *The prisoner* (pp. 13–26). Routledge.
Tronto, J. C. (2013). *Caring democracy*. New York University Press.
Turner, M., Payne, S., & Barbarachild, Z. (2011). Care or custody? An evaluation of palliative care in prisons in North West England. *Palliative Medicine, 25*(4), 370–377. https://doi.org/10.1177/0269216310393058

Wood, F. J. (2007). The challenge of providing palliative care to terminally ill prison inmates in the UK. *International Journal of Palliative Nursing, 13*(3), 131–135. https://doi.org/10.12968/ijpn.2007.13.3.23275

World Health Organisation. (2019). *WHO definition of palliative care*. World Health Organisation. https://www.who.int/cancer/palliative/definition/en/

Wrigley, A. (2018). Death, dying and maintaining hope: Ethical tensions and responsibilities for end-of-life care in the prison setting. In S. Read, S. Santatzoglou, & A. Wrigley (Eds.), *Loss, dying and bereavement in the criminal justice system* (pp. 22–31). Routledge.

6

Evaluating End of Life Care in Prison Custody

For many of the staff and prisoners involved in caring for prisoners facing the end of life in prison custody, how care was evaluated was an important issue. Invested as they were in the tasks associated with working with dying prisoners, some form of evaluation, however personal, was needed to inform ongoing care and imagined future scenarios. Such feedback, where positive, was also part of easing the emotional labour of caring in challenging circumstances. After a death, however, more formal evaluations of care occurred, with a greater focus on accountability and the performance of the prison as an institution. Three organisations have responsibility for investigating the circumstances of any death in custody: the police, the coroner and the Prison and Probation Ombudsman (PPO), but it was the role of the PPO that was most often raised by people living and working in the prisons studied when they discussed how end of life care was formally evaluated.

This chapter will explore the influence of discourses that sought to define the quality of end of life care in prison based on the ideal of equivalence, and the expectation of a post-death investigation into the care provided. It will also look at how these evaluations were experienced by prison staff and prisoners, and explore the shortcomings of current forms

C. Robinson, *Dying in Prison*, Palgrave Studies in Prisons and Penology, https://doi.org/10.1007/978-3-031-27103-8_6

of evaluating end of life care in prison custody. It will look at the recently introduced *Dying Well in Custody Charter* and also briefly consider the methods used to evaluate deaths in prison custody, especially the role of the Prison and Probation Ombudsman.

It was noticeable that those involved in or observing deaths from natural causes in prison custody were often seeking standards against which to evaluate the care provided. Conversations with prisoners and staff alike suggested this was an ongoing concern, even for those staff who had considerable experience of working with prisoners dying of natural causes. Towards the end of this study, a CM asked my opinion, seeking advice on the care they were providing for Eddie. His statement that 'most of the time they're guessing what to do' (Fieldnote, LTHSE) highlights the need for feedback, but it is striking that even in the LTHSE, included in this study because it had one of the highest rates in England and Wales of prisoner deaths from natural causes in the previous five years, there could be considerable uncertainty about what constituted good end of life care.

As Kohn and McKechnie (1999) point out, understandings of care are socially constructed. What is understood as good or bad care, or the right or wrong way to deliver care, can be specific to a particular group or setting. In the prisons studied, there were three discourses providing a means for evaluating end of life care, two of which were related to personal values and personal experience and were highly informal. These standards were loosely defined, unsystematic, subjective and often highly personal. The third discourse was based on assumptions about what a formal investigation would conclude, revealing both the importance of formal, external, feedback to those involved in caring for dying prisoners, and also the difficulties that could occur if external feedback was not constructed as available or trusted.

The most common rationale for the construction of quality care was that of 'equivalence' where the focus was on medical and social care: is the medical or social care a prisoner receives equivalent to that received by members of the community not in prison? This applied to all health-related care, not just palliative care. For many staff, constructing good end of life care was heavily influenced by this principle of equivalence, the idea that prisoners should receive the same standard of medical care as someone in the community. However, there was generally no means for measuring this and the strongly held and divergent views between staff and prisoners as to the extent to which this was achieved are discussed in detail below. The ideal of 'equivalence' of care did have some formal bearing in the official fatal incident investigations of the PPO, discussed below, but remained a highly subjective concept in discourses within the prisons.

An alternative evaluation of care, equally subjective, was provided by a more nebulous sense of what makes for a good death, described in the context of the prison setting as making death 'as good as it could be'. This was discussed in Chapter 5, where the importance of personal values and experience, particularly understandings of 'decency', was explored, and will not be discussed further here. The main aim of discourses that sought to make death 'as good as it could be' was to inform care before death. Common concerns, for example, that no one should die alone, could be mobilised to evaluate a death, but notions of decency, privacy and the sadness of a life ending in prison served primarily to inform adjustments that improved the experience of care and brought comfort, control or closure, rather than to assess care after a death had occurred.

A third, more relevant way of evaluating care was provided by the expectation of an investigation after a death, something not experienced in all deaths in the community but resulting from the prisoner's status of dying in state custody. In this context, care will be seen to be defined as meeting the standard the Prison and Probation Ombudsman (PPO) investigation will deem satisfactory, a standard that for each individual cannot be confirmed until after a death has occurred. Girling and Seal (2016) argue that "prisoners' loss of liberty places a heavy responsibility on the State to ensure that they are adequately cared for" (p. 216). The scrutiny that is part of a fatal incident investigation by the PPO after a death in custody arises from the obligations of Article 2 of the ECHR. It is important in establishing the extent to which the prison is meeting these obligations and can serve to inform practice throughout HMPPS. Whilst it is the Coroner's role, assisted by the police, to determine the cause of death, the PPO's remit is to establish the circumstances of a death in prison custody, including what care was provided and to make any recommendations for changes. Their reviews of deaths from natural causes in custody include independent assessments of clinical care (Prison & Probation Ombudsman, 2017) and are intended to contribute to safer and fairer prison custody (PPO, 2021). PPO reviews provide a formal, external evaluation of the care delivered to a dying prisoner, which includes considering whether the care received was equivalent to that available in the community. The seriousness with which PPO reports were regarded in the prisons studied led to a focus on the anticipated or expected findings of a PPO investigation. As such, the expectation of a PPO investigation served to focus attention on particular aspects of care, reflecting the perceived likely PPO priorities.

The Ideal of 'Equivalence'

The ideal of 'equivalence' was one many participants, both prisoners and staff, regarded as important in assessing the quality of care in prisons. It originates from UN and WHO instructions (World Health Organisation, 2019). Charles and Draper (2011) summarise the importance of this ideal, saying:

> the principle of equivalence assumes that, when it comes to responding to health-related needs, prisoners are equal in the morally relevant sense to those outside of prison and the fact of their imprisonment is not itself a morally relevant difference sufficiently to justify unequal treatment where unequal means disadvantageous. (p. 215)
> There should, according to this ideal, be no difference between the medical care available 'inside' and 'outside' the prison.

The ideal of equivalence is not without controversy. Charles and Draper (2011) question the focus within the UK on the equivalence of process, suggesting instead that equivalence of outcome would be a preferable measure. Lillie (2018) goes further, suggesting that although there are examples of good practice in end of life care in prisons and favourable reports from the PPO:

> Nevertheless, there is no evidence that there is systematic equivalence in care provision, and there remain significant structural barriers to ensuring high-quality palliative care in prisons. (p. 49)

Regardless of such criticism, the importance of the idea of equivalence of process in the provision of general medical care is embodied in the rules and regulations governing prisons. For example, PSO 3050 makes it clear that within a week of arriving in a prison, a prisoner should receive a primary care assessment equivalent to that given when registering with a new general practitioner in the community (PSO 3050, 2.12). Similarly, PSI 03/2016 seeks to provide social care equivalent to that available in the community, with the intention of ensuring local authority services can operate within the prison:

> so that prisoners who may have needs as a result of illness, disability or age… have equivalent access to care and support services as in the community, and are supported to live with dignity and as much independence as possible. (PSI 03/2016, 1.8)

The *Dying Well in Custody* charter (Ambitions for Palliative & End of Life Care Partnership, 2018), is part of efforts to ensure equivalence of care at the end of life in prison custody. Published in 2018, it was followed shortly after by a self-assessment tool for prison use. These publications followed nationwide discussions involving palliative care specialists and prison staff in various roles. Based on *Ambitions for Palliative and End of Life Care; a national framework for local action 2015–2020* which was developed by a partnership involving the NHS, medical organisations and the voluntary sector, they sought to achieve equivalence for palliative care in the prison setting and update existing guidance. There are six 'ambitions' for end of life and palliative care:

- Each person is seen as an individual
- Each person gets fair access to care
- Maximising comfort and well-being
- Care is coordinated

- All staff are prepared to care
- Each community is prepared to help (National Palliative and End of Life Care Partnership, 2015).

Whilst these 'ambitions' had been translated into the Dying Well in Custody Charter, they were not reflected in prison 'rules', and as such the standards of palliative care in the community were not yet formally embedded in the expectations of palliative care in the prison. This is perhaps inevitable given that, at the time of this study, none of the relevant PSIs had been reviewed since the *Ambitions* document was produced in 2015, but serves to highlight the different priorities manifested in the prison rules and regulations discussed in Chapter 3. Intended as a self-assessment tool, it is not mandatory for prisons to use the adaptions of the *Ambitions* document that constitutes the *Dying Well in Custody Charter*. The *Charter* had been trialled in the LTHSE prison but was not mentioned by healthcare staff there. Nursing staff in the Category B prison were excited by the possibilities for improvement it offered, but aware it would be "a huge piece of work" to implement (Interview 10, Category B).

In both prisons studied, participants' assessments of the quality of care provided or received relied heavily on the ideal of equivalence as the standard by which care could be evaluated, although its application was very subjective and linked to personal experience. Several references were made to care being better or worse than could be expected in the outside community (Interviews 5, 13 and 11, LTHSE; Interview 10 Category B. Fieldnotes, LTHSE and Category B). There was a clear divide between staff and prisoners in their assessments of how far equivalence was achieved. Some staff regarded the care in prison as better than equivalent and most prisoners as worse. Whilst staff and prisoners made their own assessments of whether or not a prisoner had received care equivalent to that received by members of the community not in prison, it was only after death this received external validation. The importance of the ideal of 'equivalence' is manifested in reports by the Prison and Probation Ombudsman following a death in prison custody, which explicitly specify whether or not the standard of care received by the deceased was equivalent to what would have been received in the community. In practice, however, staff and prisoners were frequently reliant on their own estimates of whether equivalence was being achieved.

Constructing Care as 'Better' in Prison

Staff in a variety of roles in both prisons presented the case for care in prisons, particularly at the end of life, actually being better than in the community. The main difference was seen as the availability of health-care professionals within the prison, able to respond whenever needed. This was contrasted to someone dying at home, where carers might visit only a few times a day, rather than the level of care or frequency of checks provided to someone dying in a hospital or hospice. Staff made comparisons with their family members who had received end of life care at home or imagined how care would be provided at home in such circumstances. Reflecting on one death, a governor said:

> Probably had more care and attention than some people would have outside. And I think I can say that for quite a lot of the men here. Y'know, for the care and attention that they get. Not everybody would get a doctor on call, not everybody would get a nurse that would deal with them, y'know if they were in their home circumstances they wouldn't have that care. (Interview 13, LTHSE)

Similarly, the prospect of death outside custody was viewed as potentially more unpleasant and less dignified for prisoners who had committed offences that were especially stigmatised or who had lost contact with their family for other reasons. Speaking of Eddie, one officer tried to describe what he imagined would be the case:

> if Eddie was in the community, he, it could be that he'd be left to… and he struggles with whether to say what he was going to say. Eventually he says, 'sit in his own shit', and then apologies to me for the language. (Fieldnote, LTHSE)

Nursing staff were aware that in the community, a district nurse would make a limited number of visits to a dying patient a day, and saw a fairer comparison as being between a hospice in the community and the palliative care suite in prison:

> For someone in a palliative care suite in one of the prisons that's already got it well established, they've always got a nurse with them 24 hours a day, who is there on hand, like in a hospice, to do exactly what they need whenever they need it. Whereas in community, from a district nurse point of view, we'd go in three, four times a day. (Interview 10, Category B)
>
> This nurse had tried to have the perceived higher standard of care in prison reflected in the PPO post-incident reports following a death, challenging the clinical reviewer to report this, but said:
>
> But when the report comes out, it'll just say that it was the same as they would have received, y'know, rather than better. And she sort of said "well we can't really put better because that would cause a riot". And it's like, "but if it is better, you should put it". (Interview 10, Category B)

The concerns raised by the clinical reviewer that it would be unacceptable to the public for prisoners to be seen to receive better care than other people are interesting. Foucault says the public believes the "condemned man should suffer physically more than other men" (1991, p. 16). This is clearly undermined by the UN and WHO ideal of equivalence of care for prisoners but lingers on in the reviewer's reluctance to report care as better. Wanting the care provided to be recognised as better was perhaps a mechanism for the emotional labour needed to find reassurance that everything had been done for someone dying in circumstances regard as far from optimal. For some staff, if the availability of professional healthcare support was better for the dying in prison, it was necessitated by the fact of imprisonment:

> And I think you've got to treat them like that because they haven't always got somebody else around and they can't just pick up the phone and call somebody. (Interview 8, LTHSE)
>
> Care in prison had to be better, in the opinion of this participant, because the prisoner was restricted in so many other ways with regard to having their needs met.

Constructing Care as 'Worse'

Prisoners also used the ideal of equivalence to evaluate the standard of healthcare available in the prisons studied but reached very different conclusions. Prisoners were generally critical of the prison healthcare provider or of the medical and social care that was offered. This is in keeping with findings from other studies. Aday and Wahidin (2016) say it is common for prisoners to mistrust medical care in what they see as a defective system, with well-documented delays and denials of treatment, and when they have seen prisoners suffering resultant pain and humiliation. Similarly, Schaefer et al. (2022), in a systemic literature review, found that prisoners believed clinicians were not adequately trained to meet their needs. In this study, one prisoner thought his peers would always regard the person who had died as not having received proper care and that "everyone will attack the staff, all staff, for people who pass away" (Fieldnote, LTHSE).

Stories about poor general medical care circulated and had currency amongst prisoners, feeding a widespread perception that care was not equivalent to that available outside. In the LTHSE prison, the healthcare provider, Care UK, was referred to by prisoners as "Don't Care UK" (Fieldnotes, LTHSE) and described as worse than useless (Fieldnote, LTHSE) and lacking compassion (Fieldnote, LTHSE). Specific examples of poor care were readily shared. The treatment of chronic conditions in particular was compared unfavourably to the care received before imprisonment. This is in keeping with Condon et al.'s (2007) study which found examples of prisoners who had entered prison with conditions such as diabetes, Crohn's disease and incontinence not being able to access the same food or medical equipment as they had relied on in the community. In the LTHSE prison, one prisoner spoke about having to walk, outside, the 200 yards to the healthcare centre in his pyjama trousers since no wheelchair was available on his return to the prison after seven weeks in hospital (Fieldnote, LTHSE). Another spoke of a prisoner complaining of chest pains not being seen in a timely manner (Fieldnote, LTHSE). In the Category B prison, one prisoner said his monthly pacemaker checks before he came to prison had been replaced by one check-up in 10 months (Fieldnote, Category B). Another had written to his solicitor about problems getting regular medication when shortages of pharmacy staff had resulted in him receiving only two doses of a medication a day when he should have had four (Fieldnote, Category B). A prisoner in the Category B prison reported having two different forms of cancer, but having missed a planned operation because the prison authorities had got him to the hospital too late (Fieldnote, Category B).

Both prisoners and some staff, including healthcare professionals, attributed problems with healthcare to a lack of training (Interview 11, LTHSE and Interview 1, Category B). Some also added in a lack of equipment and a lack of ability, with one officer concluding that far from care being equivalent, "it's unfair, it's unfair" (Interview 11, LTHSE).

The Expectation of Investigation

Deaths in prison custody, even when anticipated, are always subject to investigation by the police, coroner and Prison and Probation Ombudsman (PPO). The process can be lengthy but should include the causes of death as well as the circumstances of death, and in the case of the PPO report, explicitly address the quality of care provided to the prisoner and where relevant, their family (PPO, 2021). As such, when a death had been anticipated, the PPO reports can be a tool for assessing how far the WHO vision of palliative care has been met. Furthermore, the findings of previous investigations after deaths from natural causes and the awareness of future investigations offer prison staff another means of evaluating the care being provided to those approaching the end of life in prison.

The expectation of an investigation was taken very seriously by prison staff and could direct priorities in the care of the dying prisoner as prison staff anticipated possible criticism, based on previous reports. Whilst prison staff expressed concern about having to appear in the coroner's court, it was the PPO investigation, and particularly their report, which was most frequently mentioned by prison staff in a variety of roles, including governors, officers and healthcare professionals (Interviews 5, 13 and 11, LTHSE; Interview 10, Category B. Fieldnotes, Category B; Fieldnotes, LTHSE). This aspect of evaluating end of life care, through the investigations and report of the PPO, is specific to the prison setting. Responses to the prospect of external scrutiny reflected the differing priorities of different occupational groups, with healthcare professionals focussed on evidencing care plans (Interviews 1 and 10, Category B), family liaison officers being concerned that family care should be exemplary (Interviews 3, 9 and 16, Category B; Interview 15, LTHSE) and governors and senior officers focussed on the correct application of restraints (Interview 7, LTHSE; Fieldnote, LTHSE).

Preparing for an expected investigation could influence any aspect of care for the dying prisoner. Uncertainty in the LTHSE about where to keep, and whether to display, Eddie's signed forms requesting cardiopulmonary resuscitation should not be attempted directly related to anxieties about future investigations. Concerns were expressed about how investigators would respond if resuscitation was attempted against Eddie's wishes (*Fieldnote, LTHSE*). Staff reported colleagues having been criticised by the coroner in the past for not attempting resuscitation (Fieldnote, LTHSE) or being sued by prisoners for having resuscitated them (Interview 9, Category B) and there was a belief that attempting resuscitation on a prisoner with a DNR request in place would be illegal (Interview 9, Category B). One senior officer spoke about attending the coroner's court and seeing staff be criticised for not attempting CPR. A fieldnote records:

> he's seen the prison service leave officers out to dry over issues like this, and doesn't want him or his staff to get the blame. … He'll take any blame on the chin, but doesn't think it's fair to put his staff in that position. (Fieldnote, LTHSE)
> The issues around communicating a prisoner's requests for resuscitation not to be attempted should they collapse became more fraught because of the investigation that would follow a death. There was a concern, beyond respecting his wishes, to provide clarity for officers, so they would not be put in a position where a subsequent inquiry might blame them for their actions (Fieldnote, LTHSE).

The expectation of an investigation also served to increase the importance of documenting and measuring care. When a death was anticipated, accurate record keeping became important because all records were likely to be included in the ensuing investigations (Fieldnotes, LTHSE and Category B; Interview 11, Category B). Collating all of a prisoner's record and sending copies to the PPO, the Coroner and the prison service solicitor was in itself a huge task (Interview 13, LTHSE). An awareness of the burden to be carried by accurate record keeping after a death was demonstrated by a governor who, on the day he was interviewed, had visited the hospital to review the use of restraints on a prisoner who was terminally ill. He said:

> When I'm writing that up, I'm writing my sort of authoritative assessment of that risk, knowing that within 6 months that's probably going to be in front of the PPO, or copies of that, and the coroner and everyone looking and assessing my decision. So my decision's got to be defensible, right? (Interview 7, LTHSE)

There were other ways in which an expected investigation increased the importance of record keeping. The *Dying Well in Custody Charter*, discussed above, was also seen as part of record-keeping at the end of life, with a nurse seeing it as a tool for evidencing the work done by healthcare staff for the investigation following a death (Interview 10, Category B). On 'bedwatches' the senior escorting officer was usually given responsibility for record-keeping (Fieldnotes, Category B; LTHSE). One participant spoke about this task, placing a noticeably different emphasis on its importance in later investigations:

> If the doctor comes in and says "Right, this procedure" or gives an injection, you document everything, exactly what's happening, bit by bit so you've got an ongoing occurrence record of who the doctor's name is, what he's done. Not what the drug is but just "was given an injection at such and such" er, and just keep an ongoing record and a log, just in case anything does at a later date happen or the prisoner passes away or escapes, that you've known what has happened at any one time.... Because then you've got an ongoing record if it goes to the coroner's court in three years' time. (Interview 11, LTHSE)

The expectation of an investigation shaped the care given to dying prisoners by encouraging staff to prioritise the issues they knew would be the focus of the investigators. Attempts to find a dying prisoner's next of kin could be informed by an awareness that the PPO would be critical of a lack of family contact (Interview 13, LTHSE). In the case of Neil in the LTHSE prison, where a family member had been allowed to sit with a dying prisoner for the first time, there was a belief this would happen again because it would be positively received by the expected investigation: "we'll get relatives in again. It makes us look good" (Interview 12, LTHSE). Other interactions with prisoners' families were also informed by an awareness on the investigation to come. One FLO spoke about his frustration with the prison administration team's reluctance to meet the costs of the families of prisoners at the end of life:

> She's getting a taxi to A&E. She doesn't work, she's on benefits and I'm mindful that come later down the line, when he does pass away, she'll be interviewed by the PPO "What care was given to you? What did the prison do for you? What did you do for them?" And it's all about the PR side of it, and the bean-counters forget the PR side of it. ... I mean it's about funeral expenses. We used to pay, we didn't question it. It was paid. A lot of the theory behind that was the fact of when we come to coroner's court, or investigation, they look at that – "did the prison offer funeral expenses?"; "the prison paid in full". (Interview 9, Category B)
> Getting a favourable report from the PPO and a positive comment in the coroner's court was in his view sufficient justification for providing financial assistance to a prisoner's family.

In part as a response to the expectation of an investigation, staff and prisoners put considerable emphasis on the need to have a care plan in place for a dying prisoner. This might result from a 'case conference' or 'multidisciplinary team meeting', but getting a plan in place was seen as important (Fieldnotes, LTHSE). For healthcare staff, this included liaising with specialists outside the prison (Interview 1, Category B) and attending meetings at outside hospitals, if that was where the prisoner was being treated, to ensure continuity of care when they returned to the prison (Interview 12, LTHSE). Other caring actions might be speeded up because of an awareness of a likely investigation. In the LTHSE prison, when Eddie needed handrails fitting on his cell, this was done by the Works department very quickly. When I commented on the speed, a senior officer said: "even Works aren't stupid, they know he's going to die and no one knows when" (Fieldnote, LTHSE). The clear implication was that there was a need to forestall the potential criticism to be expected if delays meant he died without the handrails having been fitted.

Anticipating an investigation could lead to unexpected actions in a prisoner's last few hours. One officer recounted having been an escort on a 'bedwatch' and encouraging nursing staff in the hospital to remove the syringe driver that was no longer needed from the prisoner's room before he died, so police would not seize it as part of their investigation. He had previous experience of the police keeping a syringe driver, an expensive piece of equipment, for over a year after the prisoner's death and did not want the hospital to be inconvenienced in this way (Interview 2, Category B).

The expectation of an investigation could also change the care given immediately after a death, in ways which staff found emotionally challenging. One nurse found it difficult that the expectation of an investigation meant she was not to be permitted to wash the body or provide the final stages of care she was used to delivering in her previous work outside the prison (Interview 12, LTHSE). Similarly, Neil's wife was told she had to leave his bedside immediately after his death because the cell would be regarded as a crime scene (Interview 13, LTHSE). However, at times, the concern about a future investigation was put aside in order to do what was regarded as the right thing, even if it wasn't the mandated behaviour. A nurse spoke of being helped by an officer to move a prisoner after his death. She knew he should be left where he was but was anxious to restore some dignity by moving him into bed from the commode where he had died. In this instance, the value placed on dignity overrode any scruples about complying with the needs of an expected investigation. Another officer reported working with a nurse to straighten a body and place a white sheet over it:

> And the police said 'Who's done this? Who's done that? Have you touched the body?' 'Yeah (laughs) 'yeah, it were me'. And we'd got last rites in as well. (*Interview 2, Category B*)

> Confident in his occupational identity and clear about what constituted 'decency', this officer was unconcerned by the expectation of an investigation.

Despite the emphasis placed by prison staff on the importance of the investigations that would take place after a prisoner had died of natural causes, there was surprisingly little engagement with the investigation findings. Prison officers acknowledged they rarely saw or read the full report (Interview 11, LTHSE). Instead, they developed a subjective understanding of the standards expected by investigating bodies, especially the PPO, based on previous experiences and often on hearsay and rumours. As a result, interpretations of what an investigation would evaluate as 'good' care, varied.

Furthermore, evaluations of desirable end of life care based on the perceived priorities of past reports were potentially of limited use given that prisoners' needs vary and prison staff inevitably face new situations. These evaluations, whether by the police, coroner or PPO were only available after an individual's death; too late to make specific improvements to their care. When informed by perceptions of an anticipated investigation, the care of the dying individual came for some participants to be defined as meeting standards unconfirmable until after the death had occurred.

Conclusion

Prisons have their own particular understandings of what constitutes quality care, including palliative care. The aims enshrined in the WHO definition of palliative care, and to a lesser extent in the *Ambitions for Palliative and End of Life Care,* were often part of this understanding, but in the prisons studied they were rarely referenced. Instead, many staff and prisoners were instinctively seeking to care about and take care of dying prisoners in ways that met their physical and psychosocial, and to a lesser extent, spiritual needs. These efforts were informed by often very personal evaluations of what constituted quality care, used to provide some sort of standard against which to judge the care offered.

The ideal of equivalence was important to the understandings of quality palliative care in both the prisons' studies and was a standard shared by both staff and prisoners. However, there were differing interpretations of what equivalence of care meant and incidences where prisoners, and some staff, felt the care received had fallen short. The *Dying Well in Custody* Charter, which offered a tool for evaluating and encouraging equivalence between palliative care in the community and in prison custody did not, at the time of this study, appear to be being used. A second, parallel understanding of quality palliative care in prison, of making it 'as good as it could be', discussed in the Chapter 5, served to inform personal definitions of care and resulted in adjustments being made to the regime when a prisoner was dying. Both of these approaches to understanding what constitutes care relied on informal, subjective definitions and were internal to the prison establishment.

External evaluation of the quality of end of life care in prison custody is clearly important, aside from the fundamental issue of whether the death could have been prevented. Dying from natural causes in prison is not the same as dying from natural causes in other settings, and the need for, and nature of, investigations after even expected deaths, served to highlight this further. The responsibility of the state to ensure prisoners are adequately cared for should be the subject of scrutiny. Investigations and reviews are needed to ensure the actions, or inactions, of prison staff and prison regimes have not pre-empted a death, or adversely affected the circumstances of a dying prisoner and their family. Investigations and evaluations have the potential to inform future practice, as some of the staff interviewed expressed, but also served an important function in terms of accountability.

Post-death investigations were not the only way in which the quality of end of life care was evaluated, but, as seen above, they had a limited direct impact on the care of the dying. Where investigations were discussed by prison staff, it was with reference to an anticipated future investigation, indirectly influencing the care of a dying prisoner as staff imagined what the PPO would scrutinise after his death. Good standards of palliative care could be defined in the context of an expected investigation. Staff were aware of the aspects of the treatment of a dying prisoner that would be important in the investigation, particularly the use of restraints, and the awareness of an impending investigation did affect perceptions and delivery of quality care. Engagement with the findings of PPO investigations was limited, and when it did happen, staff reported that they did not always agree with the findings, or feel that the investigation recognised the care achieved. Whilst the demands of the coroner, PPO and prison service lawyers after a death presented a burden to staff in preparing the seemingly endless paperwork, the final reports gave some external evaluation of the care provided, but were perceived by some staff as being of limited usefulness.

References

Aday, R., & Wahidin, A. (2016). Older prisoners' experiences of death, dying and grief behind bars. *The Howard Journal of Crime and Justice, 55*(3), 312–327. https://doi.org/10.1111/hojo.12172

Ambitions for Palliative and End of Life Care Partnership. (2018). *Dying well in custody Charter*. Ambitions for Palliative and End of Life Care Partnership, UK. endoflifecareambitions.org.uk/tag/prisons

Charles, A., & Draper, H. (2011). 'Equivalence of care' in prison medicine: Is equivalence of process the right measure of equity? *Journal of Medical Ethics, 38*, 215–218. https://doi.org/10.1136/medethics-2011-100083

Condon, L., Hek, G., Harris, F., Powell, J., Kemple, T., & Priscoe, S. (2007). Users' views of prison health services: A qualitative study. *Journal of Advanced Nursing, 58*(3), 216–226. https://doi.org/10.1111/j.1365-2648.2007.04221.x

Foucault, M. (1991). *Discipline and punish: The birth of the prison* (A. Sheridan, Trans.). Penguin Books.

Girling, E., & Seal, L. (2016). Introduction: The deathscapes of incarceration. *The Howard Journal of Crime and Justice, 55*(3), 267–277. https://doi.org/10.1111/hojo.12169

Kohn, T., & McKechnie, R. (Eds.). (1999). *Extending the boundaries of care*. Berg.

Liebling, A. (2017). The meaning of ending life in prison. *Journal of Correctional Health Care, 23*(1), 20–31. https://doi.org/10.1177/1078345816685070

Lillie, K. (2018). Loss at the end of life: Palliative care in prisons. In S. Read, S. Santatzoglou, & A. Wrigley (Eds.), *Loss, dying and bereavement in the criminal justice system* (pp. 43–53). Routledge.

Prison and Probation Ombudsman. (2017). *Independent investigation into the death of (name) a prisoner at HMP Wakefield on (date).* Prison and Probation Ombudsman, UK. https://www.ppo.gov.uk/document/fii-report/

Prison and Probation Ombudsman. (2021). *Terms of reference.* Prison and Probation Ombudsman, UK. https://s3-eu-west-2.amazonaws.com/ppo-prod-storage-1g9rkhjhkjmgw/uploads/2021/12/PPO-2021-Terms-of-Reference-with-cover.pdf

Schaefer, I., DiGiacomo, M., Heneka, N., Panozzo, S., Luckett, T., & Phillips, J. L. (2022). Palliative care needs and experiences of people in prison: A systematic review and meta-synthesis. *Palliative Medicine, 36*(3), 443–461. https://doi.org/10.1177/02692163211068278

World Health Organisation. (2019). *Prisons.* World Health Organisation. https://www.who.int/topics/prisons/en/

7

After a Death

This final analytical chapter builds on understandings of care developed in the preceding chapters to explore what care is extended to the deceased and how care is received, or not received, by the bereaved family, prison staff and other prisoners after a death from natural causes in prison custody. It will consider how the dead prisoner was constructed, revealing how aspects of the construction of the dying individual, examined in Chapter 4, persist or change after their death. The dead prisoner is seen to take on new identities, as a potential victim of crime and as a possibly estranged family member, which influenced how they are treated after death.

Death may be a great leveller, but in many regards the status of the deceased as a former prisoner could not be overlooked. This chapter considers what influenced understandings of the prisoner's worth after death, and how this was reflected in whether they were regarded as 'grievable' or deserving of memorialisation. The need for memorialisation is seen to arise out of a construction of a prisoner as someone who is deserving of respect after death, regardless of being incarcerated at the end of life. The increasingly frequent task of memorialising the dead was a new role for prison staff in the prisons studied, observed closely

C. Robinson, *Dying in Prison*, Palgrave Studies in Prisons and Penology, https://doi.org/10.1007/978-3-031-27103-8_7

by prisoners aware they may one day die in prison custody. Increasingly frequent deaths from natural causes also led to new challenges in caring for those affected, whether the prisoner's bereaved family or the staff and other prisoners who had known him. How people were supported after a death reveals practices within the prison of care giving and care receiving (Fisher & Tronto, 1990).

Lastly, this chapter considers the position of death within prison culture, drawing on findings which show the frequency with which deaths from natural causes occur in prison has reduced the taboo around the subject.

Constructing the Dead Prisoner

The constructions of dying prisoners used by officers, healthcare professionals and other staff, discussed in Chapter 4, continued to be relevant after a prisoner's death from natural causes, whether the death was anticipated or not. In Chapter 4, it was seen that the dying individual might be figured as a 'prisoner', 'patient', or less frequently, a 'person', typically in association with the occupational identity of the staff member. As a 'prisoner' they were someone who was stigmatised and potentially posed a risk to security; as a 'patient', they were more deserving of compassion. Chapter 4 showed that the humanity of the individual could become more obvious after a terminal diagnosis, but that this was not universal. Some sympathy could be extended to the dying individual, but it was often associated with them having been a 'decent' prisoner, who had not presented challenges to prison staff, or with their comparative youth, or with having committed a less stigmatised offence. Constructing the individual in prison as a family man could also enhance the ability of staff to extent sympathy to the dying prisoner.

These constructions also informed assessments of whether or not it was appropriate to feel grief for the deceased and influenced how the body was treated and disposed of after death, including what memorialisation was judged relevant. The 'grievability' or otherwise of a deceased prisoner was indicative of how they had been figured by others during their life. Prisoners watched staff responses to a prisoner's death, particularly those of officers, to gauge how much value they placed on the living prisoners. Some staff did mourn prisoners who had died, especially when they had known the prisoner for many years. For healthcare staff, it was an occupational norm to feel and show some grief at a death. Prisoners also said they had felt grief after a prisoner they had known had died. They appreciated informal opportunities to grieve the deceased, but expected the prison to also provide formal memorial services.

The Status of the Dead Prisoner's Body

Immediately after any death in prison custody, the location of the death was regarded as a potential crime scene, sealed off pending a police investigation. PSI 64/2011 mandates that "all deaths in custody are treated as suspicious by the police" and details the actions that must take place to facilitate the investigation. The expectation that all deaths will be investigated reflects the importance placed on security within the prison. Commenting on how this affected her nursing, one healthcare professional said:

> That's the one thing that I find quite strange because when you're in hospice and on a ward we do the last offices and we wash them, wrap them up. Here, when they die, you just leave them. And that's quite difficult, because you just think, "no, I need to get him sorted out". But because it's a crime scene, as soon as they have died, you have to come out. (Interview 12, LTHSE)
>
> It is clear there is a distinction between the body of the deceased prisoner and that of people who die in the community. Once a death has occurred in the prison, the fact of the investigation reconfigured the prisoner, formerly seen as someone who has committed a crime, into someone who was potentially a victim of a crime, but nevertheless denied them the same care as would have been available after death had they died of natural causes in the community.

There were other ways the deceased prisoner could continue to be affected by the incarcerated status accorded to them during their life. It was notable that in some circumstances, the deprivation of autonomy associated with imprisonment (Sykes, 1958) could continue after death. When prisoners were planning ahead, telling staff how they wanted their remains to be handled, staff had on occasions to tell them that because they were a prisoner, their plans would not be possible (Interview 5, LTHSE). Prisoners without a next of kin could not be cremated, even if they had expressed this wish before death, in case family members later contacted the prison service to claim the body (Fieldnote, LTHSE, Interviews 13 and 5, LTHSE). In this way, the deceased prisoner was reconfigured as a member of an unknown family which might become known in the future.

Grievable or Not?

The importance of constructions of the prisoner after their death was also evident in whether or not they were regarded as 'grievable'. Butler (2016) says, "only under conditions in which the loss would matter does the value of life appear. Thus grievability is a presumption that life matters" (p. 28). In the context of attitudes to deceased prisoners, the converse was seen to be sometimes true; if a loss of life was not defined as 'grievable', then that life could be seen not to have mattered, or at least not to have mattered as fully as other lives.

Prisoners were very alert to this, seeing examples of their deceased peers being treated as 'ungrievable' as indicative of the low value placed on the lives of those who survived (Fieldnotes, LTHSE). They were highly critical of actions such as not putting a screen in place after a sudden death or leaving a wrapped body where it was visible to prisoners looking through the cracks in their cell doors (Fieldnote, LTHSE), desiring that their dead peers should not provide a spectacle for others. Prisoners also regarded delays in arranging memorial services in the prison chapel or errors in the information about such services as unacceptable (Fieldnote, LTHSE). These incidents offended a sense of what it was to treat someone with respect after death. They were interpreted as demonstrating the deceased was not valued by the staff responsible for making arrangements, by implication because the deceased had been a prisoner. It was felt that if staff did not show respect after death to someone who had been a prisoner, there was little hope of it being available to prisoners during their incarceration. When prisoners thought officers regarded the deceased as simply 'one off the roll', they equated this with themselves being 'ungrievable' and unvalued (Fieldnotes, LTHSE).

Prison chaplains in the LTHSE prison made a similar comparison to that of prisoners, interpreting the failure of officers to attend memorial services within the prison as indicative of a lack of value placed on the life of the individual who had died (Fieldnote, LTHSE). Staff in other roles contextualised prison officers' attitudes to deceased prisoners as part of a traditional 'macho' occupational culture, not limited to male officers, which meant grief at the death of a prisoner was not shown (Fieldnotes, LTHSE). It was rare for officers to visibly behave in a way which might suggest to their colleagues they were grieving for a prisoner, or imply that they were paying their respects for him. When they did so, they could find themselves being criticised. This is in keeping with other studies about the emotional labour of prison officers around deaths which have established that the 'feeling rules' lead to feelings of sadness around a prisoner's death being hidden (Tracy, 2005) or moderated (Robinson, 2020) to avoid condemnation from colleagues. One officer spoke about a colleague who had gone off sick after a prisoner had died, saying "he got a ribbing for it" (Fieldnote, LTHSE). Another officer in the Category B prison had attended a memorial service within the prison for a prisoner whose death was self-inflicted. He said it had been a lovely service, and had stayed to talk with the prisoners who had attended. However, he was aware how exceptional his attendance was, rooted in his own willingness to subvert or ignore occupational norms: "He said staff don't go because they fear being criticised for being there by colleagues — but he doesn't care" (Fieldnote, Category B).

In the LTHSE prison studied, a member of staff reported telling prisoners about an officer who was the driver for colleagues required to attend Eddie's funeral. The officer had asked if he could also be at the graveside during the service to pay his respects. The member of staff had been touched by this, and said that when he had mentioned the incident to prisoners who had known Eddie, they had said "can you tell us who it is so we can shake his hand?" (Interview 5, LTHSE). Both the staff member and the prisoners he shared this experience with regarded it as unusual for an officer to seek to pay his personal respects in this way. It was a measure of the esteem in which Eddie was held that the officer was willing to deviate from occupational norms, albeit in a setting where very few colleagues were present.

In contrast, officers themselves said it was impossible not to feel some emotion at a death (Interview 11, LTHSE), especially in the LTHSE prison, where there were a large number of long-term prisoners and long-serving officers:

> If we've had staff who have been here 30 years plus, and they'll have, they'll have known that prisoner for all that length of time, worked with them, they'll be on first name terms, whatever. And it, it will affect people. (Interview 7, LTHSE)
>
> This is in keeping with Crawley's (2004) suggestion that there is inevitably a degree of intimacy between prison officers and prisoners, especially when the prison officer has worked with the same prisoner through a variety of difficult and disappointing experiences in their sentence.

Officers and senior managers were aware officers were often criticised for not showing grief but contested the idea that this was the case for most officers: "Y'know everybody is different, some, it's just a number, but it's not as a rule" (Interview 13, LTHSE). It was accepted there were differences in how officers were affected by a death (Fieldnote, LTHSE) and that they had different strategies for dealing with emotions after a death (Interview 2, Category B; Interview 6 and 11, LTHSE) which will be discussed below in the context of the care afforded to affected prison officers. Some at least said they remembered the face of every prisoner they had worked with who had died (Interview 6, LTHSE).

Experiencing and expressing grief for a deceased prisoner was more acceptable amongst healthcare staff. The different dominant status awarded by healthcare staff to the terminally ill individual, discussed in Chapter 4, was again apparent. Healthcare professionals spoke about forming a bond "as if they are a 'normal' patient" (Interview 12, LTHSE) and in Neil's case, the presence of his wife at his bedside in the LTHSE prison at the end had heightened their emotional responses (Interview 12, LTHSE). Nursing staff in the Category B prison attended every funeral for prisoners they had cared for, even though this could be quite emotionally taxing. Attending the funeral was also seen as a form of supporting the prisoner's family (Interview 10, Category B). This was in contrast to their actions in previous nursing roles in the community, but indicative of the closer bonds they had formed:

> I don't know, I just feel, because I've looked after them for so long, and I know their family, I just think it would be wrong not to go. I mean on the community we rarely went, but on here, I know it sounds really lame, but up here especially, it is like a family up here. (Interview 10, Category B)
> Again, the relationship with the prisoner's family was important in shaping how staff regarded prisoners. Furthermore, constructing the dying individual as a 'patient' rather than as a 'prisoner' had a lasting effect, influencing a relationship extending after death. It resulted in the individual being seen as a 'grievable' patient rather than a prisoner unworthy of such emotion.

Caring for Those Affected

Deaths from natural causes in prison custody typically affected three groups of people: other prisoners, especially friends and contacts of the deceased; prison staff who had worked with the deceased and the prisoner's bereaved family, if there was one.

Caring for the Family

The WHO definition of palliative care emphasises the importance of improving the quality of life of both the patient and their family. As discussed earlier, a terminal diagnosis for a prisoner or an unexpected death from natural causes led to a new form of relationship between prison staff and the prisoner's family. These relationships were based on prison staff caring about and taking care of prisoners' families, seeking to make a distressing time as easy for them as possible. Family liaison officers (FLOs) led on this, but prison chaplains also built relationships with the families of dying prisoners, especially in the Category B prison (Interview 8, Category B). They and other staff talked about what they were doing for the family as 'support' rather than 'care'. For FLOs, this included breaking the news appropriately, being a single point of contact within the prison for any questions, arranging or helping arrange funerals and significantly, shielding the family from media intrusion or further distress.

Much of the care provided was directed by PSI 64/2011. This states that prisoners with a terminal diagnosis must be encouraged to engage with their nominated next of kin and that the prison must have an appropriate member of staff to engage with this next of kin (PSI 64/2011, Chapter 11). The caring role of this member of staff is apparent in the PSI, which emphasises their role in minimising the family's distress:

> Where the prisoner is hospitalised, it may be helpful for the nominated member of staff to meet with the family to provide information, which may include discussing the escorting arrangements including whether the prisoner is handcuffed or not. This information will reduce the distress of the family and aid their understanding of prison escorting procedures. (PSI 64/2011, Chapter 11)

The PSI also specifies the next of kin should be given accurate information, recognising that any failure to do this can increase their distress:

> It is vital that accurate information about the prisoner's death is given to the next of kin. Inaccurate information given at this stage can cause unnecessary distress and suspicion and can undermine the prison's ability to build a relationship with the family. (PSI 64/2011, Chapter 13)

It specifies the Governing Governor must write to the family to offer condolences and invite them to visit the prison if they wish, and contact them again after the draft PPO report into their relative's death has been agreed (PSI 64/2011 Chapter 12). The Governing Governor is also tasked with offering to contribute to funeral expenses, and the PSI details what this can include, up to a maximum of £3,000. The care to be provided is therefore structured as a series of tasks. In the prisons studied, FLOs were performing these tasks by building relationships with the prisoner's family in which their support was offered organically, moving on to the next stage of the post-mortem process as the prison and family required, but still with an awareness of the mandated tasks (Interviews 9 and 16, Category B; Interview 15, LTHSE).

The PSI specifies the role of the FLO starts when the family is informed of a death. In practice, in both prisons studied, when a death was anticipated the FLO made contact with families much sooner. In some cases, discussing a Do Not Resuscitate request was regarded as indicating an FLO was needed (Interview 16, Category B). If a prisoner was approaching death, FLOs were often involved in supporting families at the bedside. Examples of this include the FLO who sat with Neil's wife overnight in the LTHSE prison, and the FLO from the Category B prison who accompanied Iain's wife to sit with him while he was dying in hospital. Other staff did this too, including governors (Interview 7, LTHSE). It was regarded as better for the family to be involved sooner rather than later, to prepare them for receiving the news and to start building a relationship (Interview 2, Category B).

FLOs kept in regular contact with family members. The contact could continue for several months, up to and beyond the coroner's court and final report into the death from the PPO (Interview 16, Category B). They spoke about this contact in terms of meeting the needs of the family member, of asking how they were feeling, rather than simply contacting them when there was question (Interview 15, LTHSE). They tried to be responsive to the family's needs, asking them what they would like and were often aware the family member had no other sources of support (Interview 16, Category B). Considerable sensitivity was needed from FLOs. They were aware when the conviction was for child abuse the family members could experience shame, thinking staff would probably know what had happened to them (Interview 15, LTHSE). FLOs were also aware it could be difficult for the family to have to explain who was or wasn't attending the funeral. FLOs recognised the particular importance of building up trust in these circumstances (Interview 15, LTHSE).

FLOs and other staff within the prison often sought to protect the family as part of caring for them. They were aware that media interest in the prisoner's death could be particularly distressing, reopening the stigma the family had experienced at the time of the conviction (Interview 7, LTHSE). At funerals, governors attending from the prison knew sometimes not all of the mourners would have been told the deceased had been in prison at the time of the death, and they sought to shield the family by encouraging funeral directors to conceal this information (Interview 13, LTHSE). Sometimes officers struggled with what to tell the family, because they feared the prisoner's behaviour, unrelated to their death, might add to the family's distress. One FLO spoke of responding to a death that was not from natural causes. The family asked for his watch. The FLO knew the prisoner had traded the watch for a mobile phone, found taped to his penis when he was taken to hospital, and knew this would upset them (Interview 13, LTHSE). Other staff were conscious actions such as forwarding a prisoner's education certificates could cause distress, and sought advice about how to do this sensitively (Interview 13, LTHSE).

Although their work arguably protected the prison from hostile criticism after a death, FLOs cared about the families they had supported. When interviewed, they often spoke at length about the families, regardless of the cause of the prisoner's death, remembering cases long past. For them, seemingly it mattered less how the prisoner had died, and more how the family was coping. They took pride in taking care of practical arrangements for the family, especially around the funeral. For FLOs, their managers and others involved in supporting prisoners' families, their understanding of quality care were based only in part on whether the tasks specified in PSI 64/2011 had been completed. Definitions of care relied more on the levels of satisfaction expressed by the family and the quality of the relationships developed. One chaplain recounted being able to chat with the wife of a terminally ill prisoner, who was very happy with the care he was receiving, and then after his death, meeting the extended family to plan the funeral held outside the prison. The care provided for the family could be evaluated as good because the prisoner's wife was content (Interview 8, Category B).

Providing, Receiving and Not Receiving Support in the Prison

In addition to prisoners' families, deaths from natural causes also affected both prison staff and prisoners. They found deaths upsetting, sometimes stirring strong emotions, unconnected to any relationship with the individual who had died.

There is a lack of research about the impact of deaths in prison custody on other prisoners which is in keeping with the relatively scant attention paid to prisoners' experiences of other bereavements, including those of friends and family members who die while the prisoner is incarcerated. A number of authors (Aday & Wahidin, 2016; Hendry, 2008; Masterton, 2014; Olson & McEwen, 2004) have noted this omission, with Olson and McEwan stating "very little information can be found in the literature on bereaved prisoners, and it appears their grief may not be of great concern to others" (p. 226).

When prisoners' experience of bereavement is the subject of research, the focus is typically on the effects of losing a family member whilst imprisoned (Masterton, 2014; Hendry, 2008; Olson & McEwen, 2004; Schetky, 1998) rather than on the death of a fellow prisoner. There are arguably some similarities between experiencing the death of a family member and the death of a fellow prisoner, with prison policies restricting prisoners' access to the normal rituals of grieving, the space and privacy to grieve, mementos of the deceased and social support, regardless of the identity of the deceased. Bereaved prisoners will be expected to return to normal prison routines immediately after a death, with no opportunity to mourn (Aday & Wahidin, 2016). Schetky (1998) argues it is not just the prison regime that affects the grieving process, but also the prison culture: "the unwritten code of behaviour in prison is antithetical to the mourning process" (Schetky, 1998, p. 384). Aday and Wahidin (2016) and Taylor (2002) support this, claiming a key characteristic of prison culture is that it does not welcome expressions of emotion. Similarly, Masterton (2014) who draws on her experience of providing bereavement counselling in a Scottish prison concludes prison culture is not conducive to expressions of distress. Hendry (2008), writing about grief in prisons in New Zealand, links this to a more general masculine culture, not limited to the inside of prisons.

Whilst these studies illuminate the difficulties in general facing bereaved prisoners, they do not address directly the impacts on prisoners who have experienced the death of a fellow prisoner. One of the striking aspects of this omission is that the literature does recognise long-term prisoners may be living with their only friends in the world (Aday & Wahidin, 2016) and that prisoners with life sentences in particular do worry about the health of other lifers (Schetky, 1998). Due to their imprisonment, the social world of long-term prisoners may be limited to other prisoners. Aday and Wahidin (2016, p. 318) summarise this situation, writing:

> Losing close friends in prison may also be a harrowing experience for prisoners who frequently establish close kin relations with prison peers. In many cases, such losses are considered more significant than family on the outside.

In practice, however, as Olson and McEwen (2004) find, "prison inmates and their relationships are often not well regarded by others. They may be considered disenfranchised grievers" (p. 226). Doka (2002) describes disenfranchised grief as that which occurs when a loss is devalued, perhaps because the life lost is seen as less valuable. This could apply to any prisoner, whose crimes and imprisonment frequently lead to stigmatisation and rejection by wider society. Disenfranchised grief can also occur when those around the grieving person do not acknowledge their relationship with the deceased person, do not recognise the meaning to them of their loss or do not believe the person to be capable of feeling genuine grief (Doka, 2002). Masterton (2014) suggests anger can be intensified by disenfranchisement. In a wider context, the idea that flawed grieving processes have long-term impacts on prisoners is supported by Schetky (1998) who finds unresolved grief is common amongst prisoners, but may be hidden by disruptive behaviours and Hendry (2008) who describes unresolved grief as affecting prisoners' ability to cope with prison life. The impact of the death of a fellow prisoner can also be seen in prisoners facing the prospect of their own death in prison (Aday, 2006; Aday & Wahidin, 2016).

Staff and prisoners in this study spoke about the impact on other prisoners of a death, especially in the LTHSE prison, where it was recognised prisoners could have been neighbours on the wing for many years, and a death would have an effect, even if prisoners would not admit it (Interview 13, LTHSE). Other staff felt the impact of a death would be limited to only prisoners who had been close to the deceased (Interview 6, LTHSE). This was in one instance explained away by a construction of prisoners as uncaring:

> Prisoners are prisoners. Prisoners do their own thing. If a prisoner died on the wing, some of them wouldn't bat an eyelid. It's just, somebody else'll fill that bed tomorrow. It's just the nature of, it's the nature of how prisons work and it's the nature of prisoners. (Interview 11, LTHSE)
> In this way, prisoners can be seen to become disenfranchised grievers, believed incapable of feeling grief or experiencing the bereavement as meaningful.

In contrast, prisoners themselves gave many examples of grieving for deceased peers. One spoke about having been too upset to eat for a week after the death of a prisoner he was close to, and having struggled again at the anniversary of the death (Fieldnote, LTHSE). Another, speaking about two people he had met in prison who had subsequently died, had to acknowledge his eyes were filling with tears as he talked about them (Fieldnote, LTHSE). The deceased prisoner did not need to have been regarded as 'grievable' for a death to have an impact.

Prisoners expected staff within the prison to support them when they needed care. This included prison officers and chaplains, and there was criticism of both when care was thought not to have been provided (Fieldnotes, LTHSE). Chaplains in particular sought out prisoners they thought may be affected by a death. During Eddie's illness and after his death, chaplains made an effort to meet up with his main carer to check how he was feeling and raised any concerns with senior members of staff (Interview 5, LTHSE, Fieldnote, LTHSE). Prisoners expressed gratitude that chaplains were on a wing after Eddie's death, appreciating the care this suggested, even if they did not personally need the chaplain's pastoral support (Fieldnote, LTHSE). Staff could list formal sources of support for prisoners affected by a death, including the prison chaplaincy, the Listeners scheme and the Samaritans (Fieldnote, LTHSE; Interview 13, LTHSE) but thought prisoners often preferred informal sources of support:

> There'll always be somebody, unless it's that person who has passed away, there'll be somebody that they can go to. (Interview 13, LTHSE)
> Often, however, it was the perceived absence of support from staff that resulted in prisoners turning to fellow prisoners (Fieldnote, LTHSE) with certain prisoners being regarded as particularly good at providing care (Fieldnote, LTHSE). Support could come in subtle ways, such as making sure other prisoners, employed as carers, had a break. In one meeting observed, where a prisoner struggled not to cry, another patted him firmly on the knee a couple of times to provide reassurance (Fieldnote, LTHSE).

What was harder for prisoners was finding people to talk to whom they trusted. Here the distinction between 'prison acquaintances' and 'prison friends' was relevant, as was the awareness that the people surrounding them were convicted criminals. Prisoners were wary about which of their peers could be trusted not to break confidentiality. This could be a barrier to seeking informal support:

> I'd talk to the inmates, but as soon as you start talking, there's a thing called trust. You talk to someone, they talk to someone else, they talk… And all of a sudden everybody knows your problems. (Interview 14, LTHSE)
> Lillie (2018) suggests the lack of privacy and personal space in prisons makes it harder to grieve the death of fellow prisoners. In the LTHSE prison, where cells were single occupancy, this was less of an issue. One prisoner there, talking about dealing with difficult feelings and the need to hide them behind a mask, said simply "happiness is door-shaped" (Fieldnote, LTHSE). He welcomed being locked behind his door. There was no one he would turn to for support; only solitude would be effective.

For staff, formal support was also available from a variety of sources. In each prison this included a staff care team, a group of colleagues from different departments who volunteered to provide support. There was also an employee assistance programme for help with any work or personal issue which could be accessed by phone or online, as well as line managers, occupational health and staff associations such as the Prison Officers Association (Interview 7, LTHSE; Interview 2, Category B). In the Category B prison, the staff care team also provided support for healthcare professionals within the prison, employed by Care UK, because their provision relied on staff approaching their senior managers for support and was therefore regarded as less than ideal (Fieldnote, Category B). Chaplains regarded their role as including supporting officers and other staff (Interview 5, LTHSE) and healthcare staff expressed their appreciation of this (Fieldnote, LTHSE).

Despite the breadth of the formal provision, staff in both prisons often regarded it as inadequate. One officer suggested: "there's more care for prisoners from staff than there is for other staff" (Fieldnote, LTHSE). There was criticism of some staff care team members in the Category B prison as "nosy" (Interview 2, Category B), "deadwood" and "prone to gossip" (Fieldnote, Category B). Some officers highlighted the lack of training in dealing with traumatic events (Interview 11, LTHSE) or perceived a lack of care in failures by senior staff to prepare them for potentially distressing experiences, such as being on a 'bedwatch' when a life support machine was turned off (Fieldnote, LTHSE). De-briefs could fail to include key people involved in the incident, and the staff care team could be slow to approach people (Interview 16, Category B). Governors and members of the senior management team could be overlooked when staff were approached to identify support needs. Their role included prompting other staff to access the formal support available, but:

> I think we sometimes forget the people who are overseeing it because they are looking after everyone else, and nobody is looking after us. (Interview 7, LTHSE)

The formal support available was seen by several staff as failing most when it came to meeting the support needs of FLOs. At the LTHSE prison, one member of the senior management team had tried to address this by training as an FLO in order to understand the role and be better able to support them. Others felt more structured support was needed for FLOs, suggesting a regular meeting to 'offload', similar to the provision for officers working in the segregation unit with the most challenging prisoners (Interview 13, LTHSE). At the Category B prison, there was a concern that the FLOs did not have a coordinator to take responsibility for their support and workloads, and that this situation had been ongoing for a long time (Interview 9, Category B).

In the absence or perceived failings of effective formal support, staff, like prisoners, sought out informal sources of support. Often this came from talking to one of their immediate colleagues. Chaplains and healthcare staff talked about finding support within their teams (Interview 8, Category B; Interviews 5 and 12, LTHSE). This preference for seeking support from colleagues rather than the staff care team is reported in other studies of prison staff after a death in custody (Ludlow et al., 2015). Officers were often more specific in where they sought informal support. Some took their concerns home. This is not unusual amongst prison officers. Crawley (2004) finds that although some prison officers preferred not to discuss work at home, others often confided in and sought advice from their partners. In two instances, officers who participated in the research felt they had an advantage with regard to getting support when working with a dying prisoner or after a death because they had wives with healthcare expertise. As one said:

> I'm quite fortunate in the fact that when I go home I can talk to my wife and she listens. Because she used to work in a nursing home so she's seen plenty of dead people, she'd dealt with plenty of dead bodies and everything. So I get it out the system and then it's over and done with. I'm lucky. (Interview 6, LTHSE)

Other officers had one specific colleague they spoke to if they needed support. This could be a line manager, but it was also sometimes a colleague who had shared the experience. One participant spoke about going to the hospital in an ambulance with a prisoner who was declared dead when they arrived. Waiting for the mortician to return from lunch and then helping move the body and empty the prisoner's pockets had affected the other officer. He had not sought counselling but:

> Years afterwards, we'd have a little chat and he'd bring it up, so I know that it did affect him. (Interview 6, LTHSE)

The subject remained something the affected officer needed support with, years after the event and seemingly only trusted the other officer involved. As with prisoners, trust was an important factor in who officers chose to seek support from. Another officer received support from a previous line manager, someone he had not worked with for many years and who had moved to a different prison because:

> I can talk to her about things and it's not going to go any further. She can talk to me about things and it's not going to go any further. So really she's the only person I've ever really spoke to. (Interview 9, Category B)

What is striking is that there were similarities in where staff and prisoners sought support, and in their attitudes to the formal support provided. It is also noticeable that there were few differences in the care and support they sought around a death from natural causes compared to other circumstances where they might need help. The sources of support accessed and trusted remained largely the same.

Memorialising the Dead

In the prisons studied for this book, how the deceased prisoner was memorialised reflected how he was constructed after his death. Prisoners shared the view of staff that the frequent absence of mourning family or friends at funerals was a cause of sadness, a poor return on a life (Interview 13, LTHSE; Interview 1, Category B). One prisoner in the Category B prison reported on a recent funeral he had been told about by staff who attended:

> He says there were only four people at the man's funeral, and that his wife was dressed like a tramp. His eyes water up and he pauses for a moment before moving the conversation on deliberately. (Fieldnote, Category B)
> Such accounts served to emphasise ways in which the individual was not valued by those tasked, in the mind of the teller, with memorialising him.

Prisoners knew they could not attend the funeral, held outside the prison, but expected there to be a memorial service within the prison, organised by the chaplaincy team, as part of demonstrating the worth of the deceased. There was also informal memorialisation of deceased prisoners. One prisoner spoke about dedicating a music session to a recently deceased member of the group, joking he had had the worst sense of rhythm (Fieldnote, LTHSE). The same prisoner also talked about having fortuitously been in the healthcare dentist's waiting room soon after this death, with other prisoners who had also known the deceased well, and having valued time to share happier memories informally (Fieldnote, LTHSE).

In the immediate aftermath of a death, prisoners gathered for other purposes would discuss the deceased, responding with jokes if the atmosphere became too intense. The Education department was a convenient setting for this, and two staff members talked about occasions when prisoners discussed a deceased prisoner in the classrooms. One reported:

> Everyone was then quiet for a few minutes, which as you know is rare in that room. It felt as though it all got a bit intense and real for them all because very soon they started to make jokes about it to change the atmosphere. (Fieldnote, LTHSE)
> The education department was again serving the function of an 'emotion zone' as suggested by Crewe et al. (2013) and discussed in Chapter 2, but even here there were limitations on how much grief prisoners were comfortable showing; the conversation was deliberately moved on when it became too emotionally intense.

Despite these informal occasions being valued by prisoners, a formal memorial service organised by Chaplaincy had significance (Fieldnotes, LTHSE). It was seen as a crucial part of showing the deceased prisoner had value and was deemed 'grievable'. At both the LTHSE and Category

B prison, family members sometimes attended the memorial service in the prison. In this way, memorial services brought together prisoners and the bereaved families of their former peers in a manner that would not usually be expected. The presence of partners, siblings and other kin also reconstructed the deceased prisoner as a family man. Prisoners valued the opportunity to meet the families. One prisoner who had spoken at such a memorial service treasured the card he had afterwards received from the deceased prisoner's brother (Fieldnote, LTHSE). Another felt staff had deliberately only told him about a memorial service after the event, and was sad not to have met the prisoner's family; he had done some drawings for them for the prisoner to send out to them and felt a connection (Fieldnote, LTHSE).

Memorial services were not without controversy. In the LTHSE prison, some prisoners felt Chaplaincy took too long to arrange the service (Fieldnote, LTHSE) and did not do so with enough care, criticising chaplains for getting the deceased's name wrong on a 'sign-up sheet' to attend a memorial (Fieldnote, LTHSE). Prisoners were reported to remove 'sign-up sheets' in attempts to control who attended a memorial service, and to seek to limit attendance to those they felt had been friends of the deceased (Fieldnotes, LTHSE). In doing so, they were constructing the deceased prisoner as part of a particular social group. There could also be a reluctance to talk about the deceased in a more public setting. This could be for several reasons. When Eddie died, one of his closest friends was pleased to have been asked to speak by the chaplain leading the memorial event, but felt unable to do so because he did not wish to show the emotions it would provoke (Fieldnote, LTHSE). Other prisoners saw it as inappropriate to be expected to speak or withheld their testimonials as a way of claiming kinship with the deceased:

> But when they turn to us and as I say "has anyone got anything to say about him" and everyone just turned round and looked at us, I was just "Listen, my memories are my memories". And this lad at the front went "well, we want to know what he was like". "No you don't. You just want to stick your nose in. You didn't know him, you've just come down here. It's too late, the point is you didn't know him" (Interview, LTHSE)

As before, certain crimes were more stigmatised, and the memorial service could make this more apparent, suggesting some prisoners regarded certain of their peers as 'ungrievable'. In the Category B prison, chaplains were especially careful about the format of the memorial services for prisoners who had been convicted of sexual offences, aware some prisoners may make derogatory remarks (Interview 8, Category B).

The Place of Death in the Prisons' Culture

Deaths from natural causes were regarded as inevitable and as having always happened in prison custody. One participant, when asked if he had expected when he became a prison officer to be working with prisoners who were dying, summarised this by saying: "you come into it knowing that you are in a city that's behind a wall basically. That's what it is… and everything that happens outside, happens inside" (Interview 6, LTHSE). Staff coming in through the front entrance to the main building at the LTHSE prison had a daily reminder that death from natural causes was part of the history of the prison. The wooden board listing previous prison governors included: "1825 Thomas Shepherd (died of cholera in prison with 29 prisoners)" (Fieldnote, LTHSE).

What had changed in recent years was that deaths from natural causes had become a more common occurrence. Participants made a strong link between this and the ageing population of the prisons where they lived or worked. The prisons selected for fieldwork were chosen because they had experienced a relatively high number of deaths from natural causes in the five years prior to the research. The frequency of these deaths was discussed by participants, especially in the LTHSE prison studied, which had had the second highest number of such deaths in the country. At the Category B prison, comparisons were made with this LTHSE prison where it was recognised that deaths from natural causes were more common occurrences. For a staff participant at the Category B prison, he could see the trend in high security prisons such as the LTHSE prison expanding out to the local prisons like the one where he worked:

> And it's because there's not the spaces in the Cat A, Cat B estate, they're with us a lot longer than normal. I mean a lot will come to us on lengthy sentences and won't get to the next jail. … It's summat that over the coming time will need addressing, but it's going to be a national problem. It's not just a local problem, it's a national problem. (Interview 9, Category B)

What was significant at the LTHSE prison was the way in which the frequency of deaths from natural causes was shaping prison culture, as apparent in the examples below of how readily prisoners imagined their future deaths in prison custody in conversation. Staff in this prison were aware when a death occurred:

> everybody is thinking "one day is that going to be me?"… For most of our prisoners, one day, it will be them dying in custody. (Interview 7, LTHSE)
>
> When there had been a number of deaths on one wing, it was recognised that this reflection could become more pointed. In 2016, 11 prisoners died of natural causes in the LTHSE prison, the majority of whom had been resident on the same wing:
>
> I think out of the 11 we probably had six off D wing, had all originated D wing. And y'know, I think prisoners begin to think "Hmm, probably not the right place to be if I'm not feeling too well", y'know "Is it me next". (Interview 13, LTHSE)
>
> There was no indication of why this had happened, but several prisoners commented on the coincidence of so many deaths in one year being on D wing, referring to it as the 'death wing'.

At the start of the research, it was expected most people would find the subject matter potentially painful, and that the sensitivity of the subject would lead to some reluctance to participate. Instead, in the LTHSE prison in particular, there was a very noticeable willingness to talk about the subject, with prisoners often approaching the researcher to share their experiences. Staff in this prison also found the subject of dying arose at unexpected times, sometimes in casual conversation and, without any great significance being placed on it, but also more poignantly and personally. One talked about reprimanding a terminally ill prisoner for using inappropriate language in a group situation, only for him to retort:

> "What are you going to do L (first name)? What are you going to do? I'm going to die." And I'm like that "Oh, for God's sake, stop it." And then he'd just laugh and "Oh, I'm only kidding". And everyone would laugh about it. (Interview 4, LTHSE)

Another staff member reported a conversation with one of the younger prisoners about the plans to decorate the palliative care suite:

> His immediate response was dismissive "I'm not interested in that", but as we talked more about the technique that was used for the artwork he seemed to have something of a lightbulb moment. He paused and said "I should be more interested in that, because I'm going to die in prison. It's not something you should really be aware of at 25 is it? But I think I should consider that more." (Correspondence, LTHSE)
> In her account, both she and the prisoner were taken aback by the certainty a 25-year-old could have that he would die in prison. A topic neither expected to be relevant to someone of his age became significant because the length of his sentence meant the setting of his death, however many years in the future, was now known.

There are few studies addressing the concerns of prisoners facing the prospect of their own death in prison. The fear of death in prison is argued to be influenced by a number of factors, including witnessing how prison staff have treated the dead body (Aday, 2006) and seeing their peers in pain and humiliated as a result of the denial of or delays in medical treatment (Aday & Wahidin, 2016). Aday (2006) finds the fear of death amongst prisoners correlates to health variables, with those with more chronic and complicated medical conditions fearing death in prison most. Novisky et al. (2022) argue that observing death and dying were normal prison experiences amongst the 193 older US prisoners they interviewed, but that anxieties around their own deaths reflected concerns about the prison healthcare system and worries about what would happen to their personal belongings and body after death. Handtke and Wangmo (2014) suggest that when a prisoner knows their release date, their anxiety about death is reduced. It is recognised however that for some prisoners, death is seen as an escape, ending lives that have little social value (Aday, 2006), or even as an acceptable part of the punishment (Aday & Wahidin, 2016). Some prisoners, however, in order to protect themselves, remain in denial about the prospect of dying in prison (Handtke & Wangmo, 2014).

The frequency with which deaths from natural causes happened in the LTHSE prison, and the number of people known to have sentences which would likely mean they would die in prison, had seemingly reduced any supposed sensitivity about the subject. It may also have increased the need in staff and prisoners to talk with someone, the researcher, who seemed interested. This is in contrast with the typical approach of research ethics committees, where death and dying are regarded as topics participants are likely to find distressing. This willingness to talk about death and dying suggested that death had become a recognised part of the experience of imprisonment, an acceptable topic of conversation, even with a stranger. The place of death in the culture of this prison was thus different from what might be expected. Dying in this prison was regarded as a relatively normal occurrence, and discussing it was far from taboo (see Ariès, 1976; Walter 2015, 1991) on death as a taboo and death denial in modern culture and the appendix to this book for how sensitivities around the subject of death were handled with consideration for the importance of conducting ethical research).

Burles et al. (2016) argue dying prisoners are doubly marginalised, by the fact of their imprisonment and the circumstance of dying. As discussed in Chapter 2, dying prisoners could find themselves physically marginalised, separated from their peers as in the LTHSE prison's healthcare centre. The resistance to this is demonstrated in Eddie's determination to remain on the prison wing after receiving his terminal diagnosis, even when quite frail. Arguably, however, the ease with which dying and death was discussed within the LTHSE prison reduced the marginalisation of death, suggesting that the condition of dying prisoners was not culturally marginalised, but something that could be discussed and was part of the expected experience of imprisonment for many long-term prisoners.

The situation was different in the Category B prison. There were prisoners here who expected to die in prison, but there were fewer of them and death did not seem to be a topic of conversation amongst prisoners outside those immediately affected by it. A handful of prisoners in the Category B prison, all of them elderly, expressed an awareness they would die in prison. Some of them anticipated this as being in their current prison, perhaps aware, as the officer quoted above, that the lack of spaces in other prisons meant they could not be moved on. One shared a letter from his cardiologist, written prior to sentencing, which specified he had a 70% chance of living five years, odds he clearly found unfavourable. He had hoped his cardiologist's letter would influence the court, but was given a 16-year sentence. He said he had accepted he would die in prison, but he felt apprehensive about this (Fieldnote, Category B). Another prisoner in the Category B prison envisaged the exact location of his death, and in conversation said: "he hopes to just die in his sleep, pointing at his lower bunk as he says this" (Fieldnote, Category B). Prisoners also spoke to each other about expecting to die in prison, with another prisoner in the Category B prison saying, "one of the men downstairs says he's only leaving in a box" (Fieldnote, Category B), but they conversed about death less readily than at the LTHSE prison.

In both prisons studied, it was expected that deaths from natural causes in prison custody would occur. In the LTHSE prison, the frequency with which such death occurred meant dying from natural causes was no longer seen as unusual. It was an occurrence which had impacted on the culture of the prison, on what was acceptable to talk about, and what was seen as part of the experience of imprisonment.

Conclusion

It is striking that the effects of imprisonment could continue after death, particularly with regard to the status awarded to the deceased, decisions about the disposal of their corpse and how they were memorialised. Whether regarded as 'prisoner', 'patient' or 'person' at the end of life in prison custody, the individual became a potential crime victim at the point of death, with implications for how their body was treated by healthcare staff and investigators. For some, the deprivation of autonomy associated with imprisonment could continue after death. The requirement for those with no identified next of kin to be buried, in case relatives later made themselves known, meant some prisoners were not able to have the reassurance of their body being disposed of as they wished.

How a prisoner was regarded in life influenced whether they were regarded as 'grievable', but 'grievability' was also influenced by occupational culture. For healthcare staff, it was an occupational norm to feel and show some grief at a death. For prison officers, demonstrating grief was more complicated, but emotion was felt after prisoners' deaths, even if a persisting 'macho' culture sometimes made it hard to admit. Some prison officers did mourn prisoners who had died, especially when they had known the prisoner for many years. It was striking that the emotional labour of prison officers often resulted from the challenges of working with death and dying, where there was a need to maintain face or perform protective deep acting, not in response to actual grief at an individual prisoner's passing.

The increased number of deaths from natural causes in prison custody meant care needed to be extended not just to terminally ill prisoners, but also to their friends and family, and those who had cared for them within the prison. In their work with prisoners' families, family liaison officers often exceeded the expectation of PSIs. They sought to provide support from an earlier stage, making contact when a death was anticipated, and reported being pro-active in building relationships intended to help bereaved families through the complexities of coroner's courts and PPO investigations. Their role often required great sensitivity and led to efforts to protect the family, from the media or from unpleasant aspects of the deceased's life. The work undertaken by FLOs meant they often needed support themselves.

More broadly, both prisoners and staff reported that it was hard to find someone they trusted to talk to about their feelings after a death. Gaps in training, de-briefing and support, and a lack of trust in staff care teams and employee assistance programmes, meant staff tended to rely on informal sources of support. They reported choosing to talk to a trusted colleague informally, sometimes over a period of years. Similarly, although there were peer-based Listeners schemes for prisoners, and support offered by staff including chaplains, prisoners found their concerns about trust and confidentiality led them to rely on informal support. In this regard, despite being in very different positions in the prison, staff and prisoners accessed and trusted sources of support that were largely the same. When care was extended to colleagues and peers, provided formally or informally, it used existing channels, treating the need for support around death and dying the same as any of the other problems staff and prisoners faced.

Prisoners watched staff responses to a prisoner's death, particularly those of officers, to gauge how much value was placed on the living prisoners, and were very sensitive to any potential disrespect for the deceased. Prisoners said they felt grief after a prisoner they had known had died, contrary to the expectations of some staff. They appreciated informal opportunities to grieve the deceased, but expected the prison to also provide formal memorial services and to support them in their grief. For them, aware as they were of the different ways in which staff constructed them, as 'prisoner' or perhaps 'patient' and very occasionally 'person', what mattered was that dying and deceased prisoners were valued as human beings.

References

Aday, R. (2006). Aging prisoners' concerns toward dying in prison. *OMEGA Journal of Death and Dying, 52*(3), 199–216.

Aday, R., & Wahidin, A. (2016). Older prisoners' experiences of death, dying and grief behind bars. *The Howard Journal of Crime and Justice, 55*(3), 312–327. https://doi.org/10.1111/hojo.12172

Ariès, P. (1976). *Western attitudes toward death: From the Middle Ages to the present* (P. Ranum, Trans.). Boyars.

Burles, M. C., Peternelj-Taylor C. A., & Holtslander L. (2016). A 'good death' for all?: Examining issues for palliative care in correctional settings. *Mortality, 21*(2), 93–111. https://doi.org/10.1080/13576275.2015.1098602

Butler, J. (2016). *Frames of war: When is life grievable?* Verso.

Crawley, E. (2004). *Doing prison work: The public and private lives of prison officers.* Willan.

Crewe, B., Warr, J., Bennett, P., & Smith, A. (2013). The emotional geography of prison life. *Theoretical Criminology, 18*(1), 56–74. https://doi.org/10.1177/1362480613497778

Doka, K. J. (2002). Disenfranchised grief. In K. J. Doka (Ed.), *Living with grief: Loss in later life* (pp. 159–168). The Hospice Foundation of America.

Fisher, B., & Tronto, J. (1990). Towards a feminist theory of caring. In E. Abel & M. Nelson (Eds.), *Circles of care: Work and identity in women's lives* (pp. 35–62). State University of New York.

Handtke, V., & Wangmo, T. (2014). Ageing prisoners' views on death and dying: Contemplating end of life in prison. *Bioethical inquiry, 11*, 373–386. https://doi.org/10.1007/s11673-014-9548-x

Hendry, C. (2008). Incarceration and the tasks of grief: A Narrative review. *Journal of Advanced Nursing, 65*(2), 270–278. https://doi.org/10.1111/j.1365-2648.2008.04890.x

Lillie, K. (2018). Loss at the end of life: Palliative care in prisons. In S. Read, S. Santatzoglou, & A. Wrigley (Eds.), *Loss, dying and bereavement in the criminal justice system* (pp. 43–53). Routledge.

Ludlow, A., Schmidt, B., Akoewi, T. & Liebling, A. (2015). *Self-inflicted deaths in NOMS' custody amongst 18–24 year olds: Staff experience, knowledge and views*. RAND Corporation.

Masterton, J. (2014). A confined encounter: The lived experience of bereavement in prison. *Bereavement Care, 33*(2), 56–62.

Novisky, M. A., Narvey, C. S., & Prost, S. G. (2022). Older Adults' perspectives on death and dying in prison. *Journal of criminal justice*, 101930. https://doi.org/10.1016/j.jcrimjus.2022.101930

Olson, M. J., & McEwen, M. A. (2004). Grief counselling groups in a medium-security prison. *The Journal for Specialists in Group Work, 29*(2), 225–236. https://doi.org/10.1080/01933920490439392

Robinson, C. (2020). Ethically important moments as data: Reflections from ethnographic fieldwork in prisons. *Research Ethics Review, 16*(1–2), 1–15. https://doi.org/10.1177/1747016119898401

Schetky, D. (1998). Mourning in prison: Mission impossible? *Journal of American Academic Psychiatry and Law, 26*(3), 383–391.

Sykes, G. M. (1958). *Society of captives: A study of a maximum security prison.* Princeton University Press.

Tracy, S. J. (2005). Locking up emotion: Moving beyond dissonance for understanding emotion labor discomfort. *Communication Monographs, 72*(3), 261–283. https://doi.org/10.1080/03637750500206474

Taylor, B. (2002). Grief and hospice care for the correctional community: Training, nurturing and mentoring of staff. *Journal of Correctional Health Care, 9*(2), 169–174. https://doi.org/10.1177/107834580200900208

Walter, T. (1991). Modern death: Taboo or not taboo? *Sociology, 25*(2), 293–310.

Walter, T. (2015). Sociological perspectives on death, dying and bereavement. In J. Stillion & T. Attig (Eds.), *Death, dying and bereavement: Contemporary perspectives, institutions and practices* (pp. 31–44). Springer Publishing Company.

8
Conclusion

Deaths from natural causes in prison in England and Wales are not new but have become more frequent. Prison staff and prisoners alike are faced with trying to adjust their thinking and adapt their practices, with little central guidance and with rules, all-important in the prison regime, which reflect a different set of concerns. Staff and prisoners have been seen to need to create a coherent understanding of the situation. They are responding to what they regard as changing circumstances by constructing understandings of the carceral geography of death and dying, of the dying prisoner and of what constitutes quality care at the end of life.

This book has shown that deaths from natural causes in prison custody can soften the usual distinctions between what is expected or not expected, permitted or not permitted, between 'inside' and 'outside' prison. The awareness a prisoner has a terminal diagnosis or is approaching the end of life in prison custody often leads to a blurring of the practical and emotional distinctions that have marked their lives as prisoners. Within limits, the physical environment, the relationships and the regime soften. This is at times tangible, embodied, for example, by the soft furnishings and plump cushions of the palliative care suite

C. Robinson, *Dying in Prison*, Palgrave Studies in Prisons and Penology, https://doi.org/10.1007/978-3-031-27103-8_8

in the LTHSE prison studied, and the intentions for interior design in the proposed suite at the Category B prison. It is also intangible; a softening of attitudes towards prisoners, a blurring of their identities in the minds of prison staff and the emergence of grey areas in matters of discipline which are usually black and white. The blurriness can extent to outside hospitals, where the importation of a dying prisoner, escorting officers and sometimes restraints, marks the bedside as both part of the hospital and a site of prison custody. In the prison, sympathy creeps in, changes relationships and informs care. The concept of decency is repurposed to help inform understandings of how to make death 'as good as it could be'. Small changes to facilitate care soften the experience of imprisonment. The harshness of prison is never entirely dissipated, and the softening that occurs is neither dramatic nor universal. It occurs in response to factors associated with a prisoner that generate sympathy, such as his age, his previous behaviour or a concern for his family, and associated with his perceived proximity to death. It is limited by the lingering stigma associated with the prisoner and the importance of the security agenda within prisons.

This book has shown that in the perception of prisoners and staff, prison changes death, and death changes prison. The change to the prison is not dramatic; it is closely linked to the tangible and intangible softening and blurring of boundaries considered above. However, this research has identified a number of ways in which the experience of dying and death is different because of the prison setting. The prison is affected by both an individual death and the cumulative effect of a number of deaths from natural causes. In comparison with deaths in the community, those occurring in prison custody are seen by prisoners and prison staff to reflect the priorities of the prison regime, the attitudes of people within the prison, especially staff, towards prisoners, the stigma of imprisonment and the dominance of the security imperative over issues such as care. These are all factors determining the response of prison regimes and personnel to dying prisoners, discussed below, which led participants in this study to argue deaths in prison custody were different from those in other circumstances because of the prison setting. However, this research also found that although deaths from natural causes have always been part of the prison, the increased frequency with which they are now occurring has led to changes to the prison that participants regard as long-term and enduring. Participants spoke about ways in which the prison had changed as a result of deaths from natural causes. These include the repurposing of space, the changing of working practices and the development of new concerns for staff and prisoners alike. Typically, each individual death temporarily interrupts the routine of the prison. Each dying prisoner's circumstances lead to small adjustments to facilitate their care, but the frequency with which deaths from natural causes in prison are now occurring, and the expectation this trend will continue, means that staff and prisoners alike report deaths from natural causes are resulting in lasting changes to how the prison operates.

This chapter elucidates these findings in relation to the two key questions set out in Chapter 1 and explains how this research contributes to understandings of deaths from natural causes in prison. It also indicates how the conclusions reached relate to aspects of the operational practices around deaths from natural causes in prison custody that prison authorities and others may wish to address. The limitations of this research project are acknowledged, and recommendations are made for further research on related topics arising from this study which are beyond the scope of the research aims in this instance.

Key Questions

The research addressed two linked research questions:

> How do deaths from natural causes in prisons impact on prison regimes, culture and relationships?
> What determines the responses of prison regimes and personnel to dying prisoners?

How prison regimes and personnel respond to a death from natural causes is heavily influenced by the pre-existing culture, regime and relationships within the prison. However, the responses of prison regimes and personnel to deaths from natural causes also shape the ongoing culture and relationships in the prison, and have the potential to subtly and permanently change the prison regime. Prisoners notice and remember the treatment of their dying peers; if prison staff are perceived to have responded inadequately, then the stories subsequently circulating can add to tensions in staff–prisoner relationships. Adjustments made with regard to one dying prisoner can become part of a set of assumptions in the culture of the prison about how a dying prisoner should be treated or enshrined in understandings of the regime, of how the prison is operationalised. Some impacts of deaths from natural causes are long lasting, necessitating changes to prison buildings or new roles for staff, and thus affect the care of future dying prisoners. In both prisons studied, specific deaths had particular impacts and were expected by staff and prisoners to have changed future responses. Examples of this included the new ways of working introduced in the LTHSE prison, where Eddie was unusual in being permitted to stay on the wing as he became frailer and Neil's wife was permitted to stay with him overnight. Other deaths were remembered because the prisoner, for example, Dean, William or Iain, at the Category B prison, provoked sympathy amongst staff or was well-liked by prisoners, as Eddie was in the LTHSE establishment. Their deaths became part of the culture of the prison and the lived memory of the staff and prisoners who had known them.

This research has focussed on the ways in which the challenges presented by the circumstances of dying prisoners affect the physical environment of the prison, attitudes towards prisoners, the implementation of prison rules, provision of services and resourcing and on staff identities and well-being. In doing so, what is being considered is the very nature of prison. It is therefore to be expected that there were many ways in which the prison regime, culture and relationships were unchanged by a death or the cumulative experience of an increasing number of deaths. There was an imperative to keep the regime running, to minimise the potential for disruption, especially after a death on a wing. Whatever physical changes were achieved, the manifestations of carceral geography were still overtly present. The physical environment remained that of the prison, reflecting the priorities of the prison, even if of a previous prison-building era. With regard to relationships, staff and prisoners were both clear that although a terminal diagnosis may change a relationship, there was still an expected social distance which could not be bridged. The ways in which the prison regimes, culture and relationships were not affected by deaths from natural causes can be attributed to the steadfastness of the nature of prison. It is no accident that prison changes the experience of dying. Instead, it is the inevitable result of the nature of prison. Prison is after all a system of social control ("the maximum security prison represents a social system in which an attempt is made to create and maintain total or almost total social control" [Sykes, 1958, p. xiv]) which is not expected to significantly change around one prisoner because he is dying. However, even while most aspects of the prison remained unchanged, the softening described above was still evident. Acknowledging that prisons have long been considered institutions redolent with power (Foucault, 1991; Sykes, 1958), there are still a number of factors which serve to determine how power is used, and ways in which the exercise of power can negatively or positively change the experience of dying in prison. The examples of this will be considered next, before returning to the ways in which deaths from natural causes have been seen to impact on prison regimes, culture and relationships, despite the nature of the prison seemingly mitigating against this.

Factors Determining Response to Dying Prisoners

The central factor in how a dying prisoner was treated by prison staff was whether they attributed to him the dominant status of 'prisoner', 'patient' or 'person'. The statuses of 'patient' or 'person' served to ameliorate the underlying circumstance of the individual being a prisoner, someone deprived of their liberty with little hope of compassionate release despite a terminal diagnosis. Healthcare staff recognised the role of their own occupational culture in constructing the individual as a 'patient' and experienced tensions with the contrasting occupational culture of prison officers, who were more likely to regard dying individuals as first and foremost 'prisoners'. Prisoners in healthcare centres could be regarded by officers as being "patients before they are prisoners" (Fieldnote, LTHSE), but healthcare staff experienced opprobrium from officers when their nursing practices reflected the intimacy and physical contact inherent in caring for patients in the community. In this respect, a terminal diagnosis softens attitudes towards a prisoner, rather than dramatically changing opinions.

Each of these three statuses, 'prisoner', 'patient' or 'person', affected how the prison regime and personnel approached the dying prisoner or the prisoner after a sudden death. 'Prisoners' were security risks to be managed, in ways often affecting their care, especially through the use of restraints. They were extended only limited autonomy, and could be seen at death as "one of the roll", a disrespectful term that upset prisoners and some staff. They were not 'grievable', and whilst prison officers may admit finding the circumstances of a death difficult, they did not mourn a deceased 'prisoner'.

In contrast, when an individual dying in prison custody was seen as a 'person' or 'patient', informed by the occupational culture of the staff member relating to them, this served to provoke more sympathetic responses to the individual. The fact of a terminal diagnosis was itself often regarded by prisoners and staff as grounds for sympathy. Sympathetic responses were more easily generated if the dying individual was young, had good family relationships, was in prison for non-sexual offences, and was regarded as likeable. In constructing someone as a 'person' or 'patient', staff were expressing a valuation of the individual as someone deserving of respect and care. This helped inform actions to improve their circumstances, such as making adjustments to the regime and providing them with perceived quality care, the meaning of which will be discussed below. A 'person' or 'patient' was also more grievable after death.

Care in prison was evaluated by staff and prisoners in three main ways. These reflected in part the construction of dying prisoners as 'prisoner', 'patient' or 'person'. In trying to understand what would constitute quality end of life care, three discourses co-existed together: seeking to ensure equivalence with the medical and social care available in the community; seeking to match the expectations of the anticipated PPO investigation; and trying to make death "as good as it could be". Each of these discourses by which staff and prisoners evaluated the care of the dying was loosely defined and highly subjective.

There were significant discrepancies, especially between staff and prisoners, over the extent to which care met the standards understood to be part of the most commonly accepted evaluation of care, the 'ideal' of equivalence with care in the community. Efforts to make deaths "as good as it could be" were informed by notions of decency, a term that resonates within the prison service, and personal experiences of deaths in the community that recognised dying in prison was far from ideal. There were many examples of trying to make death in prison 'as good as it could be'. Attempts to make death 'as good as it could be' prioritised physical comfort, sought to ensure no restraints were used at the moment of death, valued the individual's privacy and prioritised the idea that no one should die alone. Care based on the anticipation of an investigation used understandings of the individual as first and foremost a 'prisoner', someone for whose treatment prison staff would have to account for after their death.

What was striking was the extent to which a caring culture existed in the prisons studied. Care in prison is often associated with healthcare staff, and contrasted with the discipline and control practised by prison officers. This research instead concludes that care was both a responsibility and a source of pride for some staff in all roles and for some prisoners. For staff, it was additionally a professional task. In both prisons studied, there were many examples of caring about, taking care of, care giving and care receiving (Fisher & Tronto, 1990) seriously and terminally ill prisoners. It was this caring about that could have an emotional effect on prisoners and staff, something which led to considerable emotional labour.

There were ways in which the prison regime, culture and relationship did not soften when faced with a terminally ill prisoner. As seen throughout this thesis, prisons are places dominated by security considerations, and by the actions and regulations arising from the imperative to keep the prisoner population incarcerated and to prevent them from escaping, harming the public or harming each other. Security and rules were very significant in determining responses of prison regimes and personnel to dying prisoners. Security considerations shape carceral geography around dying prisoners, resulting in a physical environment still marked as a prison even when the death occurred in outside hospital.

Staff were very aware of the limitations this posed to the care of dying prisoners, hence the desire to develop palliative care suites where regimes could be relaxed and the environment softened. The care provided in prison is subject to security considerations, through the need for approval on security grounds of actions and objects that will assist in caring for dying prisoners. The extent to which security considerations and the application of prison 'rules' determines responses to dying prisoners is ameliorated by the use of discretion, a vital tool in making adjustments to the regime, but potentially subject to idiosyncratic and arbitrary application.

Impacts of Deaths from Natural Causes on Prison Regimes, Culture and Relationships

Deaths from natural causes impacted on the prison regime, culture and relationships in several ways. Some of these impacts were tangible and visible, others were less obvious and harder for staff and prisoners to elucidate. Many of these changes were only really noticeable to those directly involved, but they all contributed to the care of a terminally ill prisoner. Deaths from natural causes in prison custody also necessitated new tasks, and tasks which whilst not always entirely new involved more staff, especially in the LTHSE prison, as a result of the elevated number of deaths from natural causes in recent years.

One of the most prominent changes to the prison regime resulting from the increasing number of deaths from natural causes in prison custody was the presence of a palliative care suite in the LTHSE prison studied and the plans for similar provision at the Category B prison. The desire to better meet the needs of dying prisoners had led to the repurposing of space within the prison and the redirection of resources towards the needs of this specific group of prisoners. Palliative care suites changed the physical environment of the prison, but were also places where there was an expectation of changes to the prison regime. They served to soften the carceral geography, to introduce softness and colour into a usually hard and drab setting. They also provided space in which the normal regime of the prison could at times be subverted by the needs of the dying prisoner, with doors being left unlocked, family being permitted to visit and stay and healthcare professionals more freely deploying touch in the administration of care. There were other changes to the physical provisions the regime made for prisoners on the wings. Doorbells were situated next to beds so frail prisoners could more easily call for help, steps lowered, and approval given for more comfortable mattresses. Each of these changes subtly affected the expected prison regime in favour of providing for the comfort and ease of physically frail dying prisoners. There were other ways in which the regime 'softened'. Small adjustments were made and normal wing routines could be speeded up or adapted. The need to make family liaison officers (FLOs) available for work with dying prisoners and their families could place an additional burden on the prison regime, as could responding to post-death investigations and attendance at subsequent coroner's court hearings where staff could be unavailable for their usual tasks for several days.

Deaths from natural causes also subtly changed the culture of the prisons studied. As discussed above, care quietly permeated the prison culture but was especially marked around those prisoners who were frail or known to be dying. It was also extended to those thought to be affected by a death, although not universally or consistently. In the LTHSE establishment especially, the prison culture was marked by an awareness of death and dying, reflected in the willingness of prisoners and staff to talk about their experiences or concerns. The experience of living and working with prisoners who had died was so common that it had changed the culture of the prison, and changed attitudes towards subjects often regarded as sensitive.

The culture of the prison was also different because new tasks were placed on or accepted by prison staff, particularly officers, who found themselves pushing wheelchairs or helping healthcare colleagues turn prisoners in bed. The care of the family, by family liaison officers but also sometimes prison chaplains, became more important, and the relationship between the family and prison altered, with far more contact and involvement with a dying or deceased prisoner's family than was usual with prisoners' families in other circumstances. Officers found themselves facilitating visits in healthcare centres rather than Visits halls. They also found themselves involved in more post-mortem investigations, in dealing with the problems regarding communicating prisoners' wishes not to be resuscitated whilst respecting medical confidentiality and in supporting their colleagues after a death.

The frequency with which deaths from natural causes were occurring had led to more 'bedwatch' duties for officers and a greater emphasis being placed on the correct use of restraints, in accordance with the accepted standards set by the Graham Judgement. Restraints had become a significant issue within both prisons studied. For staff, this was because their misuse could offend a sense of what constituted decency, but also because there was a fear that if used inappropriately the prison may be criticised by the PPO after a death. For prisoners, restraints conveyed the shame of stigma, embodied a lack of care and were an affront to their dignity. Although restraints were used on prisoners needing treatment in 'outside' hospital who were not terminally ill, cultural standards around the respect due to the dying made these issues more significant when death was expected.

Deaths from natural causes also changed relationships. In the high security prison, where prisoners may be resident for several years, there was an awareness that long-term relationships developed, between prison officers and prisoners, but also between prisoners. The circumstances of a dying prisoner provided an opportunity for his peers to express and develop their caring side, to make amends for their past, and in some cases to embody their feelings towards a prisoner in practical actions. More intimate relationships developed between prisoners as a result. Relationships could also be changed negatively when a prisoner was dying, with their frailty being regarded as an opportunity for exploitation by some of their peers. For staff, especially officers, the circumstances of a dying prisoner reduced the social distance between them. Officers felt more sympathy in their relationships with dying prisoners, although this was sometimes seen as an expected part of professionalism, to the extent that it was performed even if the officer struggled to align their deeper emotions to the perceived occupational norms. Officers reported allowing dying prisoner 'more grace', softening their discipline approaches because of the prisoner's circumstances, but struggled to show they were upset by a bereavement. For both staff and prisoners, memories of such deaths could come up years later. There was a need for support to be offered, but mixed views on what was available and a tendency to expect formal offers but in practice seek informal support.

Contribution and Impact

This research project has collected data that provides a rare insight into death and dying in prison. Whilst the need to research deaths in prison custody is recognised within prison sociology (Liebling, 2017), there have been no studies of deaths from natural causes that consider the impact on the prison as an institution. This aspect has been overlooked. Even within this study, changes to the normal regime, whilst frequently observed, were often taken for granted by participants as the right thing to do and therefore underreported by them. This made the ethnographic elements of this research more significant; only through participant observation did the extent of the adjustments being made and the impact of these deaths become apparent.

The research has identified a number of factors relevant to determining the responses of prison regimes and prison personnel to dying prisoners, and several ways in which deaths from natural causes impact on prison regimes, culture and relationships. In doing so, it contributes to prison sociology by concluding both that deaths from natural causes in prison custody soften prison regimes, culture and relationships and that prison changes death and death changes prison. The softening occurs in both visible, tangible ways, but also intangibly, and it is this blurring which informs the responses of prison regimes and personnel to dying prisoners.

The research makes a further original contribution to prison sociology by challenging and contradicting much of the existing literature, primarily from health sciences, which juxtaposes the philosophy of 'care' attributed to healthcare professionals in prison with the 'control' or 'discipline' philosophy assigned to prison officers. Instead, this research demonstrates care quietly permeating the prison culture, especially with regard to efforts, expressed primarily by prison officers and governors, to make death in prison 'as good as it could be'. This research is therefore significant because it considers palliative care in prisons more holistically than existing studies, which have often been limited to the medical care of terminally ill prisoners and tended to focus on the experiences of healthcare professionals. Prison officers are seen to be meeting the psychosocial needs of terminally ill prisoners. This finding is unexpected in the context of previous studies of palliative care in prison (Bolger, 2005; Burles et al., 2016; Lillie, 2018; Wood, 2007), which have focussed on the opinions of healthcare professionals, but perhaps less unexpected in light of previous studies of prison officers' performance of care (Tait, 2011) and their relationships with prisoners more generally (Crawley, 2004, 2005; Liebling et al., 2011; Tait, 2008). Appropriate palliative care includes meeting the psychosocial and spiritual needs of prisoners and their families. In the context of the prison, this means considering, as this research does, locations other than the prison's healthcare centre in which end of life care is delivered. It also means it is important to have considered the interactions between staff other than healthcare professionals with the dying prisoner and between other prisoners and prisoner-carers with the dying prisoner.

This research has particular relevance because the number of deaths from natural causes, associated with an ageing prison population, is predicted to continue to increase (Ministry of Justice, 2018). As a result, this research has the potential to be useful to those engaged in the management of prisons (including prison governors), in the care of prisoners, and in the support of prison staff, prisoners' families and friends. It is also of relevance to the Prison and Probation Ombudsman, as the body responsible for investigating prisoners' deaths.

With regard to operational and policy matters, these findings suggest a number of areas for attention which are likely to affect several prisons. These include the contradictions and oversights in PSIs, and the current difficulties in obtaining compassionate release for dying prisoners, both of which can only be addressed at a national level. This research demonstrates that the compassionate release system is not working, as evidenced by the way both staff and prisoners no longer expected compassionate release to be granted, even though they still completed the necessary paperwork. Reform is needed in particular to address the mismatch of expectations between the prison service and palliative care professionals with regard to the requirement to specify that death is anticipated within three months. This is at odds with current medical practice and serves as a barrier to compassionate release applications. However, granting compassionate release is politically sensitive. Prison staff are themselves aware of the risks and anxious to avoid a situation where a prisoner granted compassionate release commits further crimes. Some measure of when compassionate release is appropriate is clearly needed, although it's impossible to conclude that the current measures are suitable given how rarely release is granted. Other barriers to compassionate release, such as resolving which local authority should cover the costs, should be easier to address.

The research also highlights the continuing need, despite the Graham Judgement, to work to ensure the appropriate use of restraints when terminally ill (or other) prisoners are transferred to NHS facilities outside the prison. It also demonstrates the ways in which the expectation of an investigation after death can shape the care of the dying prisoner as the prison seeks to forestall possible criticism. This can, perhaps understandably, lead to a better standard of care for the prisoner, but it can also lead merely to better record keeping. In some cases, the expectation of an investigation had unexpected consequences such as the removal of extraneous medical equipment from the room prior to death in an attempt to avoid it being seized as part of the investigation. The expectation of an investigation also changed the care of the body after death and potentially served to make a death emotionally harder for prison staff, especially healthcare staff, and the prisoner's family, required to leave the deceased immediately after a death since the room was regarded as a crime scene.

At a local level this research shows the ongoing tensions between prison officers and healthcare professionals over the construction of the dying prisoner, which can adversely affect the care of the prisoner and employment experiences, particularly of nurses. It also highlights the need to ensure the appropriate use of discretion when adjustments are made around dying prisoners that rely on feelings of sympathy informed by the personal characteristics of the prisoner, and so risk becoming arbitrary and discriminatory. In each prison, there were aspects of practice, at the time of this study, which presented challenges that could be addressed by learning from other prisons, particularly with regard to the use of syringe drivers and Oramorph in the prison and communicating the existence of a prisoner's DNR wishes amongst staff. Lastly, the research serves as a reminder that prison staff and prisoners alike expect formal offers of support after a death has occurred, and feel undervalued if these are not forthcoming, even if the support they accept comes from informal sources.

Limitations and Recommendations for Further Research

One of the most significant limitations of this research is that although the increasing number of deaths from natural causes in prison custody makes research so necessary, it also means the situation is evolving. Prisons are amending their practice in response to a developing understanding of the needs of terminally ill prisoners, to changing external guidance (such as the *Ambitions for Palliative and End of Life Care*) and because they are simply getting more practice at dealing with deaths from natural causes and are therefore operationalising new practices and procedures. Furthermore, although the research was conducted in two prisons, carefully chosen because they had both contrasting and similar characteristics, as discussed in Chapter 1, it cannot encompass the current situation in all prisons, and only seeks to represent the impacts of and responses to deaths from natural causes in prison custody in one jurisdiction, England and Wales. It should also be noted that some of the adjustments made to meet the needs of dying prisoners were also in place for their peers who were seriously ill or frail from other reasons, and did not exist solely because of awareness of a terminal diagnosis.

The aim of this research project was to analyse the impact on prison regimes, culture and relationships of the growing number of prisoners dying from natural causes and to explore the factors influencing responses within the prison to dying prisoners. In the course of this research, related questions arose which could not be included in these aims. Firstly, this research suggests further study is needed on the experience of family members bereaved when a prisoner dies of natural causes.

This would help address whether they feel supported by the prison, including by the family liaison officer, and whether practices such as being permitted to stay in a prison overnight with their dying family member are valued. Linked to this there could also be further study on the experiences of the FLO. This project suggests the increasing number of prisoners dying from natural causes is presenting FLOs with new challenges in terms of workload, but also in terms of the emotional labour associated with the deaths of prisoners who have committed sexual offences against family members. The relationship between a prison and a prisoner's family seems to change in the circumstances of a death from natural causes, and this arguably warrants further attention. Secondly, the 'bedwatches' observed during this research highlighted the need to identify how the experiences of prisoners, healthcare professionals and prison staff can be improved when the prisoner is receiving medical treatment outside of the prison. It is clear from this study that the two sets of professionals, coming from very different institutional objectives, bring conflicting priorities to their work with the prisoner on a 'bedwatch' which can potentially affect the treatment of the prisoner. Lastly, this research has highlighted lesser gaps in the existing literature, including in the UK context how gender may influence prison officers' attitudes to sex offenders, and the role of gender in the style of caring provided by prison officers.

Final Remarks

There is, sadly, no simple answer at a policy level to what should be done in response to prisoners dying from natural causes. Some things could be improved, as outlined above, but there are more fundamental structural difficulties which are harder to address. At heart, the issue is that dying prisoners need different things. For some, compassionate release is desirable, and needs to become less rare. For others, compassionate release would remove them from the place that has become their 'home', and potentially simply move them to another institution, one where they did not have such long-term relationships with staff willing to provide their psychosocial care at the end of life. Staff and prisoners talked about an ideal 'secure hospital' where prisoners who were physically frail could be housed. Others would resent being with only their elderly and frail peers as they reached the end of life. Even if such a facility existed, there would still be the question of when a prisoner should move to it, and who would decide.

What should happen to dying prisoners is not an easy issue to address, but one where the responses reflect society's priorities and values. Prisoners' needs differ, but in meeting them, the criminal justice system has also to remember the expectations of the public, the needs of victims and the requirement to act with fairness. What is currently happening, however, presents complex moral and ethical questions which need addressing. Is prison the right place to die? Is it right to leave individual prisons and individual prison staff to try to find case-by-case solutions? Should remand prisoners be treated differently at the end of life? Further discussion at a policy level is clearly needed, both to support the staff who are trying to respond appropriately to the needs of dying prisoners in their care, but also to ensure the prison service in England and Wales continues to respect the humanity of the people it accommodates.

For many of the prisoners involved in this research project, the possibility of dying in prison was something they acknowledged, did not welcome, but often accepted. What concerned them more was how imprisonment would affect their experience of dying, the care they would receive, and the way they would be treated by those around them. The issues they spoke about reflected their situation as prisoners, and the workings of a total institution (Goffman, 1961) and the stigma associated with their imprisonment (Goffman, 1963). They saw contrasts with how dying in the community might be envisaged. They recognised being in prison would change the experience of dying, as did the prison staff, officers, governors, nurses and chaplains who worked with them. Their willingness to participate in this research reflects the urgency with which the challenges arising from prisoners dying of natural causes need to be addressed. They knew the experience of dying and death to be different because of the prison setting and saw ways in which, for the immediate moment or in the longer term, prison regimes and culture were altered by responding to the needs of dying prisoners. Deaths from natural causes in prison custody soften prison regimes, culture and relationships and this blurring informs the responses of prison regimes and personnel to dying prisoners. In this respect, prison changes death, and death changes prison.

References

Ambitions for Palliative and End of Life Care Partnership. (2018). *Dying Well in Custody Charter*. Ambitions for Palliative and End of Life Care Partnership, UK. endoflifecareambitions.org.uk/tag/prisons

Bolger, M. (2005). Dying in prison: Providing palliative care in challenging environments. *International Journal of Palliative Nursing, 11*(12), 619–621. https://doi.org/10.12968/ijpn.2005.11.12.20227

Burles, M. C., Peternelj-Taylor, C. A., & Holtslander, L. (2016). A 'good death' for all?: Examining issues for palliative care in correctional settings. *Mortality, 21*(2), 93–111. https://doi.org/10.1080/13576275.2015.1098602

Crawley, E. (2004). *Doing prison work: The public and private lives of prison officers*. Willan.

Crawley, E. (2005). Institutional thoughtlessness in prisons and its impacts on the day-to-day prison lives of elderly men. *Journal of Contemporary Criminal Justice, 21*(4), 350–363. https://doi.org/10.1177/1043986205282018

Fisher, B., & Tronto, J. (1990). Towards a feminist theory of caring. In E. Abel & M. Nelson (Eds.), *Circles of care: Work and identity in women's lives* (pp. 35–62). State University of New York.

Foucault, M. (1991). *Discipline and punish: The birth of the prison* (A. Sheridan, Trans.). Penguin Books.

Goffman, E. (1961). *Asylums: Essays on the social situation of mental patients and other inmates*. Penguin.

Goffman, E. (1963). *Stigma: Notes on the management of spoiled identity*. Penguin.

Liebling, A. (2017). The meaning of ending life in prison. *Journal of Correctional Health Care, 23*(1), 20–31. https://doi.org/10.1177/1078345816685070

Liebling, A., Price, D., & Shefer, G. (2011). *The prison officer* (2nd ed.). Willan.

Lillie, K. (2018). Loss at the end of life: Palliative care in prisons. In S. Read, S. Santatzoglou, & A. Wrigley (Eds.), *Loss, dying and bereavement in the criminal justice system* (pp. 43–53). Routledge.

Ministry of Justice. (2018). *Prison population projections 2018 to 2023.* Ministry of Justice.

Sykes, G. M. (1958). *Society of captives: A study of a maximum security prison.* Princeton University Press.

Tait, S. (2008). Prison officers and gender. In J. Bennett, B. Crewe, & A. Wahidin (Eds.), *Understanding prison staff* (pp. 65–91). Willan.

Tait, S. (2011). A typology of prison officer approaches to care. *European Journal of Criminology, 8*(6), 440–454. https://doi.org/10.1177/1477370811413804

Wood, F. J. (2007). The challenge of providing palliative care to terminally ill prison inmates in the UK. *International Journal of Palliative Nursing, 13*(3), 131–135. https://doi.org/10.12968/ijpn.2007.13.3.23275

Appendix: Researching Dying Prisoners

Any researcher has responsibilities to participants, key informants, funders, gatekeepers and future researchers to conduct ethical research (O'Reilly, 2012). Part of this responsibility is captured by the requirements of research ethics committees. In this appendix I will set out the ways in which the research that informs this book was designed to be ethical and to address the expectations of ethical research held by the three relevant ethics committees: the NHS Health Research Authority, Her Majesty's Prison and Probation Service and the University of York. In doing so, it is crucial to recognise the difference between 'paper ethics' and 'ethics in practice'.

Throughout this study, ethical challenges arose from both the circumstances of the research participants and the sensitivity of the research topic. These included ensuring participation was informed and voluntary and protecting the well-being of all participants and the researcher. For prisoners, their incarcerated status means there are additional issues around giving informed consent, and vulnerabilities, particularly with regard to confidentiality and anonymity. This appendix will reflect on

C. Robinson, *Dying in Prison*, Palgrave Studies in Prisons and Penology, https://doi.org/10.1007/978-3-031-27103-8

those challenges and suggest that they should always be welcomed, not just as a way to honour our research participants but also because they provide illumination on the research topic.

Ethical Issues in Researching End of Life

One important ethical consideration in a study of this nature is whether to seek to include terminally ill prisoners as participants, and if so, to what extent any risks can be minimised. For some researchers (De Raeve, 1994; Hammersley & Atkinson, 2007) involving people at the end of life in research is unethical. For others (Barnett, 2001; Lawton, 2001), having the opportunity to participate in research can be therapeutic for people at the end of life, or serve as a way to avoid social death by providing "an opportunity to be an active and participating citizen again rather than an invalid or patient" (Kendall et al., 2007, p. 527). Excluding the terminally ill from research about an issue that concerns them deeply is paternalistic (Barnett, 2001; Lawton, 2001). When qualitative research includes terminally ill participants, Kendal et al. (2007) advise researchers to avoid asking direct questions about death and dying.

Bearing this conflicting advice in mind, it was decided to focus on conducting participant observation in the locations within the prison where interactions between staff and terminally or seriously ill prisoners take place, rather than on identifying individuals with a terminal diagnosis. This included the prison healthcare centre and any accommodation units adapted for this prisoner group, as well as prison wings. It was felt to be unnecessary and unethical to request access to prisoners' medical information or to seek to identify which prisoners were medically diagnosed with a terminal illness. Furthermore, the research questions included situations when a death from natural causes was unexpected, where no previous diagnosis may have been made. The aims of the research could be adequately addressed by looking at cases where prisoners were regarded by staff and other prisoners as seriously or terminally ill, without this being medically confirmed, even if a diagnosis had been possible. Given the nature of the research questions, it was not felt necessary to interview terminally or seriously ill prisoners, although the chosen methods allowed for ethnographic conversations which could, with the prisoner's consent, be included in the research data, but which were likely to be less burdensome for a physically frail prisoner than a more formal semi-structured interview.

Risks to Participants and Researcher

Crewe (2009) says one of the first things he learned when conducting an ethnography in a prison was that the prison was a safe environment. As an insider, I had the advantage of being familiar with prisons and having worked within other prisons, in a different role, safely. I already had training from HMPPS in personal protection, security awareness and anti-corruption practices, and a good awareness of the rules and practices in place to ensure safety. This included not being alone with prisoners regarded by the prison authority as not safe for one-to-one meetings. My willingness to conform to the security practices I knew to be expected, such as staying in sight of prison officers when on a wing, may have placed limitations on the research, but was essential to maintaining credibility with 'gatekeepers'.

The principal risk to participants in the project came from the sensitivity of the research topic. Discussing death and dying may be upsetting. Whilst I had experience of talking about these topics with prisoners and prison staff, from my role as a prison chaplain, from facilitating death cafes in the prison where I work and from previous research with prison officers, it was important to have other sources of support available to participants. Briefings were provided for each prison's Listeners and staff care team. In the LTHSE prison, I attended meetings of the Listeners, prisoners trained by the Samaritans to support their peers, so they could ask questions. This was not possible at Category B, where meetings were not held for Listeners, so each Listener was met individually at the start of the first period of fieldwork, something repeated with the Listeners on the relevant wings at the beginning of subsequent fieldwork periods. Listeners and members of the staff care team were given details of the research in advance (but not told who was participating) in the hope they would be better able to support anyone who had been upset by the research. Because the subject of death and dying could be particularly upsetting, the Safer Custody Team in each prison was asked to identify any prisoner they felt should not be approached about the research. In practice, they typically felt unable to do so. I was aware I might also find the topic upsetting at times, and so support, including non-managerial supervision from a trained counsellor with experience of working with staff in the criminal justice system, was in place before the fieldwork commenced.

Informed Consent

Hammersley and Atkinson (2007) claim ethnographers rarely tell their participants everything about the research, partly because they may not know the detail of the study at the start, but also because participants may not be interested in the project and to give them unwelcome detail would be intrusive. The freedom to follow their advice in this project was curtailed by the requirements of the NHS Health Research Authority and HMPPS. A detailed participant information sheet was produced, and, in recognition that not all prisoners (or indeed prison staff) would have the ability or time to read it, potential participants were also talked through the research. These explanations were inevitably partial, but the potential participants were given copies of the PIS and consent form and asked how long they needed to decide whether to participate.

Informed consent, especially in ethnography, is problematic. It needs to be recognised, as Miller and Bell (2002) suggest, that the formality of consent forms may alienate some people. This was felt to be particularly the case for prisoners, for whom a signature on a consent form may be more associated with signing something away, with a loss of power, rather than with giving their consent. However, it is expected by ethics committees. Miller and Bell (2002) also suggest there may be problems telling where 'participation' begins and ends, something particularly acute in ethnographic research where the researcher aims to fade into the background such that participants may forget they are there. Murphy and Dingwall (2007) say consent in ethnographic research is based on trust and is relational, rather than contractual. During the course of the fieldwork, two participants explicitly explained their willingness to participate as originating from having decided I looked trustworthy (Fieldnotes, LTHSE). However, Murphy and Dingwall (2007) suggest that as such, consent can be withdrawn at any time. This fits closely with other writers (Hammersley & Atkinson, 2007; Miller & Bell, 2002; O'Reilly, 2012) who say informed consent in ethnography needs to be ongoing and renegotiated. It was important throughout this research to check with participants whether something could be included in the data collection, reminding them that their interactions with me were with a researcher.

The importance of informed consent being an ongoing process was especially relevant to this research given the topic being studied. It was possible some participating prisoners could lose the capacity to give informed consent during the course of data collection, in which case it was intended that no further observations would be conducted unless and until the prisoner regained the ability to consent. Participants were informed of this on the information sheet and asked in advance to give their consent to the data collected before they lost capacity being retained in the study. In practice, there was no ambiguity regarding a participant's ability to consent and any observations with a participant were completed before their capacity to consent became doubtful.

Prisoners participating in the research were also vulnerable because of the power structure of the prison. However, as Fielding (2001) says, groups that are powerless or vulnerable still have a right to be researched. Chan (2012), writing about researching police officers, suggests this is not just a problem for prisoners, but can affect staff in command and control settings such as police forces. This arguably also applies to prison staff. The participant information sheet was clear that participating or not would not affect a prisoner's chance of parole or their treatment in the prison, and that it would not count towards the prison's targets for 'purposeful activity'. This did not stop one prisoner from feeling having a copy of the signed consent form helped him secure re-categorisation as a lower risk (Fieldnote, LTHSE). It was also emphasised that anyone could withdraw from the research at any time, without having to give a reason. To try to ensure consent was genuine, all potential participants, including staff, were given 24 hours to consider whether to participate.

It was important even then to be sensitive to non-verbal expressions, and whether they matched spoken expressions of consent (Nyampong, 2015).

Given a prisoner population of over 700 in the LTHSE prison and over 1200 in Category B prison (where 40% of the population changed every three months and up to 70 new prisoners might be received each day) it was not practical to gain the written consent of prisoners and staff who were tangential to the research being conducted. Limited data was gathered from these people, all of it anonymous and none of it personal or sensitive. Only when it seemed likely that someone would become more significant in the research was their consent sought, an approach regarded as the only practical solution by Murphy and Dingwall (2007) to research in 'semi-public' spaces where people know their behaviour can be scrutinised in person or via CCTV. This approach was taken because it was felt a prison was such a space.

Anonymity

Whilst ethics committees encourage researchers to ensure the anonymity of their participants, Wahidin and Moore (2011) argue it is more important potential participants are informed if there is a chance they could be identifiable from the research report. Participants were reminded of how the data would be used and informed it was possible people may try to guess who has taken part in the research project. Staff participants were more likely to be identifiable if there were not many people in a particular job, for example working as family liaison officers (FLOs). For this reason, it was felt necessary to ask those at risk of identification in this way whether their role could be mentioned. Similarly, one prisoner participant was keen to check how he would be referred to in the data, anxious not to be identifiable given he was one of a small number of prisoners with a very specific sentence. An appropriate formulation was agreed with him (Fieldnote, LTHSE).

There were also difficulties in protecting participants' anonymity during data collection. In the LTHSE prison, in particular, ethnographic conversations with prisoners took place where the interaction could be overseen, and potentially overheard, by staff and other prisoners. Occasionally pre-arranged conversations with prisoners were held in interview rooms. Each time this happened, prison officers had to be told who was to be seen, then call or fetch the prisoner, and give him a rub-down search before the interview commenced. The fact the prisoner had participated in the research could not be disguised, even if the content of the conversation was confidential.

Whilst attention is often paid to the need to maintain the anonymity of prisoners in prison research, the difficulty of protecting the identity of staff participants from their colleagues is rarely discussed. The participation of staff in semi-structured interviews was hard to hide, with most staff interviewees struggled to find a place to talk where we would not be either seen or interrupted. When an officer in a prisoner-facing role was to be interviewed, other colleagues had to be detailed to cover their tasks. Arrangements were agreed with the Safer Custody Team in one prison, and at the daily meeting of Residential Custody Managers (CMs) in the other for me to contact the team who prepared staff rotas to arrange cover for their tasks. Knowledge of a staff member's participation in the research could be potentially limited to a small group of colleagues, but not their anonymity could not be entirely maintained.

It was recognised that some of the data collected could be sensitive, for example, relating to criminal activities or providing personal information about prisoners or prison staff. With this in mind, as far as possible the data was anonymised when collected. When transcription was required, for example, of interview recordings, this was done by me. Interviews were anonymised as transcribed, with any names or personal details which might assist identification being removed. Names are only used in this book when it assists the reader in keeping track of cases referred to across several chapters, and are all pseudonymised. Distinctive speech patterns are not quoted verbatim, again to protect the identity of participants.

Confidentiality

In order to respect the confidentiality of prisoners, situations where confidential medical information might be overheard, for example in appointments with medical consultants, were not observed and a decision was taken not to have access to either medical or prison service records for any prisoner.

All data was handled in accordance with current legislation and guidelines from the University and the British Sociological Association. There were some exceptions to confidentiality required by HMPPS, specifically if participants shared information suggesting they intended to cause harm to themselves or to others, if there was a serious threat to prison security or illegal activities, malpractice or breaches of prison rules. In these circumstances, this information had to be shared with the appropriate member of staff, although in practice this never arose. All potential participants accepted the warning that their confidentiality might have to be breached. This was a proviso, required by HMPPS, that seemed familiar to staff and prisoners alike, yet as Israel and Gelsthorpe (2017) point out, it is one in which the researcher demonstrates a privileging of institutional loyalty over the interests of research participants. What was significant was the response this proviso elicited in some staff. They were unaccustomed to being included in the same stipulation as prisoners and some of them seemed surprised at this part of the consent form. Despite feeling uncomfortable, I continued to highlight this proviso, partly in order to fulfil the commitments to a research ethics committee but also because of a desire to treat staff and prisoners alike in this regard.

Data Storage

Three forms of data were collected that were not anonymised at the time of collection. The careful storage of this data was important to maintain the confidentiality of participants, and assurances about its protection were important to participants. Completed consent forms were removed from the prison, electronically scanned and stored securely on the university's filestore, with the originals being destroyed as confidential waste. Selection questionnaires, completed by staff willing to be interviewed, were stored in a locked drawer in the prison, anonymised as transcribed within the prison, with any personal identifiers removed, and the transcription emailed to be stored securely on the university filestore. Originals were then destroyed using the prison's confidential waste system. At the request of HMPPS, the Dictaphone used to record interviews was encrypted and password protected. Interview recordings were transferred to the University filestore within two days and then deleted from the Dictaphone. Whenever the Dictaphone included interview data, it was either kept with me (travelling between the prison and the university) or in a locked drawer in the university, to which only I had access.

When participants gave permission, an anonymised written transcript of the interview was submitted to the UK Data Service, with limited access to other accredited researchers permitted. The UK Data Service will store this anonymised information for a maximum of 10 years.

Ethical Approval

Ethical approval for the research was complicated by the requirement for three bodies (the National Health Service, Her Majesty's Prison and Probation Service and the University of York) to review the research proposed in detail. Although these processes were bureaucratic (the final application to the NHS Health Research Authority amounted to 91 pages), they reflected real concerns that participants should be able to make informed decisions about consent, that the risks to participants (and the researcher) should be minimised as far as possible and that the limitations on anonymity and confidentiality should be understood.

One of the key descriptions of ethnography used by O'Reilly (2012) is that it is "iterative-inductive" and as such the design of a research project changes and evolves as fieldwork progresses. This is challenging in the context of a research climate that demands ethical approval for research projects in advance. The nature of the chosen research questions was such that fieldwork needed to be undertaken in hospitals as well as prisons, compounding the challenge by requiring ethical approval from the NHS Health Research Authority whose processes are primarily intended for clinical trials. Writing about conducting ethnographic research in healthcare settings, Murphy and Dingwall (2007) state:

> Informed consent in ethnographic research is neither achievable nor demonstrable in the terms set by anticipatory regulatory regimes that take clinical research or biomedical experimentation as their paradigm cases. (p. 2223)

Although processes exist within the Health Research Authority's framework for research projects to be subsequently amended, this is not straightforward and can further delay research plans. Instead, there seems to be an assumption inherent in the process that all possible scenarios will be known in advance. With this comes an assumed relationship with the research participants; they are to be the subjects, not the co-creators of research knowledge. This echoes Murphy and Dingwall's (2007) suggestion that the power relationships between doctors and research participants/patients and ethnographers and their participants are very different. They argue the potential harm of ethnography to participants is considerably different, and less, than the potential harm to participants in the biomedical experiments for which such ethical review processes were originally established.

In addition to the NHS Health Research Authority, ethical approval was also required, and obtained, from HMPPS and the University of York. Unsurprisingly, there were occasions when the expectations of the three ethics committees were incompatible, for example, with regard to what contact information should be included in the participant information sheet. HMPPS was anxious that contact details for external people, such as academic supervisors, must not be included on participant information sheets; the NHS expected these details would be available on the PIS; the university wanted email addresses only, but HMPPS rules prevent prisoners from having access to email. Instances such as this resulted in a much longer PIS than had been intended, something which was far from desirable given not all prisoners are confident readers, and may actually have reduced the likelihood of participants giving fully informed consent had I not decided to talk through the PIS with all participants as well as giving them a copy of it.

Hammersley (2009) questions whether any ethical committee has the expertise to make a reliable judgement on any particular research project:

> There are good reasons to believe that ethics committee are incapable of making sound—and, even less, superior—ethical decisions about particular research projects. Given this, the exercise of their authority will not improve the 'ethical quality' of social science research. (p. 212)

This was demonstrated during the process of obtaining approval for the research from the two separate NHS hospital trusts involved. One NHS Trust subjected the proposal to a further ethical review after the Health Research Authority's Research Ethics Committee had approved it, and asked questions about the aspect of the fieldwork that would be conducted within the prison, not the hospital, which revealed the committee members' ignorance of prison matters.

Ethics in Practice—Ethically Important Moments

Once ethical approval has been secured and data collection can commence, the social researcher is often faced with navigating between 'procedural ethics' and 'ethics in practice' (Guillemin & Gillam, 2004) otherwise referred to as 'paper ethics' and 'real world research' (Armstrong et al., 2014). It is inevitable that researchers in any social settings will encounter people, behaviour and interactions that could not be anticipated (Katz, 2006), even with the most meticulous planning and intense ethics committee scrutiny, and that some of these will situations will be ethically uncomfortable (Hammersley, 2015). Often presented as ethical dilemmas, in reality, unexpected scenarios which raise ethical issues are unlikely to be suited to one simple answer, and "multiple ethical considerations may be involved that pull in opposite directions" (Hammersley, 2007, p. 5). I found Guillemin and Gillam's

(2004) concept of ethically important moments a more useful framing than 'ethical dilemmas' for these dissonances between 'procedural ethics' and 'ethics in practice'. Ethically important moments can be defined as occasions which were not anticipated by the ethical review process, but which are times when ethically informed choices became more crucial for the well-being of participants.

When an ethically important moment arises, the researcher's 'ethical competence' (Guillemin & Gillam, 2004, p. 269) becomes more important. Murphy and Dingwall (2007) say that in such instances research participants are "likely to be served less well by procedural ethics embodied in regulations requiring fully informed advance consent than by researcher's conscientious commitment to avoiding exploitative and potentially harmful relationships" (p. 2229). The researcher's ethical competence is called upon to ensure the ethical important moment is recognised and responded to appropriately, with a conscious and honest attempt to avoid harm to research participants. Moore and Wahidin (2017) say that 'considering their vulnerable situation, and the harms to which prisoners are routinely exposed, it is imperative that researchers do not compound this suffering, even unintentionally' (p. 57). The researcher's 'ethical competence' (Guillemin & Gillam, 2004, p. 269) must therefore come to the fore in prison research. It is arguably equally important in any social research setting, but fieldwork in prisons presents particular challenges with regard to anonymity, confidentiality, informed consent and protecting vulnerable participants. Ethnographic fieldwork in prisons around a sensitive subject such as death brings further challenges. However, recasting these as 'ethically important moments', as times when the 'ethical dimension of ordinary everyday research practice' (Guillemin & Gillam, 2004, p. 276) are most obvious, helps avoid seeing these occurrences as problems to be solved. They are still times when there is a possibility that an ethical wrong could be done, but they are also an opportunity for a better understanding of the field and our position in it as researchers.

Underpinning any response to an ethically important moment has to be the recognition that the researcher can never be a neutral influence on the fieldwork site, especially when an ethnographic approach is being taken. In this respect, not only are my personal characteristics and approach to the research relevant, but also my 'insider' status as an experienced prison chaplain elsewhere in the prison service. My relationships with research participants, built up over 12 months, and influenced by personal experiences, values and characteristics, inevitably led to ethically important moments. Some ethically important moments highlight an exception to the envisaged research methods, the research relationship with participants that was envisaged or perhaps the gaps in research ethics committee's expectations (see Bowtell et al., 2013). Others reveal important aspects of the research setting that might have otherwise been overlooked, especially given how accustomed I was to operate in similar settings for different purposes. The ethically important moments that caught my attention show the relationships between staff and prisoners, the assumptions inherent in prison culture and my positioning as the researcher. Negotiating ethical challenges is not simply about finding a way to collect data in an ethical manner, but revealing something about the field which might otherwise have been overlooked (Robinson, 2020).

Although the expectations of ethics committees were that researching the end of life in prison is a sensitive subject, with the potential to upset research participants, it is potentially erroneous to think of all people being upset by the same topics, and risks belittling the autonomy of the individuals if it was assumed that they would find participating in research about death distressing. The ease with which many people, especially in the LTHSE prison, discussed death and dying did not prevent me at times from feeling uncomfortably aware of the potential pain that reminders of the topic could inflict on prisoners. However, the ethically important moments encountered in practice were very different from those anticipated by the ethical approval process. There were many occasions when participants approached me and started discussing the research subject, without any opportunity for me to seek advice from the Safer Custody Team in advance, as had been agreed. Negotiating the ethically important moments that arose from the willingness of participants to talk about death and dying made me realise that these subjects held a different place in prison culture than that which had been expected.

Other ethically important moments, arising from the differences between procedural ethics and ethics in practice, highlighted key features of inter- and intra-relationships between prisoners and prison staff. Some staff felt they could direct me towards particular prisoners, confident that their participation was guaranteed. I had each time to work out how best to respond, to minimise any harm and to respect the prisoner's wishes. The assumptions in the actions of some staff member (including one time offering to show me a prisoner's medical record) served to highlight the prisoner's dependency on staff on a new way. A further example of the power differentials between staff and prisoner arose from my uncomfortableness when staff baulked at being included in the proviso that their confidentiality might have to be breached in some circumstances. The ethically important moment I faced in deciding whether to persist in highlighting this aspect of the consent form served to emphasise that prison staff were not used to being treated in the same way as prisoners.

The constant struggle to keep participation in the research anonymous within the prison highlighted the diminished importance of anonymity for both staff and prisoners. Prisoners' expectations of being constantly observed shaped their understanding of anonymity, in ways that were sometimes challenging to me as a researcher. On one wing in each of the prisons, prisoners in trusted positions as wing reps or Prisoner Information Desk workers took it upon themselves to create lists of names of prisoners who wished to speak to me. In the Category B prison, this was a 'sign-up sheet' openly displayed on the Prisoner Information Desks, so that anyone passing could see who had expressed an interest. These lists were seen as normal part of wing life and their production assumed to be helpful to both me as the researcher and potential participants. Similarly, striking was the willingness of prison staff to volunteer, in front of colleagues, and on one occasion, in front of prisoners, to be interviewed. I felt uncomfortable that the participation of prisoners from these wings, and of some prison staff, was now public, but realised that the 'normal' expectations of research ethics committees about anonymity had no bearing on the real world of people in the prison setting.

Conclusion

Researching a sensitive subject with vulnerable participants inevitably presents ethical issues, for which there is no simple solution. Research ethics approval processes cannot envisage all circumstances that will arise, and in some cases, ethical approval panels are ill-suited to the task of advising. In researching dying prisoners, there were particular risks to the participants (and to a limited extent, to me as the researcher). There were also problems arising from the prison setting which negatively affected the possibility of maintaining anonymity, confidentiality and informed consent. The gap between 'procedural ethics' and 'ethics in practice' (Guillemin & Gillam, 2004) or 'paper ethics' and 'real world research' (Armstrong et al., 2014) is inevitable, and researchers need to develop ethical competence in order to find an appropriate response. Framing these instances as 'ethically important moments' is more useful, and more accurate, than seeing them simply as dilemmas.

Each of the ethically important moments experienced in undertaking this research required me to draw on what ethical competence I had developed as a researcher, in order to avoid harm to research participants. However, ethically important moments also serve as tools in data collection, highlighting a dissonance between procedural ethics and ethics in practice which in this study forced me to consider why it was this particular ethically important moment that had arisen. Reflecting on these moments revealed more about the practice, culture and assumptions of the research setting. In responding to an ethically important moment, the researcher is no longer simply a bystander, but sees the behaviour, assumptions and motivations of other people afresh.

References

Armstrong, R., Gelsthorpe, L., & Crewe, B. (2014). From paper ethics to real-world research: Supervising ethical reflexivity when taking risks in research with 'the risky.' In K. Lumsden & A. Winter (Eds.), *Reflexivity in criminological research: Experiences with the powerful and powerless* (pp. 207–219). Palgrave Macmillan.

Ayete-Nyampong, L. (2015). Changing hats: Transiting between practitioner and researcher roles. In D. Drake, R. Earle, & J. Sloan (Eds.), *The Palgrave handbook of prison ethnography* (pp. 307–325). Palgrave Macmillan.

Barnett, M. (2001). Interviewing terminally ill people: Is it fair to take their time? *Palliative Medicine, 15*(2), 157–158. https://doi.org/10.1191/026921601666846232

Bowtell, E. C., Sawyer, S. M., Aroni, R. A., Green, J. B., & Duncan, R. E. (2013). "Should I send a condolence card?" Promoting emotional safety in qualitative health research through reflexivity and ethical mindfulness. *Qualitative Inquiry, 19*(9), 652–663. https://doi.org/10.1177/1077800413500927

Chan, J. (2012). Researching police culture: A longitudinal mixed method approach. In D. Gadd, S. Karstedt, & S. Messner (Eds.), *The Sage handbook of criminological research methods* (pp. 301–311). Sage.

Crewe, B. (2009). *The prisoner society: Power, adaption, and social life in an English prison.* Oxford University Press.

de Raeve, L. (1994). Ethical issues in palliative care research. *Palliative Medicine, 8*, 298–305. https://doi.org/10.1177/026921639400800405

Fielding, N. (2001). Ethnography. In N. Gilbert (Ed.), *Researching social life* (pp. 145–163). Sage.

Guillemin, M., & Gillam, L. (2004). Ethics, reflexivity, and 'ethically important moments' in research. *Qualitative Inquiry, 10*(2), 261–280.

Hammersley, M. (2009). Against the ethicists: On the evils of ethical regulation. *International Journal of Social Research Methodology, 12*(3), 211–225. https://doi.org/10.1080/13645570802170288

Hammersley, M. (2015). Research 'inside' viewed from 'outside': Reflections on prison ethnography. In R. Earle, J. Sloan, & D. Drake (Eds.), *The Palgrave handbook for prison ethnography* (pp. 21–39). Palgrave Macmillan.

Hammersley, M., & Atkinson, P. (2007). *Ethnography: Principles in practice.* Routledge.

Israel, M., & Gelsthorpe, L. (2017). Ethics in criminological research: A powerful force or a force for the powerful. In M. Cowburn, L. Gelsthorpe, & A. Wahidin (Eds.), *Research ethics in criminology: Dilemmas, issues and solutions* (pp. 185–203). Routledge.

Katz, J. (2006). Ethical escape routes for underground ethnographers. *American Ethnologist, 33*(4), 499–506.

Kendall, M., Harris, F., Boyd, K., Sheikh, A., Murray, S. A., Brown, D., Mallinson, I., Kearney, N., & Worth, A. (2007). Key challenges and ways forward in researching the "good death": Qualitative in-depth interview and focus group study. *BMJ, 334*(7592), 521–524. https://doi.org/10.1136/bmj.39097.582639.55

Lawton, J. (2001). Gaining and maintaining consent: Ethical concerns raised in a study of dying patients. *Qualitative Health Research, 11*(5), 693–705. https://doi.org/10.1177/104973201129119389

Miller, T., & Bell, L. (2002). Consenting to what? issues of access, gate-keeping and 'informed' consent. In T. Miller & L. Bell (Eds.), *Consenting to what? Issues of access, gate-keeping and 'informed' consent* (pp. 54–69). Sage. https://doi.org/10.4135/9781849209090

Moore, L., & Wahidin, A. (2017). The role of ethics in prisoner research. In M. Cowburn, L. Gelsthorpe, & A. Wahidin (Eds.), *Research ethics in criminology: Dilemmas, issues and solutions* (pp. 55–76). Routledge.

Murphy, E., & Dingwall, R. (2007). Informed consent, anticipatory regulation and ethnographic practice. *Social Science & Medicine, 65*, 2223–2234. https://doi.org/10.1016/j.socscimed.2007.08.008

O'Reilly, K. (2012). *Ethnographic methods* (2nd ed.). Routledge.

Robinson, C. (2020). Ethically important moments as data: Reflections from ethnographic fieldwork in prisons. *Research Ethics Review, 16*(1–2), 1–15. https://doi.org/10.1177/1747016119898401

Wahidin, A., & Moore, L. (2011). Ethics and prison research. In P. Davies, P. Francis, & V. Jupp (Eds.), *Doing Criminological Research* (pp. 287–306). Sage.

Glossary

1s, 2s, 3s etc. Used to refer to the floor levels within prison buildings, especially in accommodation units. The 1s is the first/ground floor, the 2s is the floor above, the 3s is the floor above that etc.

Basic Part of the Incentives and Earned Privileges scheme (see below) which governs prisoners' entitlement to privileges including extra visits, access to television, the right to wear their own clothes etc. Basic is the lowest level, used as a punishment for not complying with prison regulations or for bad behaviour.

Bedwatch Slang term for the prison officer escort of a prisoner who is an in-patient in a hospital setting.

Cat A A classification, formally *category* A, used for prisoners whose escape would be highly dangerous to the public or the police or the security of the State and for whom the aim must be to make escape impossible (Garton Grimwood, 2015).

Cat B A classification, formally *category* B, used for whom the very highest conditions of security are not necessary but for whom escape must be made very difficult (Garton Grimwood, 2015).

Centre The central atrium of a radial prison design linking the wings. In both the prisons studied, this was a large area, the full height of the prison.

C. Robinson, *Dying in Prison*, Palgrave Studies in Prisons and Penology, https://doi.org/10.1007/978-3-031-27103-8

Cleaner's Office The area or office in a prison, typically very small, used by the prison officers with the daily responsibility for the domestic function of the wing. Often the first port of call for prisoners with queries about practical needs.

CM Custodial Manager. The senior uniformed rank amongst prison officers.

Detail The department within a prison produces the daily rota detailing specific officers to specific tasks/functions.

Escape pack The information pack taken by officers when escorting a prisoner who has been assessed as posing a risk of escape to an out-patient or in-patient appointment at a hospital or hospice outside of the prison. An escape pack must always include the prisoner's current description and 4 up-to-date photographs (From PSI 33/2015).

Escort The officers accompanying a prisoner to an out-patient or in-patient appointment at a hospital or hospice outside of the prison.

FLO Family liaison officer. The member of staff, typically a prison officer, whose role is to liaise between the prison and the family of a prisoner. In speech, each letter is spelled out.

Governing Governor The most senior member of staff in a prison, known in the private sector as the Director. Sometimes referred to as the Number One to distinguish him or her from other staff of governor grade.

H3 The area in the Category B prison used to house prisoners with medical and social care needs such that the normal wing location was not suitable for them. 'H' refers to the block, '3' to the landing.

HMPPS Her Majesty's (or His Majesty's) Prison and Probation Service. The executive agency, which includes HM Prison Service, Probation Service and Youth Custody Service and is responsible for running prisons and probation services within England and Wales.

IEP Incentives and Earned Privileges. A tool of prison management that gives prisoners the opportunity to gain benefits, based on their good behaviour, participation in constructive activity and work towards their own rehabilitation. Includes an entry-level together with three levels of privileges; basic, standard and enhanced.

Listeners Used to refer to both the peer support scheme and the individual prisoners providing peer support aimed at reducing self-harm and suicide in prison. Listeners are prisoner–volunteers trained and supported by the Samaritans.

LTHSE Long-Term and High-Security Estate. The directorate within HMPPS which includes 13 establishments accommodating the most challenging Category A and Category B prisoners.

Natural causes Deaths that are *not* suicides or unlawful killings and do not result from accident or misadventure or the misuse of drugs or alcohol. Deaths from natural causes may be expected or unexpected, and result from physical health issues such as cancers, organ failure, strokes or degenerative disease.

Patrol State The condition of a prison in which all prisoners are locked in their cells, typically following a roll check, overnight or to facilitate staff breaks and the handover between staff shifts.

PID Desk Prison Information Desk. The base for PID workers, usually somewhere conspicuous in each residential unit.

PID workers Prison Information Desk workers. Prisoners tasked with communicating information and responding to queries about the regime from prisoners.

PPO Prison and Probation Ombudsman. The official body tasked with independently investigating complaints made by prisoners, and investigating the deaths of all prisoners.

PSI Prison Service Instruction. Part of the rules, regulations and guidelines by which prisons operate. Typically organised thematically with a separate PSI for each topic and a fixed expiry date by which they should be reviewed (Ministry of Justice, 2019).

PSO Prison Service Orders. Issued until August 2013, PSOs are long-term mandatory instructions intended to last indefinitely. Some have subsequently been cancelled or replaced by PSIs (Ministry of Justice, 2019).

Servery The area on a wing from which prisoners collect meals.

SO Senior Officer. The uniformed prison officer who supervises the work of other prison officers, but is junior to a CM.

Stores The function responsible for providing basic supplies to prisoners, such as bed linen and clothing, in line with their entitlement.

Unlock Period of time during which a prisoner's cell door can be unlocked, typically for association with other prisoners or to facilitate domestic tasks.

Visits hall The room used for prisoners' visits from family and friends. Housed within the prison walls, but in a separate building from the wings, workshops or healthcare centre and so harder for prisoners with limited mobility to access.

Wing The residential using of a prison, typically housing large numbers of prisoners.

Wing Reps Prisoners appointed to represent their peers on relevant fora as required on a range of matters such as anti-bullying, catering, equality and diversity and healthcare.

Works The department responsible for the maintenance of the prison fabric.

Index

C. Robinson, *Dying in Prison*, Palgrave Studies in Prisons and Penology, https://doi.org/10.1007/978-3-031-27103-8

Kolibri 360 GmbH
Ferdinand-Jühlke-Straße 7
99095 Erfurt, Deutschland
produktsicherheit@kolibri360.de